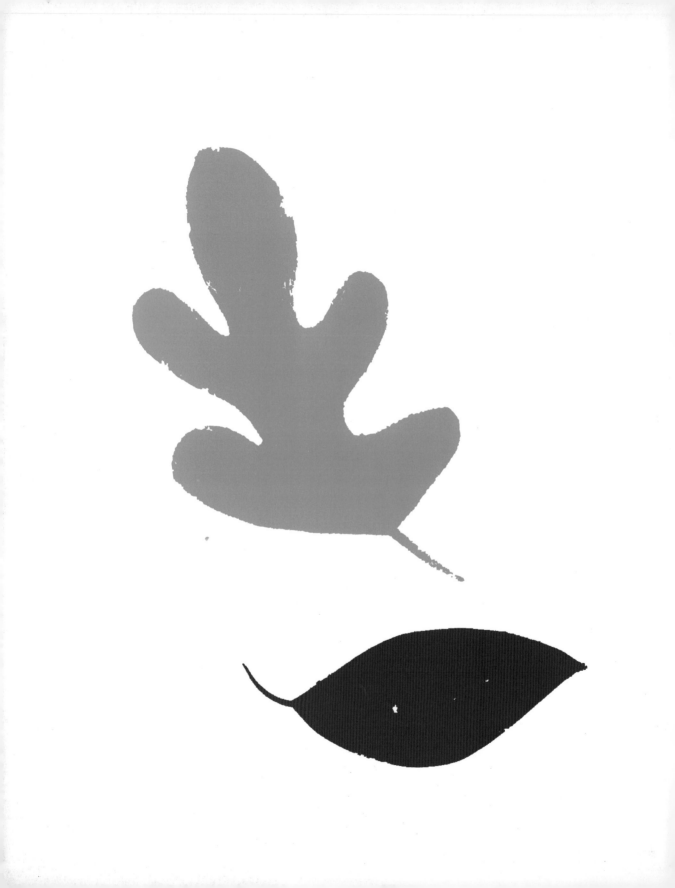

GROW

The Modern Woman's Handbook

GROW

Gorgeous Real Original Woman!

www.growexperience.com

GROW

The Modern Woman's Handbook

*How to Connect with Self,
Lovers, and Others*

Lynne Franks

HAY HOUSE, INC.
Carlsbad, California
London • Sydney • Johannesburg
Vancouver • Hong Kong

Published and distributed in the United States by: Hay House, Inc., P.O. Box 5100, Carlsbad, CA 92018-5100 • *Phone:* (760) 431-7695 or (800) 654-5126 • *Fax:* (760) 431-6948 or (800) 650-5115 • www.hayhouse.com • **Published and distributed in Australia by:** Hay House Australia Ltd., 18/36 Ralph St., Alexandria NSW 2015 • *Phone:* 612-9669-4299 • *Fax:* 612-9669-4144 • www.hayhouse.com.au • **Published and distributed in the United Kingdom by:** Hay House UK, Ltd. • Unit 202, Canalot Studios • 222 Kensal Rd., London W10 5BN • *Phone:* 44-20-8962-1230 • *Fax:* 44-20-8962-1239 • www.hayhouse.co.uk • **Published and distributed in the Republic of South Africa by:** Hay House SA (Pty), Ltd., P.O. Box 990, Witkoppen 2068 • *Phone/Fax:* 2711-7012233 • orders@psdprom.co.za • **Distributed in Canada by:** Raincoast • 9050 Shaughnessy St., Vancouver, B.C. V6P 6E5 • *Phone:* (604) 323-7100 • *Fax:* (604) 323-2600

Editorial supervision: Jill Kramer   *Design:* Amy Gingery

Library of Congress Cataloging-in-Publication Data

Franks, Lynne.
  Grow, the modern woman's handbook : how to connect with self, lovers, and others / Lynne Franks.
    p. cm.
  ISBN 1-4019-0226-X (pbk.)
  1. Women—Psychology. 2. Self-actualization (Psychology) 3. Interpersonal relations. I. Title.
  HQ1206.F684 2004
  305.4—dc21

                        2003012885

ISBN 1-4019-0226-X

07 06 05 04   4 3 2 1
1st printing, March 2004

Printed in Thailand

(**Author's Note:** This book is being simultaneously published throughout the English-speaking world, which is why the spelling is in colloquial American English, for which I apologize to my fellow Brits.)

INTRODUCTION

Have you ever been telling a story to a group of women, and they begin nodding their heads, saying how similar things have happened to them? As each woman begins sharing her experiences, an energy gets created that spreads around the group like wildfire. Whether the discussions are about our lovers and husbands, our health, our beliefs, our kids, our work, or how we want to create value in our local and global community, we women empathize, connect, and resonate with each other.

GROW—The Modern Woman's Handbook is aimed at women of all ages who wish to get back in touch with their feminine centers; that is, the place where we all remember how to connect: first, with ourselves and the divine; second, with our families and loved ones; and third, with our local and global communities. I believe that the emergence of feminine values in society must be the way forward if we're to create a positive future for humankind.

This book is based on my own experiences, which have been both good as well as challenging, and which I believe can be used by others as a guide when facing their own challenges. My life as a post-war baby boomer, child of the '60s, wife and mother in the '70s, successful career woman in the '80s, and divorced single parent in the '90s now has me moving into my true feminine self as I continue to seek and learn in the 21st century.

1.

Learning to juggle career and family while living a healthy, fulfilled life has created a whole new set of circumstances that are unique to the modern woman. We put ourselves under a tremendous amount of pressure as we try to be perfect in every situation, usually at great cost to ourselves. I know that when I was trying to create this balance, I always felt as if I were throwing up lots of balls in the air at the same time, rushing from one to another just before they dropped.

The intention of this book is not to create even more balls for you to juggle, but to learn how to gain clarity and strength in living your life to its fullest potential. I have written *GROW* as a guidebook, not a rulebook, so please use the information and exercises as tools to help navigate the journey of your life.

There are a lot of ideas to absorb in this book, some of which may be familiar to you and some of which may be new. You may wish to do the exercises as you read along, or you may decide to focus on the subjects and areas you're particularly concerned with. Some of the exercises are deep and intense, some are light and fun, but all are meant to stimulate you to conscious awareness of the subject matter. There are no right or wrong answers, but you should be as honest as you can, as that's when the most growth will occur.

We're often so busy being busy that the one person we rarely have time to listen to is ourselves. I find that journaling is a way to reflect on new ideas in my life, so I suggest that you do the same as you work through the book—this way, your pen will reflect your process in a way that your conscious mind may not be able to do. You may also work with this book together with a woman friend, using your experiences to help each other gain perspective.

What I've learned is that the answers to so many of my questions can be found deep within me. By creating the space and time to get in touch with my higher self (that part of me that I believe is my connection with the universal source, which many refer to as "God"), I move into a place of wisdom that I rarely experience otherwise.

I believe that my higher self is my pure essence and highest potential, without all the layers of fear and ego that make up my outward personality. I think of her as my best friend, who's always there for me and never lets me down. It's this essence that can see situations from all sides with absolute clarity and without judgment. And when I consciously move into this place—by asking for help through meditation and prayer—I see my truth and intuitively know how to move forward.

My higher self told me that if I start to live according to my natural feminine flow and forget the desire to control everything and everyone in my life, I will obtain more joy and connection than I can ever imagine. I believe she told me to write GROW to share everything I have learned in order to awaken the wise woman in all of you—so that together, we women can move into our fullness of purpose and love.

2.

A Vision for the Future.

Being in public relations for 20 years was about spotting trends, new ideas, and changes in society before they happened. My work in this field wasn't fortune-telling—it merely involved being able to intuitively recognize the future in the present, by spotting shifts and signs that were already out there.

While writing this book, I used my skills in recognizing the changes in our rapidly trans-forming world to take a comprehensive look at all aspects of a 21st-century woman's life. It's only from this perspective that we can learn to flow and integrate with the future and find our source of true feminine wisdom in the present.

Our wisdom comes when we aren't afraid to combine knowledge with love. Pure knowl-edge, devoid of the spirit of love, has led us to a world of destruction and sorrow—so now is the time to recognize the sacred feminine, to recapture the essence of the human heart.

3.

Only when we learn how to get to this place of personal feminine power will we be able to move forward to create change in our communities. When women work together to take on leadership roles and make choices based on sustainable values, that's when a new progressive and enlightened society will evolve.

On a global scale, it's time to change the centuries of thought that have brought us only war, greed, and destruction. It's time for women and men to join together in a new way of solving problems: a way based on feminine wisdom, whereby compassion, grace, intu-ition, and respect can help us nurture ourselves and our planet.

I have learned so much about myself in the process of writing this book, and I hope that you will gain similar insight into your own life while reading it. So enjoy, keep turning the page, and may you join me in recognizing the courageous Goddess you truly are.

•••••

Part 1
Connecting with Self

(Where You Reveal
Your True Self and
Show the Beauty
Underneath)

Taking off the Mask

Who am I really? How do I find the courage to be myself? When will my life really start? How do I reconnect with my feminine essence?

I regularly hear questions like those above from women who may appear to have everything they thought they wanted—families, successful careers, and long-term relationships. But such outward manifestations of a happy life are not enough. We're looking for more . . . we're on a journey to life fulfillment.

As we grow to womanhood, we become a composite of our own and others' projections: the attentive student, the "wild child" teen, the ambitious professional, the loving partner, the dependable wife, and the dedicated mother. However, more often than not, we follow a path that isn't true to our real selves. Influenced by our parents, teachers, friends, boyfriends, husbands, and children—as well as our culture as a whole—we can slip into a lifestyle and career that's alien to our natural tendencies and passions. Some of us give up work to look after families and feel a loss of identity in the process. Others take on a more "masculine" role to survive and be successful in a "man's world."

We often lose sight of who we want to "be" because we're so busy "doing." We take life as it comes, making decisions based on existing behavioral patterns, beliefs, and sometimes fear. And we can often experience years of accumulated dissatisfaction before we take a step backwards and say, "Stop the world—I want to get off and find *me.*"

8.

My Story: Absolutely Me!

It's so easy to lose touch with our true selves . . . I know I lost touch with mine. That was far from my thoughts when I passionately, but naively, started my own public-relations agency from my kitchen table when I was 21 years old. I loved what I was doing, but building up what became Britain's foremost PR firm by the time I was 30 took more out of me than I would have ever anticipated.

I was born busy. Since I was a small child, I remember always rushing somewhere, finding something to do, filling my life with people, noise, and activities. My mother said that as a teenager I rarely sat down to a family meal; instead, I paced around on the telephone eating junk food on the run. As an adult, I was always either working, getting on an airplane, planning more projects, or busy being very social. And wasn't I lucky when e-mails and cell phones came along—I had even more ways of distracting myself! If I happened to find myself with some quiet time, I could always overeat, have obsessive relationships, or throw another party. It took me many years to realize that, yes, I was energetic and creative, but all this activity was just a way to escape from connecting with myself.

My experience is that deep change generally comes during the hard times, rather than when you're coasting along, feeling content with your life. It was only when I felt my life collapsing around me that I realized my being constantly over-busy signaled the need to run away from myself.

After heading my highly successful PR firm for 20 years, having two beautiful children, and being involved in what seemed on the outside to be a good marriage, my life collapsed in one week. I left the company I founded, my marriage split up (with my husband going off with an old family friend), and I stopped practicing my Japanese Buddhist chanting, which in itself had become another form of busyness. Of course life's changes don't have to be so dramatic or painful, but my over-busyness resulted in missing the signs that my life wasn't going well. When I finally recognized those signs, it was almost too late. I had ignored the messages my body was sending me: My energy was low, I had various aches and pains, and I was often depressed. Eating unconsciously and living a hectic, stressed-out life resulted in what I now recognize as major burnout.

9.

I hadn't paid attention to my relationship with my husband, ignoring the obvious warning signals. I hadn't appreciated that I needed to invest time and effort into my marriage and my family. I was in such a state of exhausted chaos that I all I knew was that I couldn't go on as I had been. It was by letting go of everything that I believed made up my identity—my career, my marriage, and my religious practice—that I was able to learn who I really was. But that didn't make things any easier at the time.

And to add to the enormous changes I was going through, the hugely successful TV series <u>Absolutely Fabulous</u> was launched on British TV, featuring Edina, the manic Buddhist/fashionista/publicist, who was said by the media to be based on me. Now while some aspects of this character resembled the craziness of my life as the U.K.'s leading "PR guru," I never identified too closely with Edina (especially her excesses and aggressive relationships with her daughter and mother). Nevertheless, my love/hate relationship with the program was, in many ways, an extraordinary experience. Watching a parody on television that was supposedly based on my life was certainly another good reason to want to get back in touch with the "real" Lynne.

10.

I began an inner and outer journey of discovery, working with different teachers and spiritual leaders on how to connect with my true self. I saw how the simple practices of silence and regular breathing could bring me to a place of personal growth from where I could start to love myself. I learned who I was and how to be in touch with my feminine self, integrating it with my more masculine qualities.

I discovered how important it was to find the time to hear my inner voice, which would guide me through my darkest hours. I started spending quality time with myself, often going out in nature and finding real joy just walking in the mountains and noticing the beauty all around me. In other words, I learned how to be a human "being" instead of a human "doing."

Getting in Touch with the Real You.

To find out who *you* really are, you first have to learn how to listen to your inner voice, your higher self, who ultimately has all the answers to your most probing questions. You need to stretch your crowded life to find time for silence, away from all the busyness and bustle. Once you've found silence, you can then start to listen.

Meditation is the name for the quiet time when you let your mind go empty of all its usual voices, which plan and plot inside your brain. It's the space you create to connect with your intuitive self, that part of you that has the wisdom and answers to all your questions. There are many ways of going deep inside, but first you need to find some quiet "outer space."

Find a place in your home or in nature where you will be able to sit for at least 10 or 15 minutes without interruption, and take a piece of paper and pen to use after your meditation. Sit or lie comfortably with your spine straight, closing your eyes if you wish.

Relax . . . begin to breathe consciously, slowly inhaling deeply. Hold your breath for three beats, exhale slowly, letting go of all thoughts. Repeat this breathing several times.

> *Imagine a beam of light coming from the space between your eyes (or your "third eye"), connecting you with your higher energy. Breathe regularly and steadily as you come into the stillness of your mind and body. Ask only for connection with your "true" self. Whatever your belief system, there is help available to you from the highest part of your being, who is there to guide you.*
>
> *As you go deeper and deeper, ask your unconscious mind to show you who you really are. Since we're all the sum of many different aspects, the answers could be as varied as an artist, a gardener, a dancer, a sexual goddess, a mother, a good friend, a photographer, and so on. Combine your passions, your values, your gifts, and the roles that bring your real joy. You may not even wish to include your profession or responsibilities if you don't believe that they're reflections of your true self.*

Let the answers float around like leaves in the autumn breeze. Don't grasp at them—just keep yourself open to whatever comes in. As your breathing goes slower, taking you deeper into your inner sanctum, know that all is perfect and that you have the answers you need to show you the way forward.

When you feel ready, slowly bring yourself back to normal breathing, becoming aware of the room or space around you and its small background noises. Now, take your paper and pen and start writing down a list detailing every aspect of your identity, which you believe represents the true you.

If you repeat this meditation regularly, you're likely to find that it's the most effective way to allow answers to life's tough questions to come through to your conscious mind. By trusting your intuition, you can cut through illusion and live your life based on the authentic you.

Here are examples of some of the aspects of my true self:

12.

I am a lover.

Now, add your own:

I am a daughter.

_____

I am a dancer.

_____

I am a mother.

_____

I am a compassionate being.

_____

I am a visionary.

_____

I am a leader.

_____

Keep this list where you'll see it every day—on the fridge, on your mirror, or by your computer—as a daily reminder of who you really are.

The Heart of a Woman.

For years we women have fought for equality with men, in business and in life. We want our value in society to be properly acknowledged. While we may have initially taken up such male traits as confrontation and competitiveness, the last thing women want to do is "become" men. However, as society has opened up somewhat to women, many of us *have* become confused about our core gender qualities. Living in a male world and following their ways, not to mention dressing and behaving like them, we seem to have lost touch with our essential feminine selves.

Of course today we acknowledge that both women and men have "male" and "female" characteristics, which used to be thought of as belonging exclusively to one gender or the other. And we all know some men who function more comfortably in their feminine energy and some women who come from a more masculine core, regardless of their sexuality. But over the last several decades, many of us have been struck by the realization that we've come to embody a much stronger male energy than we ever intended—and that we're subsequently out of balance with our true feminine values. Living and working in today's busy, goal-orientated society can lead to our male side taking over—not only in terms of how we relate to other people, but how we relate to ourselves.

13.

Feminism taught us that we could have it all, but in our efforts to have a career, a marriage, children, friends, and a healthy lifestyle, we've often sacrificed the time and space to connect with our true selves. We've learned how to be strong, how to pursue our chosen goals, and how to balance the many demands of our frenetic lives, but sadly we're often left with too little time to replenish our souls.

I've met thousands of women around the world through my workshops and lectures over the last few years, and I've observed that 21st-century females are changing in ways quite different from those of their foremothers. Today we enter the workplace confident that we can do as well or better than men. Certainly such confidence and drive are proof of female empowerment—and that's wonderful. But don't we also too often assume a male pattern of aggressive, competitive behavior; make work our priority; downplay feminine pursuits for fear of being perceived as too soft or weak; and neglect to find the time to nurture ourselves? I recognize this pattern because I assumed it myself.

Having two children in my late 20s didn't change the fast-track, professionally driven course I was on. I adored my children, but like many professional women who came of age in the late '60s and beyond, I was so committed to proving myself in a man's world that I made work my number-one priority.

What happens to those of us who are keenly focused on our careers is that at around age 35, we begin burning out, realizing that we're not happy living a male role in a female body. A woman's natural psychological pattern is to feel contentment and fulfillment through relationships, which we might be able to obtain through our work. But when we get caught up in the more masculine process of evaluating our achievements based on power and material success, we often arrive at a stage of confusion and exhaustion.

Women have reached a crisis point, either physically or emotionally, which signals our unspoken desire to shift to a more feminine way of living and working. It's not just a question of heads hitting the glass ceiling. That ceiling, although still a harsh reality in many companies, is really a wake-up call. Many women eventually realize that the structured, linear environments of large corporations, academic institutions, or even national politics rarely reflect their values. Nor do women feel authentic, creative, and comfortable in such places. It's at this point that many women begin to acknowledge their dissatisfaction and commit to making a major change in their lives.

There are lots of women today who are in the process of leaving high-powered jobs to follow their dreams. Some decide to start a small business on their own or with friends; some set off, backpack on shoulders, to travel the world; some go into the voluntary sector; while others go for further education or, indeed, do start a family. Some move from a busy urban life to a life in the country, where they can combine a less stressful career with time to be with nature. Top accountants leave to become Reiki healers or yoga teachers; corporate executives open online flower shops; and high-powered consultants prefer to work from home, cutting their workload to study art or spend time with their families.

Hundreds of women from across the professional spectrum have told me that burnout from the frenzied, competitive, bureaucratic, workaday world has left them physically ill and sick at heart. They knew they had to do something to change their lives and return to a more feminine way of being, but they didn't know what.

Swinging Both Ways!

So how do we distinguish between being more in our masculine energy than our feminine? It certainly becomes more recognizable once we consciously decide to stay centered in our natural feminine state.

You can change your energy by dressing in a different way or changing the way you carry yourself, speak, or interact. Why not try to experiment with the outer aspects of how you present yourself and see how it makes you feel inside. Have some fun with this exercise, which exaggerates both your natural feminine and masculine inclinations. For one day, dress in your most masculine clothes. Perhaps wear some smart trousers with a "power" jacket and flat shoes, or a mannish T-shirt and jeans. Wear your hair in a severe style, with little or no makeup and no nail polish. Look at yourself in the mirror and see the "male" you. Go into male postures and see how your body language changes. Practice walking and acting in a masculine fashion, perhaps even lowering your voice when speaking.

Go to work or out for dinner in that energy, interacting with your colleagues and friends from a place of male action-oriented, logical behavior. Agree to go for a beer with the "boys" after work, try not to flirt or use your feminine wiles, and just relax into your full male energy. See how it feels, how people treat you, and how you engage with others. Does it feel natural, or are you very uncomfortable? Write down your experience at the end of the day, observing your emotions and feelings.

The following day, dress in a more feminine outfit, perhaps a softly shaped dress and some high heels. Do your hair up, put on some lipstick, and watch your body language in the mirror as you move into this feminine energy. Feel your most womanly—allowing

15.

your natural nurturing, sensual self to be seen—and observe how differently people react to you. Again, write your experience down, noting how comfortable you felt and whether it seemed natural for you.

Finally, on the third day, consciously integrate your male and female way of dressing and acting. Perhaps pair a soft, feminine shirt with a tailored suit, and accessorize with some gorgeous jewelry and red lipstick. Again, observe your energy. Note whether you become assertive or connected with your friends and workmates.

Play with your energy during the day, introducing both feminine and masculine behavior, and see how that feels. Which energy reflects who you truly are? Be aware that we all have our feminine and masculine sides that, when integrated together, can create a powerful whole. But first we need to return to our feminine core, where we can explore the dynamic of our being and how to use it to become all we were born to be.

16.

Return to the Feminine.

To make the shift from leading a masculine-centric life to one that's influenced by more feminine qualities, we need to change some of the aspects of the way we live our lives. We need to consciously surround ourselves with more feminine sensuality and beauty. We need to remind ourselves what being a woman feels like. We need to invite the feminine back into our souls.

In other words, we need to find the space for quiet walks in the country or in local parks, consciously seeing the beauty of the flowers, witnessing the scurry of the squirrels scrambling up the majestic oak trees, and hearing the songs of the birds. We need to spend time with other women, sharing experiences and ideas. We need to make it a priority to take care of our bodies and well-being. We need to remember to consciously breathe and stretch, and to try to find quality time to be on our own.

Despite still leading a busy professional life, I find it crucial for my health and sanity to find time to be in the country, observing the splendor of nature that's all around me.

This nurtures the core of my feminine being. I know that demanding young children or a busy job (especially if you live in a large, bustling city) can put time to enjoy nature very much on the back burner. But even in a sprawling, urban landscape like London, which is my home base, it's possible to walk in the parks, whether using them as a route to walk to in between meetings or collecting the kids from school. Becoming aware of the trees in the streets and the birdsong in the city is how the urban woman starts dancing her dance.

It's possible to see the beauty of nature everywhere if we open up to it, even in gray city rain, and replenish our souls by acknowledging our connection to the miraculous way that Mother Earth continues her cycle of renewal and rebirth.

Bring Nature into the Home

We women need to surround ourselves with natural beauty. Healthy green plants, which reflect life itself, need to be nurtured with good light and water, much like we do. Fresh flowers also brighten our environment as their sweet scents nurture our souls.

Surrounding ourselves with natural beauty—such as treasured pieces of driftwood or shells from favorite beaches, stones and pebbles found on special walks, and crystals discovered when traveling in exotic places—can make the inside of our homes and personal sanctuaries blossom in harmony with our feminine selves.

There's no better way to stay grounded with our feminine energy than by growing and nurturing living things. So for those of you lucky enough to have a garden, plant seeds, grow a tree, have an herb garden in a window box, produce your own vegetables, smell your jasmine, trail your roses, and take pride in the earth under your fingernails.

By connecting with the beauty of this planet, we become more loving to ourselves and to everyone we connect with. Nature gives us more energy and enthusiasm to follow our passions and reclaim the feminine.

Dance, Cook, Paint, Create

I have rediscovered cooking since I've been living my life in my feminine energy, and I enjoy nothing more than to prepare a simple meal for family and friends. The act of nurturing and feeding others from a place of love brings me rewards a thousand times over.

Dancing can also help us get in touch with our sensual, feminine selves. When I ask groups of women during my talks and workshops if they love to dance, they always say yes . . . but admit to rarely doing it. Self-consciousness may often mean that many women decide to leave dancing behind in their youth. Well, now is the time for us to get back in touch with the rhythm of the drums and let our hearts soar. We need to put on our dancing shoes and some great music and shake up our feminine energy.

We can also get connected with our creative feminine source by writing in a journal; painting; or making collages, pottery, or jewelry. By getting back in touch with our childhood love of creating beautiful objects, we can become the artists we were always meant to be.

So grow your hair; wear feminine clothes; enjoy the sensuality of smell, touch, and sound; and learn to love the feminine, gorgeous goddess that you truly are.

Living Life in the Feminine

There are many different ways of bringing the feminine back into our lives, but what would work for *you?* Would it be dressing a different way, changing your hair, having more quiet time, being in nature, dancing, bringing out your creative artist, cooking, gardening, or creating a beautiful sanctuary for yourself? Or perhaps a mixture of all the above?

We're going to be looking at many ways of developing aspects of your spiritual, sensual, healthy, wise, and feminine self through this book. Why not make a start with some small life changes? Take some quiet meditation time, then fill in the following spaces with five activities you could introduce regularly into your life that would make your heart sing with joy.

19.

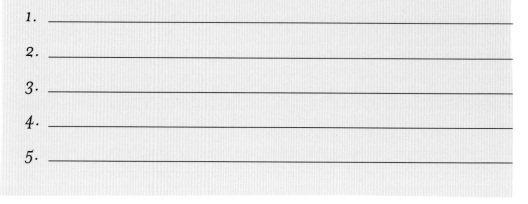

I am going to celebrate the glory of my true feminine being by finding space in my life to:

1. _____

2. _____

3. _____

4. _____

5. _____

The Power of the Feminine.

20.

Living our lives from our feminine strengths, instead of constantly trying to fit into more masculine roles, can give us the necessary tools to connect with our authentic selves. Living this way means being creative, sensual, compassionate, intuitive, nurturing, aware women, acknowledging that our feminine strengths form the path to a fulfilled life.

When I think of my feminine strengths, I'm aware of my compassion, my ability to connect and empathize easily with others, my nurturing tendencies, my intuition, my sensuality, and my love of dance. All of these qualities have helped me get in touch with my feminine core and move away from the more masculine Lynne that ran my life for so many years. Now I'm more physically affectionate, I express myself more easily, and I truly listen to others. While retaining the qualities that made me a successful businesswoman in my 30s, such as my energy and vision, my focus has shifted to a more open, flowing attitude to outcome. By letting go of some of my more masculine control tendencies, I'm more creative, yet still able to "make things happen."

Of course it's equally important to recognize our male tendencies—that is, our more action-orientated, linear side—because what we ultimately need to do is integrate our masculine and feminine energies to create our "whole" being, while remaining aware of our core gender qualities. For example, by consciously moving into my feminine strengths, I've retained the role of a leader in my professional life while coming from a place of love, openness, and peace. I've learned that humor, grace, and respectful communication can inspire women and men to far greater achievement in building a better world for future generations than the old paradigm of money and power could ever do.

I believe that through our feminine strengths, women can work toward creating awareness of spiritual and sustainable values in local and global communities, through business, grass-roots politics, and networking.

Your Feminine Strengths.

Acknowledging the power of your feminine strengths and how to use them consciously will bring benefits into all areas of your life. See how certain feminine qualities that you may have previously thought of as weaknesses are in truth your strengths. You may have thought that your need to chat was a waste of time, for instance, but it's really a natural female quality in connecting with others. Or perhaps you felt that your ability to do lots of things at the same time meant a lack of focus, when it really means that you, like most women, are a natural multitasker.

Here are some examples of some of our feminine strengths, but do add your own:

Feminine Strengths:	How It Works in My Life
Nurturing	Makes me a caring colleague, employer, mother, and friend.
Empathy	Means I can identify with others.
Networking skills	Connects me with like-minded souls, both personally and professionally.
Intuition	Helps me make wise decisions.
Sensuality	Brings pleasure into my life.

Feminine Strengths:	How It Works in My Life

Facing Our Fears.

It's so easy to put off the commitment to live the rest of our lives in the fullness of our wise and feminine glory. For a long time, I wondered what I'd be doing or where I'd be based when I started to live my real life. Just like many single women I'd met, I believed that once I was in a happy, loving relationship, the rest of my life would pan out perfectly. (Or for some it's a belief that they can't start being who they truly are until they've had a baby, or their children leave home, or they've lost 20 pounds, or they finally receive that promotion at work.)

Well, I finally got it—these are all excuses! This is no rehearsal. I was already living the rest of my life every single day, and like so many women, I was using these excuses to put off the responsibility of moving into my full potential.

So why do so many of us do this? What is the common female trait that holds us back in so many areas of our lives? It is, of course, our own fears.

Getting Out of the Comfort Zone

Lack of self-confidence and self-esteem are at the core of most women's fears and insecurities. We don't believe we can be everything we want to be, nor do we think we're good enough to deserve success or happiness.

To open up to new possibilities for our lives, we have to transform our beliefs. We must let go of the negative thought patterns about ourselves that we most likely acquired in childhood. Of course, this isn't so easy. Facing our deepest fears can be a scary proposition—it takes courage and conscious awareness to face these patterns and shift our negative beliefs into positive ones.

We're often afraid of facing our true selves because we know that if we do, it will bring about change and uncertainty. After all, it always feels more comfortable to stay in familiar territory, even if it doesn't make us happy, than to step into the unknown. And there's no guarantee that life becomes easier once we've embarked on this journey of positive growth. The reality is that many more challenges will crop up as we continue along this path. But by keeping ourselves present and open, we will stay connected with our truth.

We have to be mindful that, even if we're momentarily thrown off center, we're going to experience a process of learning and development. We're moving into the fullness of our being, creating a relationship (in the truest sense of the word) with ourselves and the divine spirit in us all.

23.

By facing our fears, moving through them, and connecting with our courage, we *can* break old patterns. And the rewards when we do are so fulfilling that we'll wonder what took us so long.

For many of us, facing our fears is something we do every day of our lives. It's by acknowledging ourselves for having the courage to step up and deal with life's little challenges (as well as its big ones), that can make us appreciate how truly brave we are. For others, it can sometimes be advantageous to get some professional help from a counselor or psychotherapist to help break through fears.

There are many forms of professional help available, so finding the right person for you usually occurs through personal recommendation and trial and error. You need to feel comfortable with your therapist and his or her methods, so meet with a few different ones before you decide which one you most resonate with. Your intuition will let you know whom to trust—who will be right for you.

If you have large blockages from childhood that are stopping you from moving ahead—and many of us do—then psychotherapy can be of enormous help. Recognizing our patterns for what they are, and how they got there, is already a major part of the healing.

Another approach is to find yourself a life coach or mentor who's able to give you a more objective perspective on your life. This type of support can work both in groups or individually, giving you the foundation to enable you to break through the barriers and fears that are holding you back. Once you've made the decision to live life to the fullest, you can truly connect with your deepest potential for joy, allowing your talents and wisdom to shine, while learning to love yourself respectfully yet shamelessly.

Fun, laughter, connection, and life fulfillment are all there for the taking if we open up to our authenticity and move into a space of wholeness and trust. Of course it can be unsettling to accept ourselves in all our rich complexity, but it is so much worse to hold back and lose out on all the joy that's ours for the asking.

24.

Shine a Light on Me.

Being in the spotlight is never easy—in fact, for most people, standing up in front of a group and talking is a chore to be dreaded. I once read that public speaking ranks as the number-one fear for most people. And talking about oneself seems to conjure up even greater anxiety.

This exercise is about pushing past both of these fears, but there's a little safety net involved. Invite three or four close friends over for a girls' night. Explain that this will be a special evening full of surprises. Once they arrive, have a warm environment waiting, perhaps a room full of candles and throw pillows—a place where you can get comfortable and open up to each other.

The agenda for the evening is simple: Each woman, including you, will get up within the circle of the group and talk about herself openly and honestly without interruption for at

least 5 (but no more than 15) minutes. The only requirement is that everyone speak from their hearts, not hiding behind any masks or presenting a front, either positive or negative.

You can talk about your dreams, your hopes, your ambitions, what brings you joy, what brings you sorrow, and what your accomplishments and disappointments have been. You can talk about relationships with men, your parents, or your children, but you should especially talk about your relationship with *yourself.* What do you like most about your-self, and what do you like least? What are your inner strengths and your inner fears? What qualities in yourself have given you the impetus to succeed, and what have held you back in certain areas? Find the courage to be vulnerable.

After you finish, take a few moments of quiet time to let your words and emotions res-onate with all present, then invite your girlfriends to reflect on what you said. The only requirement is that what they say must be both honest and positive—no false encour-agement, but no harsh critiquing either.

26. When all the women have spoken, let the rest of the evening unfold naturally. Some women may want to keep talking and sharing, while some may want to kick off their shoes, put on some music, and dance with celebration. Whatever happens, know that everyone in this circle has met their fears and opened their souls to be witnessed, and that, in and of itself, is an incredible act of courage.

Falling in Love with Yourself.

One of the biggest fears we women have is the fear of not having someone to love us. While having a partner is very natural and can offer tremendous rewards, many of us are partnerless at one time or another in our lives. Does that lessen our womanhood? Of course not. Often, having a partner is just another mask behind which we hide our full identity. So many women come into their own after the breakup of a long relationship. The fact is, it's not about the partnership at all—the ability to truly love ourselves and our lives, first and foremost, determines whether we live life to our full potential or not.

For example, a couple of years ago I persuaded my sister, Sue, to come with me to a natural-health retreat in Southern California from her home in Toronto. It was around the middle of February, and my sister's loving husband of some 30 years, Murray, had given her not one, but three valentines to open on the 14th. As a single woman, I decided that the only way to deal with the dreaded Valentine's Day was to look at the whole experience as an opportunity to show love to myself.

I took to the retreat some pieces of white posterboard, lots of snapshots of me with the people and places I love, some old magazines to cut up, a bunch of little multicolored heart stickers, and gold and silver felt-tip pens. I then took tremendous delight in making myself several poster-sized valentines, as a constant reminder of how loved, and loving, I truly am.

I used different themes for each poster, representing various aspects of my life. I made one that had a great shot of me in the center and focused on the many locales I love in the world, places of natural beauty that gave me so much joy. I added photographs of my "heart" home in Deià on the Spanish island of Mallorca, where I've spent so many happy times, together with words and affirmations that were appropriate to my connection with the beauty of Mother Earth.

27.

I made another "Valentine poster" featuring lots of photos of me with the people I love most. I included my mother, my children, and other members of my beloved family; my godchildren; my women friends; and particularly, some of the wonderful men who have contributed so much to my life as lovers and friends. Again, I used appropriate affirmations and words to remind myself of my good fortune in knowing and loving so many wonderful people and being loved by them in return. I reminded myself with words and phrases that I am also loved by the divine in me.

Even though I did receive several "e-valentines" from thoughtful, loving friends that particular year, most of all I appreciated the cards I'd made for myself, which looked great on my studio wall when I returned home.

Don't wait until February 14th to make a valentine for yourself. Use any opportunity you have to make celebration collages and posters—which include pictures of glorious *you*—surrounded by the people, places, animals, and activities that fill your life with love.

Learning to Say "I Love Me."

Love is like a muscle, and it needs to be exercised regularly—yet learning to love and appreciate yourself can often be the hardest part of your life journey. By acknowledging your feminine strengths and courage, you're on the right road, but you so often need to reaffirm your love for your feminine self.

Positive affirmations repeated aloud can be the most powerful way of reminding yourself how special you are. These are particularly effective when combined with physiology and integrated into your muscle memory by moving your body at the same time.

28.

Whether you're jumping, running, dancing, walking, or even standing still looking into a mirror, make repeated positive affirmations a key part of your daily routine.

Your Daily Affirmation Workout

These are some of my personal affirmations. Why not start repeating them aloud to see if they fit, and then develop some of your own?

- *I am a wise, beautiful, sexy woman.*
- *I am a leader, committed to building a better world.*
- *I love myself more and more every day, in every way.*

- *I am a beloved child of God.*
- *I live my life based on love, not fear.*
- *I live my truth, I walk my talk.*
- *I am open, optimistic, and flexible.*
- *I am the fulfilled, joyful woman I was born to be.*

Taking off the Mask.

Now is the time to take off the mask that you've been wearing all these years, and reveal yourself in all your splendor. With the removal of this mask, a whole new world will unfold, because once you start living in complete truth and authenticity, there will be a new freedom to your life. You won't have to hide from anything—and you won't have to try to be anyone but yourself, with all your beauty and your flaws. Showing your vulnerability as well as your strength makes you far more human and appealing as a person. And when you come from a place of openness, people usually respond in turn. Once you take off *your* mask, they will find it safe to take off theirs.

You'll also find that it's easier to make deeper levels of connection. There will never be a need to try to impress others, because living in your integrity and truth without a mask is, in and of itself, impressive in our world. Those who do it stand out and shine like diamonds.

Action and Exercise

When you decide to make a significant shift in your life, it's often good to symbolically mark your transition.

Go to a store and buy at least two inexpensive clear or white masks, the type they sell at Halloween. Also buy a small paint set.

With the first mask, paint the "old you" upon its face. Think of the qualities that you want to get rid of, such as fear, fault-finding, obsessiveness, and insecurity. Let the colors and shapes that represent these traits flow onto the mask. They might come out as realistic symbols and designs or abstract swaths of color. When you finish, let the paint dry and then put the mask on.

Go to the mirror and look at yourself. See all the traits you wish to bid good-bye to. If you want, have a final, departing dance with this mask, then take it off and destroy it. If it's hardened plaster, you can break it with a hammer; if it's paper, you can burn it; if it's plastic, cut it into little pieces.

Now take the second mask and paint the new traits you're taking on. What does openness, truth, ease, and integrity look like? After this mask is ready, put it on as well. Dance with it, and let these new traits permeate into your soul. Go to a mirror and look at this mask, seeing how the "new you" is represented. Then take this mask off and see yourself: a reborn woman shining in her true beauty. Destroy this mask as well, because now there is no need for masks at all.

The GROW Commitment.

Repeat this final affirmation, knowing that you've broken through your own boundaries to the glory of your true self:

I have taken off the mask of illusion and see the beauty and grace that is me.

• • • • •

Chapter

2

Your Body Is Your Temple

(Where You Learn
That Loving Your Body
Is Loving Yourself)

Am I as healthy as I could be? Do I put self-care on the back burner compared with the other aspects of my life? Do I love myself enough to nurture my own body? Do I realize just how beautiful I am?

One of our most important tasks as women is to learn to love and connect with our bodies. By taking responsibility for our health and well-being, we can manifest the strength and focus to help create the life of our dreams. But if we don't truly love ourselves or believe that we are worthy of self-nurture, we can take on a negligent attitude toward our upkeep.

My Story: My Wake-Up Call

The reason I know that stress, negativity, and guilt can undermine the pursuit of self-care is because I've struggled with this pattern myself. When I ran my business, I lived a pressurized life—I was always rushing off to the acupuncturist or masseur, thinking that if I could take my body in to be "serviced," it would take care of any ill health I was experiencing. I was always late for my appointments; I'd arrive feeling stressed and then run out to yet another appointment. No wonder any benefits from the treatments didn't seem to last very long!

My head felt like the "real me," while my body was simply the vehicle that carried me around. Unfortunately, I was so into my head that I got completely out of touch with my body. I kept planning to start a regular exercise routine—I even did so now and then—but I just didn't give my own self-care enough of a priority to plan it into my life in a nonstressful way. At that point in my life, I ate without thinking, I wasn't in touch with my sexuality, and I'd even stopped my beloved dancing. I periodically dove into dietary fads: macrobiotic diets; all cabbage soup or watermelon diets; lemon-water, maple-syrup, and cayenne-pepper fasts; food combining; and the Atkins, Pritikin, Zone, and Beverly Hills diets—you name the program, I probably tried it. I learned a lot about what worked for me and what didn't. The problem was that after I finished a particular diet, I'd go straight back into bingeing.

I'd also try the latest vitamin supplements; buy, but never have time to read, the newest books on health; and was a sucker for whoever was the holistic practitioner of the moment. I thought I could pay others to sort my health out and I'd just come along for the ride. Sure, much of what I tried was helpful, but I missed out on the most important key to good health: I needed to love myself sufficiently to be willing to take personal responsibility for my well-being. I had to create a lifestyle where I didn't feel so stressed, where I had time to breathe good air, and where I appreciated my body and all the hard work it performed on my behalf.

The realization that it was time to change my lifestyle came when I lost my two best female friends to cancer within a couple of years of each other. Both lived healthy lives, didn't smoke, and ate sensibly. Of course, there could be many different reasons why they got sick, but the only thing I know for sure is that they both held a lot of stress inside their bodies. Like me, they ran their own PR agency and juggled a demanding business with motherhood and marriage. I loved them deeply and was devastated by losing them—so it was time for me to take a deep look at my own habits.

Soon after this wake-up call, I moved from London to California for five years, where there are huge industries devoted to staying youthful and healthy. I became aware of alternative ways of eating and exercising, learning the importance of consuming organic vegetables and fruit, the power of a raw or even semi-raw diet, the need to drink a lot of pure water, and the positive effect on my body by exercising in some way almost every day. California has the greatest natural-food stores and farmers' markets in the world—together with a wonderful climate, this greatly encouraged my living healthfully.

Now that I'm based back in London, I realize that I can create a healthy lifestyle wherever I am. By staying aware of my body's needs, I care for myself sufficiently to prioritize my physical well-being on a daily basis. Of course I slip up: I love good food and confess to being a seasonal chocoholic. But I'm stronger and healthier than I've ever been in my life, and I'm finally appreciating my body for the fine, healthy service it has always given me.

Living Life to the Fullest.

Women, on average, live long lives, so it's up to us to live as healthfully as possible. With all the knowledge available to us about the importance of good nutrition, exercise, and lifestyle, we have the opportunity of living a youthful, vital existence for many years.

Each one of us has a unique body with its own individual health requirements. But there are some important commonalities and general guidelines that can help prevent disease and sickness for us all. Throughout this chapter, we're going to discover how to create a harmonious, balanced life by listening to, respecting, and loving our bodies. We're going to learn how to nurture ourselves with healthy nutrition, exercise, and meditation, and to recognize the physical and mental bad habits that may be causing us harm.

Joy, laughter, and an optimistic attitude are the keys to enjoying good health. Sharing our experiences with others, giving and receiving loving touch, and creating an environment that feeds our sensory needs are all elements of healthy living. However, fear, anxiety, worry, and anger are some of the biggest causes of toxic stress in the body, which can lead to sickness. We need to learn to listen to our bodies and recognize the situations that create emotional discomfort and potential ill health.

Acknowledge Your Beauty, Inside and Out.

I need to get rid of my wrinkles. I'm too fat to find a man. I look too old to get the new job I want. I hate my nose, mouth, eyes, legs, stomach . . .

How many of us have had these thoughts or heard them uttered by our friends? The constant need we women have to be reassured about our looks goes beyond any boundaries of age or experience. And it just doesn't make any sense. Yet, even though it affects our judgments and decisions and is totally disempowering, this kind of thinking can be quite difficult to shift.

There are various psychological reasons for women's problems with self-esteem in today's society. When it comes to our looks, it's so easy to get caught up in the images of beauty perpetuated by the media and advertising industries. They want us to believe that only when we appear to be young, slim, and perfect will we be considered beautiful. Well, having worked in beauty and fashion for many years, I have news for you: You *are* beautiful. Perfection is a myth—even supermodels have cellulite!

Ideas about what constitutes beauty not only change over time but vary considerably from culture to culture. Some of the most beautiful and sexy individuals I have ever seen are in the New Zealand city of Auckland, which is also the unofficial capital for the South Pacific Islands. Natives of Samoa, Tonga, Fiji, and other Pacific Islands are clearly identified by their confident, larger-than-life bodies, which are wrapped in bold island textiles. They certainly don't resemble the skinny, pubescent bodies we see on the pages of fashion magazines, but they're simply gorgeous. The same goes for many women from Africa, the Caribbean, and Latin America, where beautiful, round bodies are considered sexy and desirable. So why are we women of the Western world obsessed with being abnormally thin?

38.

We all have different body shapes, so it's important to love and accept what we've got. Our responsibility to ourselves is to care for our bodies so that we can enjoy optimal health and not worry whether we fit in with the latest dictates of the fashion and glamour industries.

And what about our obsession with looking older? Clearly our bodies and faces change as we age: Lines appear, wrinkles show up, and we don't look at all like we did at 18. But none of the signs of aging can stop us from being in our true beauty. Yes, it's a hackneyed phrase, but *beauty comes from within*—not from a bottle, an injection, or the latest face cream.

I would never try to suggest that you shouldn't try plastic surgery or any other cosmetic procedure to change your looks, if that's what will make you feel more confident. I had my nose straightened when I was 19 for breathing as well as cosmetic reasons. I certainly felt better about myself afterwards, although my boyfriend at the time loved me just as much before I had the operation as he did after.

Many years later I tried Botox, which was a total disaster for me. Botox uses the poison created from botulism bacteria to paralyze facial muscles. After the toxic injections in my forehead seeped through the targeted area, my right eye began to droop severely. It appeared (fortunately, only temporarily) as if I'd a stroke. I have subsequently heard many similar or worse horror stories from other women. I also realized just how bland and characterless we can look when our muscles are frozen. It sure cured me of wanting a wrinkle-free forehead!

I do suggest that you thoroughly research any cosmetic changes you may be planning: Look on the Internet for negative stories as well as successful ones, ask your friends if they know others who have already tried the same procedure so that you can see how it worked for them, and check out which wrinkle-banning injections contain toxic poison or are animal based. Also, be aware that plastic surgery is usually extensive, invasive surgery; protect yourself by taking arnica (a natural remedy for healing the body's tissue that's available in any health-food store), as well as consuming healthy foods and lots of water during the weeks leading up to the operation. And remember that breathing fresh air, drinking lots of water, following a healthy diet, and getting regular exercise are much cheaper and more effective ways of looking radiant!

Taking Care of Ourselves Lovingly.

As I wrote in *The SEED Handbook,* "There is nothing more sexy than confidence." This is so important it's worth repeating: *There is nothing more sexy than confidence.* When we feel happy and confident in who we are, and when our energy is strong and our spirits are good, that's when we appear to be our most attractive—and sexy. And we feel like this when we're taking care of ourselves lovingly and respectfully. We feel strong when we put that extra effort into exercising, eating well, and nurturing ourselves. If we love ourselves, others will respond positively.

We modern women have to learn to nurture ourselves, which is always a challenge with our busy agendas. Juggling a career, running a home, looking after the family, and keeping a relationship going leaves little time to look after ourselves. We often feel guilty about time away from our "responsibilities," yet taking care of ourselves has to be the priority if we're going to be able to do anything else properly.

Simple Ways to Nurture Yourself

It's often the simple things that can create a feeling of self-love. Why not make a list of some of the things you could do regularly that will give you a sense of balance and well-being? These are some of my suggestions, but please add your own. I know you have some!

Bathe regularly in oils and candlelight

Dance with abandon

Walk in nature

Fill the house with flowers and plants

Wear sensual fabrics

Regularly cook a healthy, delicious meal

Make a vegetable or fruit smoothie every morning

Write in my journal

_____

_____

_____

_____

_____

40.

On the other hand, don't let self-nurturing become another way of getting stressed. If you regularly run late in heavy traffic while trying to get to the gym or your yoga class, you could be putting toxic pressure on your body that more than negates any good the exercises themselves could do for you. By the same token, if you're so rigid about your dietary habits that you worry you won't be eating exactly the right food if you visit friends, you could create a negative mind-set around eating, which will create acid. It's all about balance.

Healthy Mind, Healthy Body.

An essential element of maintaining a healthy body is a healthy mind and a healthy attitude. The cycle of well-being is reliant on the balance of our emotions, stress level, and physical condition. Most of us are aware of the mind-body connection, but do we fully appreciate how the mind—including our thought patterns, beliefs, and attitudes—can truly be instrumental in creating physical well-being, even in treating physical disorders?

42.

Meditation, visual imagery, and deep breathing are all recognized techniques to transform negative thought patterns and alleviate stress. As I mentioned in Chapter 1, meditation, together with conscious and deep breathing, is a great way to relax and has a strong, positive effect on your health. If you can build up to around 15 minutes or more in the morning, with various mini-breaks during the day, this quiet "inner time" will create substantial physical as well as psychological changes. Physically, it will lower your heart rate and blood pressure as well as improve your oxygen circulation. Psychologically, meditation and mind relaxation will give you the peace and wisdom to get rid of stress, fears, and anxiety.

One of the best ways to get used to going to a place of inner healing is by listening to tapes or CDs, where you're taken through a guided journey to a place of stillness and reflection. I've listened to many of these through the years and particularly enjoy those spoken by Sister Jayanti, a senior teacher in the female-led spiritual and meditation network, the Brahma Kumaris.

B.K. Jayanti uses her eloquent, soft voice to take the listener to a deep place of connection with the self. She believes that meditation and life are intertwined. In her book, *God's Healing Power: How Meditation Can Help Transform Your Life,* she writes:

> As the first step in meditation, I give myself the luxury of looking at what is going on inside me at a deeper level. I don't want to be a stranger to myself any longer, but to know myself, value myself, respect myself, and even love myself. I want to learn to use my thoughts in the most effective way possible. I want to make my mind my friend.

Daily meditation, along with using visual imagery and deep breathing, will develop your mind/body connection and give you tools to help create the healthy, vital body you deserve.

Gratitude is also a great healer, so why not take this opportunity to thank your inner body for all the hard work it's doing on your behalf? The following meditation will accomplish just that.

43.

Thanking the Body: A Meditation

Once again, find your quiet place and sit or lie comfortably with your spine straight. Let your thoughts come and go as you relax into your breathing. Then go deeper by picturing a beam of light coming from the sun and going directly to your forehead, just above and between your eyes. Now, drawing particular attention to your breath, go even deeper. Feel that golden light spread from the middle of your forehead (your third eye) through your entire body. Imagine that light as a golden ray of sunshine, warming your body from the inside.

And now, as you glow from within with this golden light, bring to mind your organs, one at a time, and send them their deserved "thank you" for working to keep you a healthy, functioning woman.

Thank you, skin, for being the conduit to the outer world of sensation and the gateway to my inner health.

Thank you, lungs, for breathing in the sweet air so that I might fill my body with life-giving oxygen.

Thank you, heart, for beating so regularly, for being my engine by pumping life-blood through my body.

Thank you, liver, for being my body's purifier, filtering toxins from my system.

Thank you, kidneys, for regulating the water flow and maintaining my equilibrium of fluids.

Thank you, intestines and colon, for efficiently breaking down food and carrying away waste.

Thank you, uterus, for being the magical incubator of life.

Thank you, genitals, for giving me the joy and pleasure of being a woman.

As you send your gratitude to those places of your body that are seldom acknowl-
edged, reflect on the miracle of how they work in concert to allow you to live a full
life each and every moment. And then, slowly, with your spirit full of gratitude, bring
your attention back to your breath and ever so slowly return to the present moment.

Toxic Meltdown—Acid Overload.

Toxic accumulation—whether emotional, environmental, nutritional, or spiritual—has serious repercussions on our health and quality of life. We're bombarded with toxins from every direction: from the increased use of pesticides on non-organic vegetables, fruit, and textiles; from domestic cleaning materials containing harmful ingredients; from hormone-laden water; and from the very air we breathe—in other words, toxic chemicals enter our bodies every day. And if we combine these toxins with insufficient oxygen and water in the body, a stressful lifestyle, low nutrient intake, and inefficient elimination of waste, we will create an ideal environment for disease to develop.

According to Dr. Robert Young, one of the world's most respected nutritional microbiolo-gists who specializes in the field of cellular biology, the most crucial factor that affects our health is the breakdown of our immune system due to an acid/alkaline imbalance in our bodies. In his book, *Sick and Tired?: Reclaim Your Spiritual Terrain* (written with his wife, Shelley), Dr. Young explains that excessive acid accumulation in the stomach, intestines, and other crucial organs comes from unhealthy foods—and it combines with stress and negative attitudes to create a lack of energy and even sickness in the body.

Dr. Young (along with an increasingly growing number of health practitioners and scien-tists) believes that the presence of germs or viruses alone does not cause disease because such substances are often present when the carrier is healthy—instead, disease develops when someone creates the unhealthy terrain inside their body through excessive acid buildup. Dr. Young's years of extensive research have led him to the conclusion that a change to a more vegetable-based, alkaline diet and sprouted wheatgrass-based

45.

supplements, along with regular exercise and a positive belief system, can create the necessary alkaline balance to eliminate the possibilities of a variety of illnesses.

My own visits to the Optimum Health Institute in San Diego, California, have introduced me to the value of eating raw, "living" vegetables and fruit, together with the importance of drinking wheatgrass. My visits have been purely to detox and get back to eating healthfully; however, I've seen many cases of seriously sick people get cured, simply by following the right nutrition and regular elimination in this nonmedical, not-for-profit institute. It's not for everyone, but as David Wolfe, the raw-food guru who's also based on San Diego, says in his book, *Eating for Beauty:*

> One who eats for beauty becomes a work of art in progress. Nature's paintbrush immediately sets about applying food-mineral cosmetics to the inner tissues, which become visible externally in the warm, vivid, youthful freshness of the hair, nails, and skin.

It's not too hard to see from your own body what makes you feel good and what doesn't. If you eat a load of acid-forming fare such as fried foods, heavy red meat, and rich desserts; and then mix in alcohol, coffee, and cigarettes, chances are you won't feel too good the next morning. That's why big holidays like Christmas, Thanksgiving, and birthdays, with all their associated overeating and celebratory drinking, can literally make you sick!

As far as your nutritional intake is concerned, Dr. Diana Schwarzbein, one of the U.S.'s leading authorities on metabolic healing, says in her bestseller The Schwarzbein Principle: The Truth About Losing Weight, Being Healthy, and Feeling Younger (co-authored with Nancy Deville): "If you are aging rapidly on the cellular level, you are going to look older and feel older much faster."

Although you cannot change normal metabolic aging, you do have control over accelerated metabolic aging. In fact, it is possible to stop and even heal some of the damage done to your body by the accelerated metabolic aging process. Some things that are scientifically proven to age our bodies faster are:

46.

- *Alcohol*

- *Artificial sweeteners*

- *Caffeine*

- *Lack of exercise*

- *Poor nutrition*

- *Prescription or over-the-counter drug use*

- *Steroids*

- *Stimulants and other recreational drugs*

- *Stress*

- *Tobacco*

Of course our bodies all differ, but if you feel sluggish or bloated in any way; or you're suffering from poor digestion, headaches, aching joints, stuffed-up sinuses, fungus under your nails, and/or a general lack of energy, it's probable that you're ingesting something that doesn't agree with you. It also probably means that you have *candida albicans,* or yeast, growing unchecked in your body.

Candida is often a normal component of our bodies and can live in harmony with acidophilus, the "good bacteria" that aids digestion and elimination. But antibiotics, hormones, birth-control pills, and steroids can suppress acidophilus, allowing yeast to grow unchecked. And once the little candida bugs are running riot through our digestive systems, they crave the very foods that will spread them even further. Wheat, sugar (including fructose), alcohol, refined carbohydrates, and overprocessed foods will encourage yeast to grow.

The good news is that we can reverse the situation of yeast, toxicity, and acid overload anytime we want by changing our unhealthy habits and lifestyle to a more balanced way of living.

47•

Colonics-Cleaning Out the Waste.

One of the keys to good health is proper elimination—what goes in should come out in a regular and healthy fashion. Unfortunately, our modern diets and stressful lifestyles hinder healthful digestion to the point that we suffer a variety of related maladies. The problem originates in our colon. The purpose of this five-foot-long coiled tube located below our stomachs is to absorb essential vitamins and minerals through its dense vascular lining and, at the same time, push through waste matter that is to be expelled. When the colon's walls narrow because of waste-deposit buildup, the difficulties begin, including constipation, irritable bowel syndrome (IBS), and even toxic seepage into the body, which can lead to headaches and fatigue. One expert in this field estimates that 80 percent of critical illnesses have a basis in a malfunctioning bowel.

Colonic irrigation (or if you prefer, a self-induced enema) has been around in one form or another since the Egyptians practiced it in 1500 B.C. As performed by therapists today, it's an easy, safe, and painless procedure in which a speculum sends a gentle, warm stream of water through the colon, cleaning out the buildup of waste material. It's like getting your insides showered—afterwards you feel cleansed, light, and energized. I've tried it and highly recommend it.

48.

The Modern Woman's Well-Informed Diet.

Our bodies are miraculous. If we listen to them, they will tell us practically everything about their wants and needs, their sense of well-being, and when they're out of balance. The body tells us when we overeat, when we're tired or stressed, when we're getting sick, and when we're getting well. The problem is that while our bodies can give us symptoms that tell us whether or not we're in a healthy balance, they don't spell out the *hows* and *whys* of maintaining themselves. Fortunately, there has been extensive research and, in recent years, groundbreaking discoveries in the areas of diet and exercise as they relate to health.

Everyone knows that "you are what you eat," yet we still continue to indulge in unhealthy eating habits. Junk food, alcohol, fatty red meats, processed foods, caffeine, sweets . . . the road to an unbalanced, unhealthy diet is paved with temptation, mostly originating from the vast commercial food industry that profits every time we partake of their heavily advertised products.

There *is* an alternative. And it's not about depriving ourselves—it's more about making sensible (and even new and exciting) choices based on the latest scientific evidence. We have the information and the knowledge to know which foods suit our bodies. Now we have to apply our wisdom to create the optimal health we deserve.

There are many different theories about healthy eating, from food combining to blood types; vegetarian, vegan, macrobiotic, wheat-free, dairy-free, sugar-free diets; and others. Try what you feel is appropriate for you. There are a number of tests available to find out what suits you, but if you're tuned in to your body, it will tell you what works and what doesn't.

50.

The first step in finding the right combination of foods for you is to become consciously aware of what you're eating and how you feel afterwards. I've found that when I pause before a meal, and either silently or aloud give thanks for the wonderful food on my plate, I become more aware of what I'm about to put in my mouth.

From my research, both personal and professional, there are certain foods that every-body agrees are always good, not so good, and flat-out unhealthy for you.

YES, ALWAYS GOOD FOR YOU	IF YOU MUST . . . EAT ONLY OCCASIONALLY	YIKES! TO BE AVOIDED AT ALL COSTS
Green vegetables[1] including celery, broccoli, zucchini, lettuce, beet greens, cabbage, chard, endive, kale, spinach	**Organic poultry**	**Cakes and biscuits**
Yellow vegetables including carrots, pumpkin, sweet potato, winter squash	**Lean organic meat**	**Caffeine**
	Starchy vegetables including corn, green peas, potatoes, and some root vegetables	**Alcohol** (except red wine)
Red vegetables including beets, eggplant, red cabbage, red peppers	**Eggs**	**Refined sugar**
Freshwater fish[2] (especially salmon)	**Potatoes**	**White flour**
Soy[3] including edamame beans, tofu, seitan, miso soup, soy milk	**Whole-grain wheat** including whole-wheat breads, pasta	**Hydrogenized oils, trans-fatty acids, and margarine**
Fruits[4] including apples, oranges, grapes, papayas, mangoes, tomatoes, avocados, melons (melon should always be eaten by itself)	**Natural sweeteners** including honey, molasses, maple syrup	**Animal fat**
	Fruit juices[1]	**Yeast**
Beans and legumes	**Red wine**	**Artificial sweeteners/ diet drinks**
Whole grains including brown rice, flaxseed, buckwheat, quinoa, millet, kasha	**Chocolate/carob**	**Sodas**
	Dairy[2] including milk, cream, butter, cheese, yogurt	**• • •**

51.

YES, ALWAYS
GOOD FOR YOU

Nuts and seeds

Ginger

Cold-pressed oils

Drinks

  including vegetable juices,
  wheatgrass,[5] green tea,[6]
  purified still water

Notes:

1. Almost all vegetables are a
    source of energy and give you
    enzymes, minerals, carbohy-
    drates, and fiber. Green veg-
    etables also alkalize the body.
    Vegetables are best juiced,
    steamed, or raw.

2. Fish is probably the best choice
    for animal protein, and most
    fish are relatively low in fat.
    Sea fish are packed with
    positive nutritional extras,
    such as omega-3 oil and vita-
    min D. (Be aware that many
    sea fish also contain large
    amounts of mercury.)

3. Soy condiments are not
    recommended. Soy sauce,
    tamari, and other soy-deriva-
    tive dressings are high in
    sodium content and fer-
    mented. I recommend Bragg
    Liquid Amino condiment,

which is made from soya, is
low in sodium, and is far healthier.

4. Fruits are an excellent source
    of vitamins, minerals, and
    other nutrients, but many
    contain high concentrates of
    sugars and acid. Be selective.

5. Wheatgrass is loaded with
    natural vitamins, minerals,
    chlorophyll, and enzymes,
    which feed your cells and
    help rid them of toxins. It can
    be found at most juice bars
    and although it doesn't taste
    great, it's really worth the pain.

6. Good quality green tea oxy-
    genates the blood, as well as
    refreshes the body. Far supe-
    rior for the body than other
    non-caffeinated beverages.

•••

IF YOU MUST . . .
EAT ONLY
OCCASIONALLY

Notes:

1. Fruit juices taste great and
    have many essential vitamins,
    but are very high in natural
    sugar and calories.

2. Dairy products contain butter-
    fat, which is an unsaturated
    fat and a health detriment.
    While dairy products do have
    calcium, they also contain
    lactose sugar, which can strip
    calcium from bones. It's bet-
    ter to get calcium from other
    sources. Dairy also creates
    mucus, so it's better avoided
    if you're prone to getting
    stuffed up.

•••

Wake-Up Morning Juice.

A self-nurturing and healthy way to start your day is to make some vegetable juice, which will give you many of the vitamins and minerals you need to get through the day. You have to mix up the ingredients to find what tastes good to you, but the following two versions seem to work for me.

Total Detox Morning Juice

2-3 stalks of celery
2 peeled cucumbers
6 broccoli flowers and stalks
½ lemon
1 piece of ginger
Optional: zucchini, other greens

Less-Strict Detox Morning Juice

As above, adding 1 apple, 2 carrots, and a slice of raw beet.

To both juices, I add Inner Light Supergreens (which are recommended by Dr. Robert Young), together with their pH alkalizing drops. They're not sold in retail shops, so please visit **www.innerlightinc.com** to order or find a distributor. There are many brands of other supergreens powder available in health-food stores, but I find the Inner Light brand to be the best because it contains wheatgrass, barley grass, lemon grass, blackberry leaf, soy sprouts, herbs, and other ingredients from nature that alkaline our blood and keeps us healthy.

53.

The Modern Woman's Guide to Maximum Nourishment and Easy Digestion.

The following guidelines are ones that I have found particularly beneficial in aiding digestion. These suggestions are backed up by scientific and nutritional information that can be found in the fine books mentioned in the References at the back of this book. Here are some pertinent points to help you create a balanced eating program:

- *Eat organic foods as much as possible.*

- *Regularly include soy products in your diet.*

- *Eat fruit separately from other foods.*

- *Avoid drinking liquids immediately prior to, or during, your meal.*

- *Juice green vegetables regularly in the morning.*

- *Avoid eating protein and starchy carbohydrates together.*

- *Chew each mouthful at least 20 times.*

- *Don't eat if you're not hungry.*

- *Don't eat too late at night.*

- *Drink six to eight glasses minimum of pure water daily.*

- *Eat raw vegetables whenever possible; start your meal with a salad.*

- *Avoid fermented foods and dressings such as vinegar and soy sauce.*

- *Use only cold-pressed and organic oils.*

- *Take digestive enzymes with meals if you have a sluggish metabolism.*

- *Add olive oil to vegetables after cooking lightly in water.*

- *Drink wheatgrass juice regularly to add electrolytes to your system.*

- *Use enemas or colonic irrigation on occasion to clean out your colon.*

- *Avoid processed foods.*

A Fresh Start.

For one week, write down everything you consume—include meals and snacks, beverages, cigarettes, alcohol, and recreational drugs. Observe how your energy is. Do your joints ache? Do you have a headache? Do you have a bad, metallic taste in your mouth? Are you bloated? What (if any) other symptoms are you experiencing?

For the second week, experiment with some of the new, healthy suggestions found in this chapter. Make a note of the difference in the way you feel, and decide which changes you're going to incorporate into your new, health-conscious daily routine.

Jot down your findings on pages 57 and 58.

WEEK ONE

Sunday:
_____
_____
_____

Monday:
_____
_____
_____
_____

Tuesday:
_____
_____
_____

57.

Wednesday:
_____
_____
_____

Thursday:
_____
_____
_____

Friday:
_____
_____
_____

Saturday:
_____
_____
_____

WEEK TWO

Sunday:

_____
_____
_____
_____

Monday:

_____
_____
_____
_____

Tuesday:

_____
_____
_____

58.

Wednesday:

_____
_____
_____
_____

Thursday:

_____
_____
_____

Friday:

_____
_____
_____

Saturday:

_____
_____
_____

Journey to Optimal Fitness.

Given our busy lives, maintaining a regular fitness routine isn't easy. I've tried and failed so many times over the years, and I finally realized why: I didn't like what I was trying to do. I was out of shape to start with, so I found aerobics, yoga, or anything else I tried just too hard—and boring to boot! I never even went to a gym until I was living in L.A. I had depended on some good-natured personal trainers to come by my house and try to persuade me to work out. The one thing I never did realize was that *I* had to put in some effort myself!

My initial saving grace was my love of dance. I had been an enthusiastic and energetic dancer as a child and teen, but like a lot of us who abandon things due to lack of time, I let dancing drift out of my life in adulthood. In my early 40s, as I traveled around California, I came upon the books and tapes of Gabrielle Roth, the creator of the Five Rhythms method of dance, which incorporates exercise, meditation, theater, and movement based on the differing states and rhythms of the body.

At last there was something I could do that would be good for me and I could really enjoy! I was back in touch with my body; I became far more agile and energetic; my sexuality returned; and I met many great men and women, who, like me, considered dance as their physical and spiritual practice. My closest moments with my daughter, Jessica, often occur when we are on the dance floor, connecting and enjoying our Five Rhythms. (Fortunately there are now Five Rhythms teachers all over the U.S., Canada, the U.K., and Europe.)

When I started living in L.A., I also got into a routine of walking a mile or so to the beach every morning, breathing in the important iodine from the sea air and meditating while the frequently seen dolphins played nearby in the surf. Again, I had found an exercise I enjoyed.

As I got fitter and my body started enjoying the experience, I got more ambitious. I found that energy creates energy. I researched more about exercise and added variety to my program. Now that I'm back in Europe, I try to ensure that I walk for an hour early in the morning at least four times a week when I'm in my house in Spain. London is more of a problem with the weather, but I still make sure I walk as often as I can on Hampstead Heath—or I go to the gym, bike, dance, or walk/jog around the running track in the park opposite my home. If I'm really pressed for time, I find that jumping on my mini-trampoline for 15 minutes has similar effects to a brisk hour's walk, stimulating my lymph nodes and releasing my endorphins. I really try to do one physical activity for at least one hour every day.

We need to bring exercise regularly into our lives for many reasons: It creates energy; builds bone density; stimulates respiration, oxygen, and blood circulation; aids digestion and clarity of the brain; strengthens muscles; protects against heart disease; reduces the body's fat content; and from every possible perspective, keeps us healthy.

Basic Fitness Primer.

60.

Exercise is divided into two basic categories: aerobic and anaerobic. A balanced program of both types of activities, along with general flexibility exercises, will provide all you need to keep you healthy and fit.

Aerobic means "with oxygen." This type of exercise is usually only moderately strenuous, but can be sustained over a period of time. Aerobic exercise primarily strengthens your heart, lungs, and circulatory system, and also helps release endorphins—the "feel-good hormones" that elevate mood. Types of aerobic exercise includes walking, running, hiking, cycling, swimming, dancing, bouncing on a trampoline, rowing, kayaking, and aerobic classes at a gym.

Anaerobic means "without oxygen." This type of exercise involves short, intense bursts of power, but gives us strength and provides our muscles with the power that sustains our body. Weight training, isometrics, and strengthening exercises such as sit-ups and push-ups are examples of anaerobic exercise.

Flexibility exercises stretch the muscle fibers, allowing our limbs a wider range of motion. Yoga is the best known of all stretch practices. There are many types of yoga—from the traditional Hatha to the more aerobically strenuous Ashtanga—but all offer tremendous gifts of flexibility, relaxation, and balance. There are countless yoga centers and teachers out there, so check out which type suits you.

I recently added Pilates to my routine. I found that this form of physical and mental conditioning, which was originally developed to help dancers with their posture and strength, was just what I needed. It can be done on weights and pulley-type machines or on a mat—I've tried both and find them equally effective. Since Pilates incorporates breathing with exercises and stretching, it restores the body to true balance, strengthening the abdomen, lower back, and hips into a firm central support for the body.

There are many other enjoyable and exciting forms of exercise, including (but certainly not limited to) martial arts, such as judo, karate, and t'ai chi; solo sports, such as swimming or skiing; activities with a partner, such as tennis; or team sports, such as volleyball, softball, or soccer. There are also numerous forms of dance, from belly to salsa. Take your pick, find what works for you, and most important, enjoy and have some fun!

61.

"I finally have muscle definition now that I've started Pilates."

"My mind is so much clearer after my morning swim."

"I meet the greatest guys jogging around the park in the morning."

"My sex life has improved ever since I started belly dancing regularly."

"Ever since I started walking an hour every day, I can wear my favorite pair of jeans again."

62.

Natural Remedies and Complementary Healing.

Natural healing has been the domain of the wise woman since time began. Our foremothers were the healers in many cultures, gathering herbs, roots, and flowers from the fields and jungles to heal many an affliction. They believed that Mother Earth held all the answers to good health (along with the positive energy put out by their own village healers).

In the global village of the 21st century, we have access to the traditional healing methods from many countries, which, together with more modern healing techniques, offer us an effective means of diagnosis, as well as preventive and alternative healing. Most cities around the world have clinics or centers where a whole array of holistic practices are on display. If you're feeling out of sorts, ask around for recommendations for the most effective practitioners.

What follows is just a brief explanation of some of the more popular treatments.

Acupuncture: The objective of this Chinese-based medicine is to balance the two opposing forces of the body (*yin* and *yang*). This is done by stimulating your meridian points with fine needles, which are said to carry your vital energy. Acupuncture is highly effective for almost any ailment, whether you understand how it works or not. Most Chinese acupuncturists also recommend an assortment of extremely effective natural herbs and roots.

Alexander Technique: A series of lessons where your body is readjusted by the practitioner to a correct structural state, somewhat like Pilates but lying down.

Cranial Osteopathy: A very gentle technique that involves exploring the pulse of cerebrospinal fluid by means of gentle pressure on the skull and in the pelvic area. Particularly effective for migraines, headaches, and stress, as well as for babies who have had a difficult birth.

63.

Flower Remedies: The use of distilled flower essences to emotionally balance a body's system which, according to its adherents, is the root cause of physical illness.

Homeopathy: A system of treatment that uses minute distillations of plant, mineral, and chemical substances to subtly stimulate the immune system to battle sickness and disease.

Hypnotherapy: An altered state of mind created by a practitioner to help a patient relax and alleviate stress. Can also be useful to get rid of addictions, headaches, and migraines; and relieve depression.

Iridology: Diagnosis through the colors and patterns seen in the iris of one's eyes.

Kinesiology: A diagnostic form of healing, based on responses to certain remedies through muscle testing.

Natural Herbs and Remedies: Many practitioners of the treatments on this list also work with healing herbs. Herbal remedies can be found for virtually every illness and create a healthy balance when integrated with many traditional, allopathic medicines.

Psychotherapy: Also known as "talking therapy," this is the science of understanding individual behavioral patterns by discovering their root causes, which are usually based in childhood.

Reflexology: Massage and pressure on the soles of the feet to stimulate specific nerve endings. This is said to provoke a reflex action in other organs or tissues. Helps stress-related disorders, relaxes, and is particularly good for menstrual problems, menopause, headaches, and high blood pressure.

Reiki or Spiritual Healing: The transmitting of healing energy through the laying on of hands or holding the hands over problem areas. There are many reports of serious illnesses helped by this form of energy work, even during "absent healing," when the patient is not present.

Shiatsu and Acupressure: Shiatsu is the Japanese form of acupressure (which is basically acupuncture without the needles), which is used in a form of massage employing thumbs, hands, elbows, and other body parts to balance the body's energy. Relieves pain and stress and creates energy flow.

Transformational Breath Work: The practitioner takes the patient through emotional blockages with controlled, deep breathing exercises.

Vitamins, Minerals, and Supplements: Adding nutrients that are essential to a body's health that may be lacking in one's diet. For women, these include antioxidants, calcium, and omega oils for skin, hair, and nails.

The Menopause Myth

Menopause should be a time for celebration and joy among women, since that is that time when we move into a new phase of our lives where we can live at our optimal power. It is a transitional period when our creativity expands, our natural intuitive abilities are enhanced, and our understanding of life deepens. By no longer losing our monthly blood, our energy stays internal, transforming us into strong wise warriors who, instead of having babies, are able to fulfill ourselves and inspire others.

However, thanks to the drug companies who manufacture hormone-replacement treatments, the cosmetic-surgery industry, and today's youth-obsessed society, menopause is often portrayed in the media as some kind of unwelcome disease. We women are taught to take pills and put on creams and lotions to get our bodies to artificially produce hormones so that we can pretend that menopause isn't really happening to us at all. Clearly, our bodies *are* changing, and we must adapt to those changes. But before resorting to artificial methods, it's important to research what we can do for ourselves.

65.

I appreciate that different body types experience different levels of discomfort during the early stages of menopause. However, I believe that we still don't know enough about the effects of adding doses of synthetic hormones to our bodies and that most women can manage without them. There have been various medical and government reports in the U.S. since the turn of the century clearly stating that hormone replacement therapy (HRT) can actually increase risks of heart disease, strokes, and cancer, and for women over 65, it can actually double the risk of dementia and Alzheimer's disease.

When I first started having menopausal symptoms, I was told by a very reputable female doctor in the U.K. that I should immediately take HRT or my joints would be painful, I'd get very wrinkly, and I would stop enjoying sex. However, my doctor in California, Jesse Hanley, who has written two top-selling books on the subject, *What Your Doctor May Not Tell You about Premenopause* (with Dr. John Lee and Virginia Hopkins), and *Tired of Being Tired: Rescue, Repair, Rejuvenate* (with Nancy Deville), immediately convinced me otherwise. She told me that my body didn't need extra estrogen; in fact, there was a very strong tie-in between HRT and breast cancer.

66.

Fortunately, I listened to Jesse Hanley: Several years later, after following a healthy diet-and-exercise plan, and having a positive attitude to life, I'm fitter and healthier than ever. I do rub on some natural progesterone cream most days, which I trust can only do me good. My bones are strong, I don't get hot flashes, and I enjoy sex more than ever . . . and that's saying a lot!

In Japan, menopause is hardly known—there isn't even a word for it in the Japanese language. The traditional Japanese diet of soy, grains, and fish-based foods is given credit for this phenomena. However, we in the West, with our nutritional intake based on animal fat, excessive sugar, and processed foods are all too familiar with menopausal symptoms that can cause a certain amount of discomfort. We heat up and dehydrate more; we can experience severe mood swings; we can get quite vague and tired, experience weight gain, and indeed have a loss of libido. It can be frightening and depressing, particularly if we don't share our fears with others.

So often we women feel a sense of shame and don't want to talk about what we're going through, yet one of the funniest shows I ever saw was a small production in Los Angeles called *Is It Me, or Is It Hot in Here?* This musical was based on a menopause workshop, and the audience of mostly women in their middle years all laughed uproariously throughout. It was again an example of how women can get through their fears by sharing and laughing. So, if you're menopausal, get yourself together with a few other women who are experiencing the same thing, discuss what you're going through, and support each other in the experience of this exciting rite of passage.

It is clear that by taking a healthy approach to menopause—physically, emotionally, and mentally—we can create a transitional experience that is a beautiful initiation into the rest of our lives.

Creating a Healthy Plan of Action.

You should now be feeling good about yourself and ready to take on responsibility for your health and well-being. This chapter has given you a great opportunity to see what changes you want to make in your life. Why not create an action list of the different ways you're going to show love for your body?

You should aim to do two or three well-being activities every day. Maybe you could include at least one form of exercise, from walking to yoga. How about giving up an item in your diet that you know is bad for you and adding something that's better for you? What about stopping smoking once and for all? How about a daily meditation to balance your stress, or making yourself a morning vegetable juice?

Once you get into a comfortable rhythm with your well-being activities, you'll be surprised how easily they become part of your daily routine. Just take it step by step, reminding yourself at the end of the day that every gift you give to your body is a gift to your divine self.

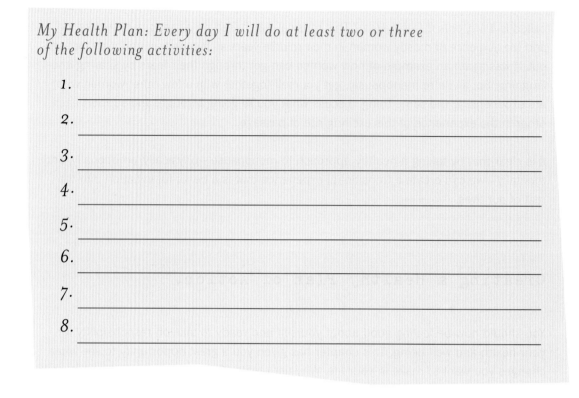

My Health Plan: Every day I will do at least two or three of the following activities:

1. _____

2. _____

3. _____

4. _____

5. _____

6. _____

7. _____

8. _____

68.

The GROW Commitment.

Add this thought to your morning meditation or as an affirmation to do when exercising:

Every day in every way, I nurture my body
to create optimal health and vitality.

• • • • •

(Where You Reclaim
Your Ancient Wisdom
and Bring Ritual and
Magic into Your Life)

Celebrating the Sacred Feminine

*Do ancient memories stir when I look up and see the full moon?
Do I feel echoes of sacred gatherings when I get together with
my female friends? When the wind from the sea blows through
my hair, do I kick off my shoes and spiral into a dance of joy?*

The sense of the sacred feminine remains in each and every one of us. We feel it, but we can't always name it. It's our inheritance as women, yet it's been so long since society has recognized the power of the Goddess and the women who serve her that we've lost touch with that side of ourselves.

My Story: Finding the White Goddess

Growing up as a young Jewish girl, I began my journey to understand where the power of the feminine lies in our modern-day religious mythology as I learned the rituals and sacred celebrations of my faith. I came across the names of queens and priestesses as I studied the Old Testament, such as Naomi, Ruth, and Miriam, but they seemed to have secondary roles compared to the many kings, generals, and prophets that made up Jewish history.

God was also projected as such a powerful, patriarchal figure that it took me quite by surprise to learn from a rabbi friend many years later that God does indeed appear in both masculine and feminine form in the Kabbalah, the mystic teachings of the Jews. The Kabbalah itself (which is traditionally forbidden to women and young men), states that peace, through the Messiah, will only return to Earth once female energy is back to its full, universal strength.

As an adult, I continued my search to find the sacred feminine—I found her presence in the myths and stories of cultures and peoples from around the world. Among Native Americans, as well as in India, Africa, and Brazil, I found worship of goddesses as strong now as it was 5,000 years ago. During my seeking, I learned to chant and pray in Sanskrit and to meditate with my eyes closed, focusing on my breath and, with my eyes open, concentrate on another's third eye in the middle of their forehead. I learned pagan rituals and how to connect with the passages of the moon. I visited sacred sites, beautiful churches, and ancient temples. I learned how to connect with the divine universal power and the divine inside me.

I first felt the energy of the sacred mother enter my life after visiting Deià for the first time. It was in this Spanish mountain village that overlooks the Mediterranean Sea that I rediscovered my feminine power, fell in love with nature, and learned to connect with a goddess energy that continues to inspire and sustain me. I saw the three faces of the Goddess (the holy trinity of the sacred feminine that is represented in so many ancient rituals) in the surrounding countryside and its accompanying seasons. In the venerable, twisted olive trees I saw the crone, the bringer of death and rebirth; in the springtime, alongside the wild flowers and newborn lambs, I saw the freshness of the maiden goddess; in the full summer moon suspended over the nearby mountains I felt the all-embracing love of the holy mother.

What I had yet to find out during my first visit to Deià was that this tiny village had also been home for many years to British poet and esoteric scholar Robert Graves, and it is where much of his family still lives. It was here, inspired in part by the beauty of his surroundings, that he wrote his opus, _The White Goddess: A Historical Grammar of Poetic Myth,_ which was a major influence on the writings and teachings of so many extollers of the return of the sacred feminine. In this complex book, Graves asserted that at the base of all human pursuit is service to the Goddess. By tying together seemingly disparate traditions, from the Celtic tree alphabet to Greek and Roman mythologies, Graves concluded that only through our union with the Goddess—through poetry, ritual, and the celebration of nature—can we find true fulfilment.

I feel honored and blessed to have a home in Deià, and to restore myself with the energy of the sacred feminine every time I return there. I have enjoyed many rituals in this magic place, particularly at the time of the full moon, when I, too, sense the presence of the White Goddess.

73.

The Return of the Goddess.

For 5,000 years or so, the majority of the Western world has lived in a so-called patriarchal society, where a detached male god has dwelled in the heavens (or in the case of Zeus or Thor, on top of a mountain), sending his opinions and orders down to the people through priests and thunderbolts.

It has been argued that, for approximately 20,000 years before that, this world lived with a far more balanced, feminine spiritual system, which brought humanity into harmony with Mother Earth. Women's roles as spiritual leaders and wise women within ancient cultures linked community with nature, brought ritual into the home, kept stories and myths alive, and offered healing herbs and midwifery to society.

A hunger for those times, when the world honored the sacred feminine and the Mother Goddess, has never been greater than it is today. Increasingly, both women and men are looking to philosophies and belief systems from different cultures and previous eras that will give them the answers they cannot find in the traditional faiths they've grown up with. Yet with the arrival of the 21st century, a new awareness of the sacred feminine is dawning. In the less traditional branches of Judaism and Christianity, steps are being taken to modernize religious practices, and women are being ordained as priests or rabbis. Many strong Muslim women are taking leadership roles in their communities, and the messages of female spiritual leaders coming from India and certain native cultures are being spread worldwide.

In this chapter, we're going to look at the goddesses of both the modern and ancient worlds. We're going to familiarize ourselves with the wonders of ritual and magic, as well as the art and comfort of a sacred sanctuary or altar in our homes. We're going to bring back the poetry and imagery of the Goddess into our lives and acknowledge the healers in us all.

I envision an elevation of goddess insight, where we as wise women can be in our full power. It is time to renew a sense of balance so that the sacred female can meet with the sacred male in a symbiotic partnership—one based on wisdom, not war; and on true equality, not the exercise of power over the other.

74.

Who Really Ate the Apple?

It all started with Eve getting Adam to eat the forbidden fruit that got us all thrown out of Eden. Bad girl . . . or was she? Like many of the myths from the Bible, the source of this story has its origins in prehistory, when Goddess worship still reigned supreme. According to various scholars, Eve was, in fact, an incarnation of the Great Goddess, the Mother of All Living Things. In varying prebiblical myths, she is said to have given birth to Adam, to all of humanity, and even to God himself. What's interesting is that the serpent is a symbol of wisdom in Goddess culture, one that's associated with the renewal of life via the shedding of its skin. That these two life-creating figures became associated with original sin marks a significant shift from the feminine world of all-encompassing sacred nature to the more masculine view, where the sacred as God is separate from nature.

By positioning Eve as literally the "fall girl" responsible for humankind's banishment from Paradise, the new masculine order not only tainted the Goddess, but by association, all women. And using that platform, they did their best to erase the Goddess from our collective memory and keep women subservient through the ages—but, unfortunately for them, our memory of the Goddess is deeply embedded.

The Goddesses of the Ancient World.

From Eve to the Virgin Mary, the various incarnations of the Goddess primarily represent the Divine Mother, who gives life to all beings, nurtures and sustains us, and offers us her compassion, strength, and wisdom. Ancient goddesses were worshiped in conjunction with the change of the seasons and fertility, and to ensure the abundance needed to survive.

The oldest known image of an European goddess was created some 25,000 years ago in what is now part of Austria. Referred to as the Venus of Willendorf, the figurine's full-breasted, pregnant features indicate a common theme among its contemporaries. Goddess artifacts have been found all over the world and reflect the characteristics of their unique societies. There is much controversy about the original use of the figurines— some early archaeologists put them down as toys, some as kitchen artifacts, and some as burial relics. However, an alternative perspective was introduced by the respected anthropologist Marija Gimbutas. In her book, *The Language of the Goddess,* she writes:

> All the Goddess images should be viewed as aspects of the one Great Goddess with her core functions—life-giving, death-wielding, regeneration and renewal. . . . The goddesses were mainly life creators, not Venuses or beauties, and most definitely not wives of male gods.

A Modern Woman's Guide to Essential Goddesses

Do you know your A to Z of indispensable goddesses? To help you familiarize yourself, here is a list of the most significant representatives of the sacred feminine throughout history and what qualities they are associated with.

Aphrodite (Greek): love, passion, sensuality

Baba Yaga (Russian): the Triple Goddess—maiden, mother, crone

Black Madonna (Christian/African): strength, passion, power

Bridget (Celtic): healing, protection, poetry

Diana (Roman): the huntress, nature, courage

Freya (Norse): love, beauty, wisdom

The Furies (Roman): anger, revenge

Gaia (Greek): the earth, abundance, creation

Hera (Greek): protection, confidence, honesty

Inanna (Sumerian): inner strength, fertility, passion

Isis (Egyptian): life, intuition, magical realms

Juno (Roman): mother goddess, childbirth

Kali (Hindu): death, destruction, release

Kuan-Yin (Chinese): compassion, mercy, peacefulness

Lakshmi (Hindu): abundance, wealth, outer success

78.   **Minerva** (Roman): wisdom, war, protection

Nut (Egyptian): the sky, mother of deities, celestial mistress

Oshun (African): healing, love, flirtation

Paivatar (Scandinavian): sky goddess, release, renewal

Shakti (Hindu): cosmic energy

Sheila-na-gig (Celtic): the vulva, fertility

Sophia (Greek): wisdom, kindness, joy

White Buffalo Woman (Native American): the earth, grace, balance

Which Goddess Are You? A Meditation

After briefly studying the above chart, take some quiet time to decide which goddess you most identify with.

Close your eyes, breathe deeply, relax your body, and visualize yourself in an ancient shrine, where an old woman sits waiting for you, wrapped in a hooded cloak. Ask her to unveil herself to you.

As she takes off her cloak, she seems to get taller and light pours from her form. When she turns to face you, you feel the love she radiates out. Is she Aphrodite, the Greek Goddess of Love; or Bridget, the Celtic Goddess of Healing and Poetry? Perhaps she's Kuan-Yin, the Chinese Goddess of Boundless Compassion; or the Virgin Mary, the Beloved Mother. . . .

80.

Once you've selected the goddess you most closely identify with, reflect on her traits and how they are manifest in you. Invite her in as your Special Goddess. Find or make an image of her to keep on your altar or in a sacred place, and honor her as the goddess inside you.

Ancient Goddesses in the Modern World.

In today's world of shopping malls, jet planes, mobile phones, and the Internet, where the mysteries of nature have been carefully dissected by science, there seems little room for the quaint mythology of the goddesses. Even my most fervent goddess-worshiping friends hardly expect to see the goddess Diana majestically riding through the woods hunting a stag, or to hear that Hera is throwing amazing dinner parties on Mount Olympus. And yet, for all of our seeming sophistication, we should realize that goddesses live and breathe as vibrantly as ever—they're still worshiped and exalted, prayed to, and celebrated in every culture on Earth. They are the Christian Virgin Mary, the Buddhist Tara, the Hindu Shakti, and the Jewish Kabbalah's Shekinah, to name just a few.

The fact that goddesses continue to live on so strongly in the modern world suggests that the role they play in our existence is far deeper and more subtle than the fairy tales of classic Roman and Greek folklore.

Mary As the Goddess

Despite exclusion from the Christian Trinity of Father, Son, and Holy Ghost, Mary has become the only officially sanctioned image of the sacred feminine in the current Western age, offering compassion, forgiveness, and unconditional love to her worshipers. Yet the early patriarchal fathers of the Christian church strongly disapproved of the worship of Mary as an embodiment of the Goddess and did everything they could to undermine the importance of her role.

Said to be a composite of older goddesses, such as Juno, the Blessed Virgin; Marianne, the Semitic God-Mother; and the Syrian Aphrodite-Mari, the image of Mary has appeared to many over the years, delivering messages of love and hope. She has become central in many countries as the embodiment of the divine on Earth and is prayed to by millions for the sustenance in their lives. The members of the male Holy Trinity are seen as remote, celestial figures, whereas Mary is the conduit for prayer on millions of women's altars throughout the Roman Catholic world.

Interestingly, many of the Catholic churches and cathedrals dedicated to "notre dame" (our lady) are built over pagan shrines to the Great Goddess, including Rome's Cathedral of Santa Maria Maggiore. Throughout Italy, churches named for Mary were built on the sites of former shrines to Isis, Minerva, Diana, and Hecate. One church was even named "Santa Maria sopra Minerva," which translates to "Holy Mary over the shrine of Minerva," and a similar rebuilding process took place at many other ancient sites throughout the world.

The Virgin Mary and Goddess folklore are intertwined in other ways as well. Over the years, various statues of Mary are said to have been found by shepherds near sacred groves of trees that were thought to have been used for ancient Celtic tree worship. One such story comes from Lluc in Mallorca, where a Moorish shepherd is said to have found the sacred

81.

image of the Virgin Mary in a rock cleft. It was taken to the nearest church in nearby Escorca and is believed to have disappeared three times and then reappeared in its original location, until it was finally decided that the image should be worshiped there. The subsequent first chapel built there was the forerunner of what has become the most revered sanctuary in Mallorca. (I was fascinated when I visited Lluc to note that near the monastery are groves of ancient trees, which are historically associated with pagan worship of the sacred feminine.) The simple carved limestone statue of the mother and child now rests in an ornate chapel and is adorned with an elaborate crown.

Even though I was born a Jew, I'm quite attracted to the qualities of the Virgin Mary. She has materialized to me during deep meditation as a figure of pure love and compassion, and I keep images of her in my home, particularly those of her Mexican incarnation as Our Lady of Guadalupe, whose folk-culture style attracted me when I lived in California. I believe that we should follow our natural instincts when it comes to images of the sacred feminine that we surround ourselves with—our higher self will always lead us to the images that resonate for us individually.

83.

Wicca Magic and Moon Spells.

Today's world is one of freedom and choice. We can pick and choose how we want to worship and can express our spirituality through an array of ancient and modern beliefs, rituals, and myths. Many of us are choosing to return to a more ancient, feminine spiritual practice of sacred magic as a source of reconnection with the natural world. Today, the witches' cauldron of the New Age brings together a potpourri of goddess traditions and rituals—from pagan to Native American, from Celtic to Greek—that empowers its followers and creates magic in the present day.

The fear that the word *witch* throws up in modern society is a throwback to the times of persecution by the churches, when witches were portrayed as cackling hags on broomsticks, servants of the devil whose spells would destroy rather than create. The reality is that witches were worshipers of the Goddess. They were the wise women of tribal communities throughout the world, followers of a feminine spiritual order where prayer and ritual were focused on a connection with nature, a full harvest, and the general well-being of the community.

The revival of Wicca, a European form of female shamanism, has brought together rituals and myths from other disparate Goddess-based spiritual disciplines while retaining many characteristics from earlier times. Wicca and other neopagan religions have their roots in nature, the changing of the seasons, and the cycles of the moon—they're about reviving conscious magical energy, where clear intention is manifested by the life force generated in individual or collective ritual.

Like Wiccan witches, we can create or adopt rituals to connect with the seasonal changes in nature or major events in our lives. By invoking the magical powers in all of us, we can move into our full power as healers and visionaries. Groups or "covens" of women of different ages can come together with the forces of nature to create magic in their lives—magic that has been happening since the beginning of time.

84.

I have connected with the power of magic on many occasions, in circles with other wise women as well as on my own. My experiences of self- or group-created ritual have incorporated the four elements of Fire, Water, Earth, and Air; the four directions of the earth: North, South, East, and West; drumming and chanting; the power of intent; and a heightened awareness of connection with nature. I have shared exciting rituals within women's circles from Jerusalem to Rajasthan, from San Francisco to Glastonbury. However, the most powerful magic I have ever experienced has been in my own garden at the time of the full or new moon, when I have been at my full strength on my own land.

Why not celebrate the next Moon cycle in your own home with meditation, followed by dancing, chanting, or drumming? It's fun, especially with other women, and connects us with the sacred feminine in all of us.

Moon Time

The different phases of the moon have traditionally been the times when women have come together in prayer and ritual, expressing their hopes and dreams. Once we flow with the cycles of the moon, often corresponding with our own physical flow of menstruation, we bring our being in touch with nature, and ultimately with the universal life force itself.

Since opening myself to the power of the moon, I have become aware and appreciative of all her phases:

- *The new moon* is a time for introspection and self-nurturing, when we plant the seeds of new ideas, projects and relationships.

- *The waxing moon* is when we start building up the strength to bring our seeds to fruition.

- *The full moon* is when we move into our highest energy and strength, when true magic is in the air and we can manifest our dreams into reality.

- *The waning moon* is a time to release and surrender to the power we've set in motion.

85.

Invoking the Power of the Full Moon

Prepare for your full-moon ritual in the hours before it reaches its zenith to ensure that your wishes are released at the peak moment, when the sway of the moon is at its most powerful. You'll need the following:

- *One white candle and matches*
- *One water bowl*
- *A notepad and pen*
- *A drum or small musical instrument*
- *A small outdoor fire (optional)*
- *The full moon*

Light a white candle for peace, to reflect the opaqueness of the moon, and to represent the element of Fire. Fill a bowl with water to reflect the moon rays and to represent the second element. Take off your shoes and walk on the ground barefoot to connect with the third element, Earth. Finally, introduce Air as the fourth element through your own breath.

Let your breathing deepen, and close your eyes, going into a silent meditation. Ask Diana, the Moon Goddess, to share her clarity and wisdom to guide your dreams. Think of your desires and needs for the next month as well as for the coming year. When you feel ready, open your eyes, take the pen and pad, and start writing down those yearnings and needs.

When you've made your list, go outside (if you're not already), and, if you're with others, have one of them slowly beat a drum while the rest of you move clockwise in a circle, perhaps with a small fire in the center. Each of you take your turn in honoring and acknowledging the beauty and power of the moon. Sip some moon water from your bowl and ask Sister Moon to help you manifest your wishes. Then take your list and light it with the candle until it burns to ashes. Blow the ashes away into the nothingness, releasing them to the Universal Mother.

Let the drumming grow in momentum with other musical instruments joining in, then start your moon dance, swirling and leaping, feeling the passion and energy that will make your dreams come alive. Dance until you can't dance anymore—and remember to express gratitude to the moon for bringing you to this place of joy and strength.

Ancient Stones and Sacred Sites.

Having been born in Great Britain, I've had the privilege of being in close proximity to the many ancient sacred sites on this island, such as Stonehenge and the Glastonbury Tor, which are connected, it is said, by invisible "ley lines" that carry mystic energy around the world. And while their mysterious origins and exact ritual purposes are lost in the mists of time, there is no doubt that these sites, with their careful construction and astonishing astronomical positioning, were focal points of the sacred to the societies that built them. To be able to witness them firsthand, to run my hands over and touch the ancient mystical symbols carved into the solid rock, was to actually get a brief wisp of the shaman's magic crossing the centuries from eons past.

While I've lived near these magnificent monuments my entire life, it wasn't until I was in my 40s that my interest was sparked and I began visiting these sites and experiencing their powers. For example, my first trip to Newgrange in Ireland had a tremendous impact on me. At its entrance, this aged stone chamber has a large monolithic stone on which is deeply carved a multitude of beautiful spirals that are thought to represent sacred feminine energy. I had been told that this site sits on one of the most powerful energy fields in Ireland. Indeed, as I stood outside the chamber, I felt a powerful band of energy around my head, causing an intense headache. I decided to wait a day to actually enter the chamber.

Dated around 5,000 B.C., Newgrange is thought to have been a transformational death and rebirth chamber and a place of initiation. While experts can only theorize about the exact ceremonies that took place there originally, today, some 7,000 years after it was built, Newgrange still functions as an astronomical marker. During the time of the winter solstice (between the 19th and 23rd of December), the rising midwinter sun casts a narrow beam down its 60-foot passage and illuminates the inner chamber.

When I finally did enter the chamber with a group of six other women, an immediate feeling of transcendence and magic hovered in the air. After some time standing silent in a circle, as if in a trance, my friend Dolores and I spontaneously began a low chant. The energy that the group of women created in this sacred space was truly magical, and that day in the chamber I experienced a deep feeling of rebirth and a release of old patterns.

I have since visited numerous sacred sites around Great Britain and have had uniquely wonderful experiences at each one. Stone circles, crop circles, and ancient burial chambers are part of the spiritual heritage of Britain, with its strong Celtic and Druid roots. Legends of King Arthur, the lost Isle of Avalon, and stories of pre-Roman prophetic, Druid priestesses come alive in romantic novels such as *The Mists of Avalon* and other great books by Marion Zimmer Bradley. No wonder so many women and men come to Britain from all over the world to celebrate the solstices, jump the Beltane fires, or drink from the holy Chalice Well at Glastonbury.

Journey to the Sacred Sites.

There are sacred sites all over the world, each with their own unique structures and legends, where the visible world connects with the mystical. Why not take a trip to those you feel most attracted to and connect with the magical energy?

Europe

Silbury Hill (England): This 4,000-year-old giant ceremonial mound rises out of the plains of the English countryside.

Stonehenge (England): The most famous stone circle in the world.

STONEHENGE

Avesbury (England): The second most famous stone circle in the world.

Glastonbury (England): This town is known for its magical energy, and it is overseen by an ancient *tor,* St. Michael's Tower.

Newgrange (Ireland): This megalith is an ancient Celtic structure.

Les Eyzies (France): These cave paintings and ancient artifacts date from the time humankind began to express its mystical connection to the world.

LASCAUX

Lascaux (France): These splendid cave paintings are possibly the most significant prehistoric expression of the spiritual known to exist.

Hypogeum (Malta): This 5,000-year-old site is used by many different cultures for Goddess worship.

88.

Neolithic Temples of Malta (Malta): These holy sites are dedicated to the Goddess.

Palace at Knossos (Crete): This spectacular Minoan palace complex honors Goddess culture.

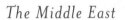

TEMPLE OF DELHI

Temple of Delphi (Greece): Home of the supreme oracle in ancient Mediterranean world; also believed to have been the seat of the earth goddess Gaia.

The Middle East

SPHINX

The Great Pyramids and the Sphinx (Egypt): These spectacular monuments date from the fourth Egyptian dynasty, some 4,500 years ago.

89.

Oracle Shrine of Didyma (Turkey): This pre-Greek goddess sanctuary was completed in the 6th century B.C.

Aphrodisias (Turkey): This ancient goddess city predates Greek culture.

Yazilikaya (Turkey): This prehistoric ceremonial sanctuary dates back to 15th to 13th century, B.C.

MT. FUJI

Asia

Mt. Fuji (Japan): The highest peak in Japan is also said to be the dwelling of a Shinto goddess.

Temples of Bali (Bali): The sacred is everywhere, as are Balinese temples.

TEMPLES OF BALI

Angkor Wat (Cambodia): This magnificent 1,000-year-old Buddhist city is set deep in the forest.

Banaras (India): Goddesses and gods abound, and devout *saddus* wander the streets in India's holiest city.

Mt. Kaliash (Tibet): "The Center of the Earth" in many traditions, this is home to the Hindu god Shiva and the seat of the sky goddess Sipaimen in Tibet's pre-Buddhist Bon religion.

Australia

90.

Uluru (Ayers Rock): This colossal outcropping rising in the outback of Central Australia is sacred to the Aboriginal people.

ULURU (Ayers Rock)

Lake Narran: According to Aboriginal myth, the creation story of the world was imparted to its inhabitants here 10,000 years ago.

Megalithic Stone Alignment (Central Australia): This is dated between 10,000 and 15,000 years old.

Africa

Binu Shrines of Mali: These are the sacred mud shrines of the ancient Dogon people, who revere the spirits of their dead ancestors.

The Americas

Chichen Itza (Mexico): This sacred center of the Mayan world has been wonderfully restored.

Palenque (Mexico): This magnificent Mayan city in the highland jungle is full of ceremonial sites and ancient temples.

MACHU PICCHU

Machu Picchu (Peru): This stunning Incan city is set on a remote mountaintop, its mystical significance shrouded in mystery.

Chaco Canyon (New Mexico, United States): The greatest architectural achievement of the northern Native Americans is the site of a great *Kiva,* which was the circular sacred den of the ancient Anasazi people.

Mt. Kilauea (Hawaii, United States): This sacred volcano is said to be where the mountain goddess Pele dwells.

91.

The Art of the Altar.

We don't have to travel around the world to visit sacred sites—we can create them in our own homes! Home altars have been the province of women since time immemorial. Even today, women all over the world continue the ancient tradition of creating sacred space in their homes, where they, together with their families, can honor the spirits of their ancestors, their teachers, and their gods.

At an altar, we can pray to the deities we follow, but we can also express through our creativity the link between the world we live in and the unseen. Making altars meaningful and beautiful is an art form in its own right—in fact, in many traditions, the home altar reflects the mysteries of that culture with images, statues, ornate fabric, and flowers. In other homes, women may not even be conscious that they have created an altar at all!

My mother, for instance, was concerned when I started talking about the importance of altars in our home. Since she was from a Jewish background, she had grown up with the patriarchal myth from the Old Testament that said God forbade the Hebrew tribe to worship idols. I pointed out that she had a whole room where she entertained and practiced healing that had crystals, flowers, plants, candlesticks, family photos, and other keepsakes arranged in various displays, which could be perceived as altars. In fact, many Jewish homes have the Menorah candlesticks and Sabbath candles arranged alongside family photographs, which constitutes a form of spontaneous altar, whether the families realize it or not.

Conscious altar making can be tremendous fun as well as a process to connect us with our most intimate feelings. It is our private space, where we can express all aspects of ourselves, including the inner child who still has fun putting objects together, creating meaning from chaos. Altars can also be used as a focus for prayer when sending healing energy to others, manifesting our practical needs, searching for answers to life's problems, and expressing love and gratitude toward the divine. An altar is where we can sit and meditate as well as partake in ritual. It's our personal space, where the outside world takes a backseat as we nurture our own heart and overcome our fears.

Your altar can be as simple or as ornate as you wish. You only have one person to please, and that's you—so create your altar just as you desire. I personally have *many* altars in my home, which represent different aspects of my life: one to honor my ancestors; one for the well-being of my children; one for romance and love; one dedicated to my personal Goddesses; one focused on planetary healing . . . the list of my altars goes on and on.

Like many, I collect small mementos from nature on my travels—crystals, feathers, shells, special stones—which I put on my altars together with photographs of my loved ones, candles, flowers, incense, and other objects and artifacts that have meaning for me.

Create that special space in your home where you can take time out of the busyness of life and expand into nothingness. Make your altar a central part of your living space. You could even have altars in different rooms: in the kitchen to welcome company, in the bedroom for your most private contemplation, and so on. (Your children can also be encouraged to designate a place in their room for special toys and beloved objects.) Make your altars vibrant and joyful, reflecting your inner thoughts together with the objects that bring you visual joy and pleasure.

93.

A wise woman grows into her strength through deep connection and love with the females of her lineage, so why not create an altar to bring together the women of your family in love and remembrance?

Honoring Your Female Ancestors

Find a space in your home for an altar dedicated to your female lineage, where you can celebrate, honor, and heal your connection with your foremothers as well as your mother, aunts, sisters, daughters, nieces, and granddaughters.

Collect photographs of your mother in the different phases of her life, and of your grand-mother, your great-grandmother, and other female ancestors. Add photographs of yourself as a child, a young woman, and an adult. If you have daughters, add their images, too, along with any items that bring back memories of your family, such as small presents they may have given you, objects of interest to them, and symbols of peace, unity, and love. As always with an altar, add candles, an incense burner, and flowers or a growing plant.

Observe and be mindful of the generations of women in your life—be aware of your relationships with them and the patterns that determined their lives, which are also reflected in your own life. When meditating at this altar, send these women love and ask that you all—from the past, present, and future—work together to heal negative family patterns and empower the generations still to come to live in their highest state of being.

The Power of Ritual.

Whether we're conscious of them or not, rituals are a major part of our lives. Celebrations for Christmas, Thanksgiving, Halloween, St. Valentine's Day, weddings, birthdays, engagements, and bar mitzvahs are when we exchange gifts, get together with our families and friends, and usually eat until we burst. We collectively say prayers at funerals, respond to a sneeze with "God bless you," and say grace before eating our meals, yet how many of these rituals do we take for granted? Do we remember why they were significant in the first place? Although nowadays our major holidays seem to be mainly about consumerism, many of them, such as Christmas, Easter, and Halloween, have their beginnings in far more ancient practices that date back thousands of years.

Ritual connects us with the deepest part of our unconscious mind, where we store our memories of ancient rites of passage that honor all aspects of human life. It helps us let go of the old and welcome in the new. It gives us comfort when we mourn the loss of a relationship or dear friend, or when we move from a beloved home. It enables us to celebrate the success of a new project, the birth of a new member of our community, or the change of the seasons.

Ritualizing the cycles of our own female bodies, from puberty to menopause, gives value and acknowledgment in a world whose main interest in these sacred passages is to sell more tampons and hormone-replacement drugs. Celebrating a young girl's first bleeding, when the members of her extended family give her gifts and the women bathe her in sweet-smelling oils and flower petals, gives her a sense of her own beauty that will last through her adulthood. I have participated in several such rites within small spiritual communities in Big Sur, California; and Findhorn, Scotland, and they were blessed, happy affairs.

Of course most of us don't reside in communities where ritual is part of the structure of our lives; instead, we live in crowded cities where most of our energy can be used up just getting through the day. Bringing ritual consciously into our daily life in a simple form that will create balance and connection between our inner and outer worlds takes thought and regular practice. But it doesn't have to take tremendous effort and time. For example, my early-morning ritual in London often includes a visit to the nearby Brahma Kumari meditation center, Global Co-operation House, where I join them in their morning prayers. The B.K.'s have brought a love of ritual and ceremony from their native India and are great believers in offering a sweetmeat or small gift to their guests while giving them *Drushti,* which is an eye-to-eye blessing. They have also taught me to take a conscious moment to bless my food.

I start my workday with the small ritual of lighting a candle. This signifies a change from leisure time to work time and moves me into a different kind of energy. I often start meetings with my team by holding hands and doing a short blessing, sharing our vision for the outcome of the meeting. Putting the candle out at the end of the working period, while giving thanks for all the positive activities of the day, also shifts me back to a leisure mode.

Bringing ritual into your life on a regular basis through meditation, poetry, chanting, and dance can provide sacred awareness in your daily life. Taking a walk in the local park can be a ritual if done with consciousness and gratitude to the divine for the natural beauty you see there. Even taking a bath or getting dressed can be a ritual if you stay aware and honor the situation. Recognize which aromatherapy oils affect your moods, which natural stones feel good as jewelry on your body, and which colors and textures bring you into goddess consciousness.

Create your own rituals to suit your life and your needs. Choose the colors of your candles and the smell of your incense intuitively; let your imagination soar; and open yourself up to connect with your favorite goddesses, angels, spirit guides, and ancestors. They are all there to work with you to co-create, to bring the sacred feminine into all areas of your life.

Wheel of the Year.

Seasonal rituals have been a way for people to connect with Mother Earth for centuries. The phases of the moon, the seasonal shifts of the sun, and the astronomical positions of the stars all helped create a natural cycle that guided and shaped the lives of our ancestors. As the cycles of nature remain, they're still governing forces in our lives. The revival of goddess religions has also revived the traditions of celebration around the annual cycle, the Wheel of the Year.

Winter Solstice—December 21

The shortest day of the year, the winter solstice celebrates the rebirth of the sun as it starts its northward journey and the days grow longer. Many ancient pagan holidays, such as Yule, were centered around this date, and it's no coincidence that modern-day Christmas (celebrating a birth) has appropriated this time of year. In addition, the new cycle and new year of nature begins on this day.

Spring Equinox—March 21

The spring equinox marks the end of winter as life bursts anew. The length of day and night are equal. In agrarian societies old and new, this date marks the beginning of the planting cycle. The miraculous resurrection of the earth and the beginning of new life are celebrated. Flowers abound and feasts are filled with fertility symbols.

Beltane—May 1

This spring holiday, our modern May Day, has only vestiges of its goddess origins left—the most obvious being the maypole. This tall, phallic symbol is planted in Mother Earth while young girls honor it through dance. The more ancient traditions featured couples leaping through a giant Beltane fire and then rushing off to the fields to have sex to sanctify and encourage the year's crops. Dating back to early Celtic times, this date stands out as one of the most joyous times of the year.

Summer Solstice—June 21

This, the longest day of the year, ushers in summer. It's a time for feasting, dancing, and lovemaking. Bonfires are burned from sunrise to sunset, marking the end of the sun's rule as the days grow shorter.

Autumn Equinox—September 21

Days of equal length again, but now the days will grow shorter. This is a celebration of thanksgiving and abundance, as altars are filled with cornucopias of fruits and vegetables. This is also a time of contemplation as dark and cold days approach.

98.

Samhain—October 31

Our modern-day Halloween was originally the Celtic feast of the dead, as indeed it still is in many other cultures. This has always been an eve of magic charms and divinations—in fact, pagans believed that during certain times between seasons, cracks to the "other side" opened and departed spirits could be contacted. Halloween is supposedly one of those times.

Moon Celebrations

There are 13 full cycles of the moon per year. The Goddess is most often associated with the moon, the shining light in the darkness of night, the regulator of the tides, and the ruler of female sexuality. There are ancient and modern rituals that celebrate each phase of the moon, from new to full. Goddesses are invoked and the aspects of the female, from her sexuality to the magic that dwells within, are celebrated.

Goddesses of the Modern World.

While there is a groundswell of women discovering the Goddess cultures of old, where does the sacred feminine reside in our modern culture? The contemporary female icons foisted onto our consciousness by the media may symbolically represent the Goddess in today's society, but rather than possessing any spiritual authority, their influence is mainly commercial. These actresses, supermodels, and pop stars are worshiped for their beauty, talent, or fame and are placed on the pedestal previously reserved for authentic goddesses who served a spiritual function. From magazine covers to television tell-alls, soft drinks to fitness videos, it seems that the essential purpose of such contemporary goddesses is to generate ever-greater amounts of publicity and money.

And then there are other icons (again, creations of the media) who have transcended their initial images to take on a more meaningful role, such as Madonna and the late Princess Diana. These two ambitious women strived for power and recognition but later expanded their roles in a way that provided, at different times, genuine inspiration to women. Princess Diana, vulnerable and complex, became a beloved symbol of a caring and compassionate goddess, willing to share her love with the world; while Madonna can be perceived as a modern-day version of the Roman goddess Diana: strong, confident, and empowering. Yet are these two celebrated women representatives of the sacred feminine in modern times? Our hunger for female icons to look up to and provide inspiration in our lives has in part been satisfied by the outward images of such flesh and blood women, but only in part.

99.

Today's woman is not satisfied with worshiping images of the Goddess, be they ancient statues or modern-day, media-created idols. It is time to take responsibility for embodying the sacred feminine in ourselves. Empowered by our feminine spiritual history, our own rituals, and each other, we can collectively contribute the strength of the sacred feminine to the future of our planet. Love, compassion, nurturing, and peaceful co-existence are what is urgently needed for the earth and all who live on it.

There are many inspiring women today who invoke the sacred feminine and guide us forward. Female role models such as Burmese political leader Aung San Suu Kyi; TV host Oprah Winfrey; eco-feminist Vandana Shiva; Indian spiritual teachers Dadi Janki of the Brahma Kumaris, Amma Ji, Mother Meera, and Guru Maya; social and business activist Anita Roddick; Eve Ensler, creator of the empowering stage show *The Vagina Monologues;* and modern-day shamans and teachers such as Starhawk, Gabrielle Roth, Denise Linn, Caitlín Matthews, and so many others, bring the sacred feminine back into society through their important work.

In today's global village, we have access to the knowledge and wisdom of such women, who can inspire us to play our role in building a more caring world. It's time for our wake-up call!

The Goddess Is in the House!

100.

Call the Goddess into your life whenever you need her, whether it's to lift your spirits, celebrate your triumphs, or give you the strength to achieve your dreams. Feel her power inside you by putting on your goddess raiments of flowing robe; beautiful jewelry; and loose, flowing hair.

Sit at your goddess altar, and dedicate yourself to bringing the energy of the sacred feminine back into the world. Acknowledge your own commitment to her love, and feel gratitude for the gifts she gives us all.

While she is still in your heart, play some uplifting music, throw back the carpet, and dance with joy and abandonment. Dance as if your life depends on it—because in many ways it does. Yell with delight and look in the mirror—the Goddess is in the house!

The GROW Commitment.

Repeat this affirmation whenever you wish to celebrate the return of the sacred feminine in yourself and the planet:

I acknowledge the power and wisdom of the Goddess within me, and commit to bringing the energy of the sacred feminine into every aspect of my life.

• • • • •

101.

Part 11

Connecting with Loved Ones

Family Connection

(Where You Examine
the Changing Nature
of the Family Structure
and Your Relationships
with Your Loved Ones)

How do I relate as a daughter? How do I relate as a mother? How do I connect with my family? How do I show them that I love them?

Whether in partnership or single, we're all constantly engaged in relationships of one kind or another: with members of our family, with our co-workers, with our friends, and with our community. The ability to maintain close connections with others is crucial to our well-being and happiness.

Relationships are particularly important for women, for we're social animals who can actually get sick if we don't engage with others. We need touch, interaction, communication, and mutual support to release our tension by sharing experiences . . . unlike men, who often retreat into themselves when stressed.

Of course, some relationships are easier than others. It's often a lot simpler to get along with our friends and colleagues than those we're most intimate with. Dealing with the complexity of the relationships with our nearest and dearest—that is, our partners and immediate family—can create the biggest challenges in life. But learning how to deepen the connection with our loved ones is how we can truly grow. In this chapter, we're going to be looking at the same principles that apply to all close relationships, which can heal any blockages related to giving and receiving love.

My Story: It's a Family Affair

I grew up in a tight family unit of a mother, a father, a sister, and an overprotective grandmother, who all lived together in regular dysfunction—as so many families do. After my first bout of going inward with therapy, I called my mother to point out my dawning realization of just how dysfunctional we all were. She agreed, but pointed out that at least no one else had ever known. I think many families experienced the same thing, particularly in the '50s and '60s, when problems were kept inside the family circle, and outside help was pretty much unthinkable.

In fact, my family really wasn't all that bad, especially when I compare them to other families. My dad was manic depressive—spending six months of the year in bed with the covers over his head, three months being fairly normal, and three months manically high, where he was incredibly sociable and spent money like water. My overpowering maternal grandmother, in whose house we lived, had difficulty communicating. She'd stuff food in the mouths of my sister and me, instilling the belief within us at an early age that a full stomach meant that we were loved. My pretty, feminine-looking mother could be fairly frightening herself when push came to shove, and spent my father's illness (which lasted most of my childhood) keeping the family butcher shop operating, which left my grandmother to keep the home operating efficiently.

These three very strong adults had major problems getting along, and looking back, I see how hard it was for them to communicate. But like all of us, they were subject to their own upbringings and influences, which were coupled with the somewhat unhealthy dynamics of living under the same roof.

Up until the last few years of his life, when he suffered severe senility, my father became a loving, connected grandfather to both my children and my sister's kids, able to show them the affection he'd found so difficult to show us. And my mother, without the pressures of work and dealing with her mother, opened into the beautiful soul she has always been, supporting me in all stages of my life.

Like my own mother, I was busy running a business throughout my children's formative years, depending on nannies for child care. I was in my 20s when I gave birth, and knew nothing about bringing up kids other than what I'd learned from my own family. My desire to have children was very strong, and I tried really hard to be a good mother. I believed I could do it all—run a demanding PR business with long hours, have a couple of kids, keep up a busy social life, and maintain a happy marriage.

My divorce and the death of my father were turning points in our family dynamics. My children were in their teens, and it was a hard time for them. We had a major shift in our relationship. Before, it had been the traditional family hierarchy, with Mum and Dad as the authority figures. And then suddenly we were three individuals going through all kinds of challenges, since their father was now mostly absent, starting a new life in Australia.

Despite having been a working mother, I invested a tremendous amount of energy in my family's well-being—perhaps I was too caring at times, which didn't always give my children their space to grow. (This is something I'm learning now.) Struggles and misunderstandings occur to this very day, but maintaining a deep bond of love at the foundation of our relationship helps my now-adult children and me overcome any difficult situations that arise. If anything, we're best friends as well as family—we spend time with each other regularly, communicate openly, laugh often, and enjoy each other's company.

Having learned that my daughter is expecting my first grandchild while I've been writing this book has created a whole new aspect to our family dynamics, bringing us even closer as we commit to the happiness and well-being of the next generation.

I believe that if parents provide constant, true love, their children will always feel it. Even within the structure of my own parents' and grandmother's somewhat dysfunctional rearing, there was always an enormous sense of love and family that I certainly inherited. I've learned firsthand that if children know that the bonds of affection within their family are unconditional and unwavering, they will always feel a sense of belonging.

108.

The New Family Dynamic.

The family structure today has changed more in the past 30 years than at any other time in history. Gone is the traditional family unit where the father works, the mother takes care of the home and children, and the kids obediently toil at school until they leave the nest soon after adolescence. And it hasn't been replaced by another basic structure—instead, families now come in a variety of combinations that pose new challenges to parents and children alike.

Today, almost 50 percent of parents are single. Often, both mother and father will commit to co-parenting, with the children spending periods of time with each. Although it's certainly not the perfect solution, children do adapt when they know that they're loved by both parents.

Obviously, divorce has played a significant role in the development of "the new family." But there are variations to even the divorced/single-parent style of modern parenting. Many women whose biological clock is ticking away are now deciding to go ahead and have a child without the support of a partner at all. They're either having a birth child, or in many cases they're adopting, as we've seen with various high-profile entertainers such as Diane Keaton, Calista Flockhart, and Rosie O'Donnell.

Then there are same-sex parents, who by various surrogate means, bring up children together. In addition, infertile couples buy young women's eggs over the Internet; dying husbands have their sperm frozen for future use; men of 60-plus have their third families with young wives; and in the not-so-distant future, babies may be cloned in a test tube.

And then we have "patchwork families," where stepchildren and half-siblings come together to create a new family unit. Keeping the continuity of family is difficult in these situations, but crucial for the stability of the children.

Because of all these changes, the psychology of the family is venturing into new and unknown territory. However, the basic challenge remains the same: how best to raise a healthy, happy child. There are lots of theories out there, but there are no hard and fast rules, except to use your best judgment possible and treat your *entire* family—children, stepchildren, parents, and partners—with love, respect, understanding, and kindness.

The Democratization of the Family

One of the key areas in how the family has changed is that today it has a far more democratic structure. Children today are both seen *and* heard—that is, they're not afraid to speak up and state their opinions, wants, and needs. For the most part, I see this as a positive development, as children have been scared into silence for too many generations. However, there has to be a balance, and in some circumstances, children can have almost too much power. Children's natural way is to push limits, and busy mothers often give in to their demands. Certainly, external influences such as the Internet, television, and pop music give children the illusion of being more adult than they are.

The solution is that new boundaries have to be created to give children structure, which is something I believe most children crave. But that structure should be based on new family values, such as mutual respect, honoring their individuality (and yours), openness, communication, nonviolence, and love.

What Is Your Family Relationship?

The unconditional love we feel for our children is a very precious feeling, but even so, other emotions and patterns can raise their heads when we deal with kids. Becoming aware of the patterns and behaviors within the family we grew up with is vital to the process of understanding ourselves.

What is your relationship with your family? It could be painful, it could be rewarding, it could be nonexistent. Take a few minutes to write down answers to the following questions about your family (where relevant), being as truthful as you can with yourself. Don't be afraid to write detailed answers—after all, family relationships are always complex.

Remember that this exercise is designed to give you a deeper understanding of your family patterns. Just be truthful with yourself and see where it takes you.

1. What was your relationship with your mother like when you were growing up?

_____

2. How has the relationship with your mother influenced the way you bring up your children?

_____

3. What was your relationship with your father like when you were growing up?

_____

4. How has the relationship with your father influenced the way you bring up your children?

_____

5. What was your relationship with your siblings like?

111.

_____

6. What influence on your life have they had?

_____

7. What is your relationship with each of your children like?

_____

8. If you could improve your relationship with any of your family members, how would you do it?

_____

9. What action could you take today to bring a member of your family closer? What can you do to bring your *entire* family closer?

_____

Conscious Motherhood.

Motherhood has never been an easy proposition—sure, it's rewarding, surprising, and even joyous, but it's never easy. Yet with the new and very different family dynamics of today, motherhood can be even more of a challenge. Fortunately for most of us, mothering is a natural part of our feminine instinct.

However, the decision to have children is not one to make lightly, so consider (with your partner if you have one) all aspects of the obligation you're taking on. Ensure that there's room in your life for a child. Personally, I don't think many young mothers appreciate the responsibility of bringing a child into the world when they first get pregnant. After all, it's a lifetime commitment. Looking back at my own experience, having children in my 20s while building a career was quite a reckless thing to do. The fact of the matter is that I hardly had time to learn to be adult, much less become responsible for new lives.

Whether motherhood is thrust upon you or is a conscious choice, and whether it comes early or late, it will take up the central position in your life. Most mothers agree that the maternal instinct takes over and you'll very quickly learn the ins and outs of feeding and caring for children, but relating to them and nurturing their emotional lives can be a little trickier. Even at an early age, it's important to connect with your child with respect—their cries are the first form of communication with you, so it's essential to learn to listen closely to what they have to say. Similarly, right from birth, children should be given a sense of safety and security, for this is the stuff that allows them to grow confident in the world.

113.

As a child grows into adolescence, pressures build and temptations multiply. Drugs, alcohol, and sexual experiences lurk, peer pressure is intense, and it's easy for children to go through an identity crisis. It makes all the difference in the world when children feel comfortable and secure enough to talk to their parents and not be judged. This feeling of safety within the family starts at the very beginning of their lives, and it influences them even when they grow into adults, which is why it's so important to establish it early.

Respecting your children's views when they're still young, and allowing them choice in deciding (within reason) what food they eat and the clothes they want to wear, are often effective ways of giving them confidence as well. Forcing your children to your way of thinking, however, is clearly not a good idea and in most cases doesn't work. For example, when my children were young, I used to make sure that we kept no junk food or soda in the house and that my son didn't play with toys that promoted violence. However, as I later found out, they would get ahold of sweets and sodas at their friends' houses, hamburgers became their preferred food, and my son's favorite toy was Action Man.

I learned that we can direct our point of view toward our kids, but at the end of the day, they follow their own path. Influencing their choices with intelligent reasoning rather than trying to control them with the "because I said so!" rule of argument clearly works far better in the long run.

Still, children should not be given *carte blanche* as far as decisions regarding their upbringing are concerned. According to family counselor Monique Duffy, who has looked after a variety of children from different backgrounds, they still need their limits. "Boundaries are important," she told me. "Children should have some input and be listened to. But there are decisions that parents have to make around safety, education, and other more important areas. If a child feels respected and listened to from an early age, then it is usually reciprocal, and the child will in turn listen to and respect their parents."

Monique and her colleagues are concerned that many young children these days are prematurely exposed to many of the hard-edged aspects of adult life. This exposure comes from different sources, including media-influenced older brothers and sisters. "The impact of the media is particularly worrying as far as encouraging little girls to dress and act in far too sophisticated a manner," she explained. "I tell the little girls I've looked after that it's okay to dress up in high heels when you're inside playing with your friends, but it's not all right to go out of the house wearing them. I think it's important to discuss with them why TV, as well as their older siblings and other influences, is not always right."

Monique Duffy and other specialists believe that there must be more honest discussions with children under the age of ten because they're exposed to more information than ever before. It's important that we're not overprotective, but we need to keep them safe without scaring or confusing them.

Working Mothers.

Many more women are working mothers than ever before, which means that the traditional role of being a mother has changed. These days, while mothers are at work, there are new alternatives for child care. In many households, fathers are playing a large part in caring for their children, sharing responsibilities that had previously been thought of as the mothers'. The concept of a "stay-at-home dad" was very unpopular until a few years ago, even though many men have wonderful "maternal" instincts and are incredibly nurturing parents.

For other families, particularly single moms, outside day care is the best alternative. The downside is that the child misses out on constant individual attention; the upside is that, from an early age, the child is involved in a social atmosphere, which, if organized properly, can be stimulating and enriching.

Another alternative, depending on financial circumstances, is a nanny. When I look back at my experiences with nannies, I shudder. I did have a number of wonderful young women living in my home and taking care of my children over the years, but I also had one or two who were irresponsible and even unpleasant to the children.

Whatever type of care you get, use agencies as much as possible and check references. Speak to as many people as you can who have used the child-care center you're interested in or know the nanny you're considering. After all, you're giving them responsibility for the most important people in your lives: your children.

115.

Mothers and Sons.

The qualities and values we need to encourage in our sons are quite different from those we should try to instill in our daughters. Being a mother to one of each, and taking into consideration the individuality of every child, it seems clear to me that young girls initially grow up far more quickly and are more confident than boys. (Considering that adult women seem to have considerable more self-esteem problems than adult men, this seems to be somewhat ironic.) Girls don't have the same pressure to prove themselves as boys do, and they have their girlfriends to fall back on. Boys are encouraged to enter competitive sports at an early age and are far more likely to get into fights as they carve out their territory on the playground.

Mothers need to instill confidence and encourage independence in their sons while letting them know that it's okay for them to have feelings and be sensitive. We need to show our sons that we value men who are balanced in their masculine and feminine energy while operating from their masculine center.

116.

The problem with so many of today's single mothers is finding an appropriate role model for their sons. We can't take a man's place in our son's life and shouldn't try—it's a different dynamic. We can nurture and support them, but our sons need men to bond with as they move into their own manhood. Some mothers are lucky enough to have the child's father around, but for many women on their own, it can be a problem finding men who can mentor their sons—and it's by example that boys learn.

There is no substitute for a loving father, but if he's not available, then it may take several men to give a boy what he needs in support and mentoring. Susanna, a single working mother and good friend of mine, brought up her teenage son on her own when his father left the country soon after he was born. She believes that a composite of male friends, together with her father, have given her son the guidance and example he needs. "When it's street-smart knowledge that he needs, he gets it from my friends. When it's problems with school, then he goes to my father," she told me. So if you have a brother, father, or good friends around, ask them to step in and take on the role of role model for your son.

Traditionally, mothers have close relationships with their sons when they're small, while daughters lean toward their fathers. Letting our sons go when they reach puberty and encouraging them to be independent can be tough. We still see them as our little boys, and we want to protect them as we've always done. Yet, as they get older, it's often our sons who want to protect *us,* which we have to learn to accept gracefully.

In ancient times, rites of passage—when young men reaching puberty went out from their tribe to hunt their first animal, fight with a lion, or experience all-night rituals of prayer—were the ways in which boys moved into manhood. We really don't have deep-seated rituals in modern society where we can prepare to let go of our sons. In fact, many times mothers and sons hang on to each other in some kind of codependency, through college and beyond, with the son living at home . . . or at least near enough to get his laundry done.

118.

Interestingly enough, it's often in societies that promote the myth of the "macho man" where a mother's influence on her son can be the strongest. In Italy, Greece, and other Mediterranean countries, men will often live at home until their mid-30s, being cooked for and fussed over until they find a wife. In India, if the boy's mother is a widow, she's expected to live with her son and his family until she dies, with the daughter-in-law treating her as the matriarch of the household.

Even in the U.K, there are more adult children living with their parents than ever before, particularly sons continuing their dependency on their mothers. In the U.S., the pattern of young people going away to college and subsequently sharing affordable rentals has meant more autonomy. But sadly, the high cost of living in the U.K., particularly in the big cities, has brought these "boomerang children" (as they are known) back home.

Showing our love to our sons when they're small is accomplished by mending their wounds and stopping their tears. Showing our love when they're older means respecting their decisions, supporting their dreams, releasing them into the world, and allowing them to move into manhood with strength and confidence.

Gifts for My Son: A Meditation

You may have one son, several, or none. But your son is also the young male aspect in you that seeks encouragement and love. Whether for your actual son or that young male inside you, there are gifts that you can give that will help him grow into his true power. You may not think that you know what these gifts are, but you already have them within you—and meditating on them will help bring them to light.

Go into a quiet place where you can let go of all the noise in your life. Close your eyes, breathe deeply, and let your intuitive voice, your higher self, give you the answers.

Go deep into your meditation, visualizing your son, the son you wish to have, or the young male inside you. Ask him what he needs from you that will help him fulfill his potential. Keep asking him softly, "What can I give you?" until you clearly hear the answers. Remember what he says, tell him that you love him completely and unconditionally and that the gifts he needs are his, open your arms to him, and feel the love between you.

When you are ready, let the vision go, pull back into yourself, and slowly come back into the present. Then write in the following space the words that came into your head. When I have done this exercise, I have realized that the best gifts I could give to my son were non-judgment, support, approval, attention, and unconditional love.

You may want to do this exercise with your son, perhaps meditating together first and then asking him what he truly needs from you. Listen to his answers with love. Then put them into practice when you're with him and when he's in your thoughts.

119.

The gifts I can give my son are:

_____

_____

_____

_____

Mothers and Daughters.

Mothers and daughters are linked together in a very different way from mothers and sons. We know what it's like to be a little girl, and we understand only too well the emotional roller coaster that adolescent girls experience. We see ourselves in our daughters—we want to protect them and keep them safe, even though we know they have to grow up on their own, no matter how hard we try to steer them in one direction or other.

Even though little girls often become "Daddy's girls," it's their mothers whom they try to copy, their mothers whom they model themselves on, and their mothers whom they go into competition with when they reach their teens. Teenage daughters are known to start falling out with their mothers as soon as adolescence takes hold. According to my mother, I was a nightmare teenager who would start yelling as soon as Mum tried to criticize me for something. Needless to say, I don't remember it like that, although I do admit to being quite a rebel.

Girls seem to want to grow into adulthood quickly. While boys are still rolling around the floor in mock fights with their friends, girls are putting on makeup and posing in the mirror in their mother's clothes. We need to encourage our daughters' self-esteem while making them aware of the realities of growing up too soon. I believe that it's important for them to understand that as much fun as dressing up can be, their true beauty comes from within; and their sparkle, like ours, happens when they feel happy and allow themselves to truly be themselves.

We modern women need to show our daughters that they're capable of being anything they want to be—and we can only do that by believing it about ourselves, too. By being in *our* strength, we can be examples of how to be in *theirs,* too. But this isn't to say that we have to pretend to be the perfect woman to our girls. We need to let our daughters learn by our experiences and our mistakes, yet we need to keep all channels of communication open, listen to them, and hope that they'll listen to us.

Much of what our daughters feel—such as fears and worries about their body images or the crisis of a pimple, pain over boys, and the drama of falling out with their school-friends—are just as common in grown women. And if we want them to move beyond these things, we need to move beyond them ourselves. I've learned that honoring the sacred feminine in our daughters, ritualizing their shifts to puberty, empathizing with them as their bodies change, talking to them about sex in a healthy and realistic way, and being their best friends when they feel they need us are our duties as mothers.

But the greatest lesson we can teach our daughters, by far, is to help them learn to love themselves. Far too many cases of anorexia and other self-destructive disorders are caused by young girls' lack of love and self-belief, combined with a need to control their bodies. Should you have teenage daughters, goddaughters, or nieces, I can do no better at this point than to proudly recommend an excellent book, *Sisters Unlimited: Every Girl's Guide to Life, Love, Bodies, and Being You,* by my daughter, Jessica Howie. Jessica's book not only advises teenage girls on how to handle their families, but it also contains general insight into how a teenage girl thinks. I only wish I'd had a copy when Jessica herself was 15—I would have understood how to communicate with her a lot easier.

The wonderful thing about daughters is how we can become close friends with them. Mothers and daughters are on a learning path together—if both stay open to seeing each other as loving, wise souls, then there's potential for an amazing and rewarding lifetime relationship.

Gifts for My Daughter: A Meditation

Since you've been both a young girl and a teenager, you know what gifts your mother gave you that made a difference in your life. And you know what gifts you wanted that you never got. Meditating on these topics will help you discover what you can do to help your own daughter.

Take yourself into a deep place of stillness and contemplation, where you can again connect with your higher self and ask for the kinds of the gifts you should give to your daughter, or if you don't have one, to the daughter that is inside you.

See her in your mind and ask her what she needs from you. If need be, ask her several times until you hear her true voice giving you the answer. When that happens, *open your arms and bring her close. Tell her how much you love her, and feel the love pass between the two of you like rays of light. When the moment is appropriate, finally let her go and slowly come out of your meditation. Write down the gifts you wish to give her in the space below. Some of the gifts I consciously wish for my daughter are <u>respect</u>, <u>wisdom</u>, <u>grace</u>, <u>self-esteem</u>, and <u>unconditional love</u>.*

If you feel your daughter is ready, repeat this exercise with her, giving her the opportunity to express her needs to you.

Gifts I can give my daughter are:

_____

_____

_____

_____

_____

Daughterhood.

We may not all be mothers, but we are certainly all daughters. It is said that we don't choose our parents, but I believe that on some soul level we do decide on the man and woman who will give us the lessons we need for growth in our lives. For better or for worse, our relationship with our parents is often the most gratifying as well as the most challenging in our lives. As much as we learn from our parents, we suffer wounds as a result of our relationships with them as well.

It can be very easy to hold anger toward our parents—after all, we put them on pedestals when we grow up and believe that they are all-wise and all-knowing. When we finally see them as human beings who are flawed and make mistakes, we tend to get angry with them and somehow feel that they've let us down.

Although it can be difficult, we need to view our parents with compassion as they wrestle with their own set of problems and fears. We need to be supportive of them and learn to communicate openly with them, for communication is how we can break through to a new understanding of each other. This isn't always easy—especially if our parents came from a generation that doesn't communicate. If that's the case, we can be there for them in other ways. We can speak to them regularly, let them know we love them, and express to them that it's okay if they show us their fears.

We cannot guarantee to like our parents, even if we do *love* them. Sometimes the misunderstandings (or in some sad cases, the abuse) is just too painful for bridges to be built. If you believe that there are too many wounds and too much pain between you and your family, be prepared to let them go. And for the sake of your own healing, you may want to avail yourself of professional counseling. Facing up to damaging patterns and pain can be healing for you, your family, and even the generations to come.

124.

With the exception of severely dysfunctional situations, our mothers are almost always there for us. As they age, I believe it's our turn to show them honor and respect. My sister and I both call our mother daily. Apart from reassuring us that she's well, she continues to give both of us the most incredible love and support. I truly value her wisdom and benefit from every conversation I have with her. It is my pleasure and good fortune to enjoy this beautiful friendship, which I believe continues to teach me the lessons I need to know.

Loving our parents and supporting them as they gradually move into their role as elders is natural and fulfilling. But it's a big psychological shift to suddenly become the caretakers of our own elderly parents. It's important for our own well-being to acknowledge if this is an act of *diligent* service or whether we can make it *joyful* service.

Like me, so many of my friends in their 40s and 50s are now becoming grandparents. We are moving into our role as family elders, alongside our parents. We can learn so much from our elders by sitting with them and encouraging our children to spend time with them, too. In indigenous villages and tribes, the whole community usually cares for the grandmothers and grandfathers, giving them respect and honoring them for their wisdom and experiences. And in turn, the elders give the children guidance. In such a cross-generational atmosphere, children are raised with love and wisdom. This is why I love the African-village adage: "It takes a village to raise a child," which Hillary Clinton adapted for the title of her first book.

A Blessing on You, Mom; A Blessing on You, Dad: A Meditation

Rummage through some of your oldest, happiest memories, either in your home, your parents' house, or even in your mind. If you have old childhood snapshots of cheerful times with your folks or some old videos or souvenirs of wonderful family holidays, spend a few quiet hours going through them.

Then take some quiet time to meditate. As you do, remember the pure love you felt for your parents when you were small. Imagine that love in the center of your heart, and feel it growing bigger and bigger until it fills your whole body.

Feel this complete, unconditional love for your parents, and ask them, in your mind, for forgiveness for any of the harsh words or harm you have caused them. Then feel total forgiveness for any pain they may have caused you over the years. If you find that this is just too difficult, put them in your prayers, send them blessings, and thank them for giving you the great gift of life.

125.

Sibling Rivalry.

We love to love 'em . . . and hate 'em, too. Our sisters and brothers were often our best friends growing up—*and* our worst enemies! Siblings can be so different, despite the same upbringing and parents, there's no guarantee you'll get along. But no matter how much you screamed at each other when you were small, you know you'll always defend each other to the death.

Friends tend to come and go, but blood ties are there forever. Value your brothers and sisters, tell them you love them, and keep in touch. Even those of us who are separated by oceans and thousands of miles of land can get on the phone or e-mail.

So stop reading this book for a bit, call at least one, if not more, of your siblings, and just remind them of some great times you had growing up—and tell them how much you love them. They might wonder what's come over you, but they'll enjoy it, mark my words.

127.

The Family of Women.

Although it isn't a blood tie, women often form bonds with other women in such close and special ways that female friends become a different type of family. We need these close girlfriends to share the parts of our lives that only other women can understand. As it is important to spend time with your family, it is equally important to spend time with your family of women to nurture and support each other. This valuable sharing time is no luxury—friendships between women have been scientifically proven to save our lives.

After extensive research, scientists from the University of California at Los Angeles (UCLA) concluded that when we women spend time with our girlfriends, it counteracts the health-threatening stress that most of us experience on a daily basis. The scientists found that the hormone *oxytocin* is released as part of our stress response, and it encourages us to tend to children and gather with other women. Then, this releases more oxytocin, which calms us down.

Additional research from Harvard Medical School shows that we also age better and lead a more joyful life as a result of having close female friends and confidantes. We have all had the experience of having our spirits lifted by our closest girlfriends. To be listened to, counseled, humored, encouraged, and loved by our women friends is a gift we should never take for granted.

Women's Friendship Circle

Think of five positive, open women whom you most enjoy spending time with, and who are on a journey similar to yours. It doesn't matter if they don't know each other, as long as you're confident that they have enough in common and will get along well. Invite them to join you for a special evening in your home to discuss the creation of a regular friendship circle. Be sure to arrange your home in an even more welcoming fashion than normal, with lit candles, beautiful flowers, and perhaps a small gift for each guest in keeping with the tone of the evening.

After greeting your friends and introducing everyone to each other, explain how even though you believe that spending quality time with your women friends is crucial to your mutual health and stress levels, it often gets left out of busy schedules. Invite them to become members of this friendship circle, where you'll share your stories, be supportive, and enjoy pleasant times. Ask them to commit to meeting at least once a month to share in a mutually agreeable activity. You could go for a walk, have dinner, or visit a health spa together, but each activity must allow you to talk to and engage with each other.

Be open to suggestions about how to develop the circle. Perhaps propose that you start your get-togethers by lighting a candle, taking turns offering a blessing, and going around the table to share what's happening in each of your lives. But be sure to let the circle evolve organically, and only invite in new members if you're all in agreement. But understand that if you do become too big a group, you'll lessen your sharing time. Try to spend at least three hours together when you meet, and treat this valuable time as sacred.

128.

Finish each circle by thanking each other, acknowledging the wise woman in each of you, and blowing out the candle until the next time you meet.

The GROW Commitment.

Repeat this affirmation when thinking of your loved ones and all the special people in your life:

I am grateful for my beloved family and friends,
and I send them unconditional love always.

• • • • •

(Where You Examine
the Nature of
Partnership and
Intimate Connections)

Wise
Loving

Am I ready to share my life with another? How do I find the right partner? What makes for a strong foundation in a committed, loving relationship? What is love?

Ever since prehistoric man chose his mate by banging her over the head with a club, men and women have been struggling to find a harmonious balance within life's greatest challenge: relationships.

My Story: Searching for Love and Romance

I moved into a small flat in London's Notting Hill with my future husband when I was 21, never giving any thought to whether this was going to be a "meaningful" relationship—or, indeed, what I wanted from the relationship at all. I had become friends with Paul through work some months earlier, and when we finally became sexual partners, I rashly packed up my suitcase, left my parents' house, and resettled myself in trendy West London with my new boyfriend.

It was the end of the '60s, and although I thought of myself as very worldly, I was still pretty innocent and knew next to nothing about relationships. I only had my parents to use as a model, and as both of them came from families (and a generation) that wasn't at ease with expressing emotional feelings, they really weren't much of an example of a fully functional couple.

After an initial romantic period, Paul and I swiftly entered a pattern of intense sexual activity along-side dramatic and violent arguments. We soon learned how to press each other's buttons, and instead of discussing what was really going on for either of us, we threw our energies elsewhere.

Although Paul was happy to be living with me and planning our future together, he started a pattern of having affairs with women in our social circle that would continue throughout our marriage. Oblivious to his philanderings, I was sure he was the man for me and didn't even think of finding out if our vision for the future was really the same. I knew I wanted a marriage; two children (a boy and a girl); a rambling, friendly house with a big red oven; and a small dog. Paul seemed to want the same things, but I was initially unaware of his additional need: sexual adventures with as many women as possible while at the same time being married to me.

With deceit underpinning our relationship from his side, and an urge for denial underpinning mine, we set ourselves up for what became the core problem in our marriage: We never learned how to truly communicate with each other, either emotionally or sexually. Sure, over the years we expressed our concerns and thoughts about our businesses, our children, our friends, and our home, and we even followed the same spiritual path for a number of years—but we were rarely able to sit down together and share how we were really feeling about each other and our relationship. We were good at staying busy, being social (in fact, we seemed to have other people around us all the time), and organizing a very full life, but our personal life was stuck. We were unable to be honest and open with each other, so lovemaking eventually became a rarity. Lack of communication kept me from expressing my needs and desires with the closest person in my life—my husband.

Finally, after more than 20 years, we split up without counseling or honest communication on either side. I assumed that I'd be meeting Mr. Right fairly soon after I got divorced. After all, I'd had years of a pretty bad marriage, but I'd learned some important lessons—I reckoned it was time to meet my prince, who would make me happy-ever-after.

After a grieving period of six months, I started off on my adventures to find him . . . and my normally good judgment of people seemed to go out the window. If I met a man socially, found him attractive, and went to bed with him, I automatically started planning our future life together. The fact that he might be totally unsuitable for any one of a million reasons seemed immaterial. I tried to make relationships work with an assortment of men of different ages, nationalities, and ethnicities—in the process, I experienced a lot of love, a lot of pain, and some really great sex. I seemed to be on a permanent emotional roller coaster, either falling in or out of love. My conversations with friends and family were pretty one-sided: Whoever was the current man was talked about exhaustively until I was banned from saying another word.

My daughter had a fairly open mind about the strange characters who appeared in our home—from an eccentric English poet to a Rastafarian drummer to a 22-year-old fire-eater—but my son was, understandably, far more disapproving. My teenage children and I were going through our puberty together, and they were far wiser and more cynical than I was.

I finally started to recognize a familiar pattern in my behavior with men: They were initially attracted to my energy and strength, but then I would become a needy little girl or controlling mother, neither of which were attractive to them or me. I recognized that both patterns were based on my relationships with my parents. My lack of loving contact with my manic-depressive father had created the needy child looking for Daddy's love; on the other hand, my ability to be the strong, controlling woman was based on the relationships my mother, grandmother, and great-grandmother had had with their husbands.

After a period of shorter affairs, I had two long-term relationships for a couple of years each, where I had time to observe my interaction with men in more depth. I saw how I had tremendous rejection issues, going back to my lack of relationship with my father in my formative years—yet I would often set myself up one way or another in similar situations. Despite my recognized professional success, I realized how low my self-esteem was. Like so many women, I felt that I needed the validation of a man to make me feel good about myself.

134.

I decided that it was time to step back from this crazy search for the perfect partner and stop wasting my energy. I started meditating with the Brahma Kumaris, which is a celibate order focused on learning to love and connect with the divine. I realized that it was necessary to respect myself if I wanted someone else to. I realized that no man could make my life complete—I had to do that myself. And I appreciated that by becoming more conscious and aware of my relationship patterns, I could change them and attract the companion I deserved into my life. I observed how so many relationships were based on expectations, illusions, and needs. And I understood, for the first time in my life, how happy I am to be single, with no expectations, yet open to love in whatever form it might enter my life.

Love Story.

The traditional pattern of relationships is undergoing a huge transformation in the 21st century. There have never been more single people, divorce has never been easier, and women are increasingly financially independent—yet we women are still conditioned to look for Prince Charming, whom we expect to ride up on a white horse and whisk us away to his castle. And what if he does? Does that guarantee we'll be happy forever? Not according to today's divorce statistics: Currently 41 percent of marriages in the U.S. fall apart (the figure is nearly that high in the U.K. as well).

I don't want to sound too cynical—a romantic wedding and living "happily ever after" *is* possible for some—but the odds are slim that the majority of romances will evolve into traditional, long-term partnerships. After all, when "til death do us part" was written into marriage vows centuries ago, most people only lived into their 40s. (And what on earth were we women thinking about when we accepted the line "to love, honor, and obey"?!) The classic story of a young couple meeting, dating, getting engaged, marrying, having children, and staying together until they die of old age is almost as unlikely in today's society as flying to Mars . . . which, thanks to author John Gray, is now thought of as the planet men come from.

Books on relationships, detailing how we should communicate and what men and women *really* mean when they talk to each other, line shelf after shelf of my library—and, indeed, they do make some sense. Women and men *are* different; we think differently, and we react in different ways. We know men are linear, rational, and not very sensitive to what we're really trying to tell them. And they think that they have to solve every one of our problems, when all we really want them to do is listen.

As for us women, however independent we may appear, there's still a part of us that defers to and wants to be looked after by a man. We're much more confident in all areas of our lives than we used to be, and that includes our sexuality. On the other hand, we often need to be assured that our worst fears about being too fat, too thin, or too wrinkled are just in our heads, and that we are truly beautiful. We want flowers, poetry, and an understanding of our hormonal problems while he does the "man thing" *and* is supportive, loyal, trustworthy, and strong.

At this point, I would like to apologize to any gay women reading this book—for the sake of convenience, I'm going to focus on and refer to the woman/man partnership, but I hope you understand that most references equally apply to same-sex love. Because whether we're gay or straight, we're all looking for the same thing: L-O-V-E. For those of us who still believe that another person is going to fill the gap inside us, I'm afraid the truth is that love is not constant, and no one can fill that gap but you. While a great partner can be a source of supreme joy and support, it's up to you alone to look inside and fit all the pieces of the happiness puzzle together. And when that happens, new relationships—if that's what you're looking for—will seem to happen by magic, and the ones you have already will tend to grow even stronger.

The Relationship Dilemma.

With the traditional structure of relationships changing, and so many single women of all 137. ages looking for a mate, how do we determine what we want, what we need, and how to go about finding it? For some of us, the search for our so-called soul mate is based on what we think is a realistic vision of the type of person who will fit into our lives. Perhaps we desire a terrific father for our children, a companion to work and play with, or a partner to build a life with.

However, in the back of our minds, no matter how realistic we seem to be, we all end up wishing for "the perfect man"—that is, someone who's going to sort out *all* of our problems and make us incredibly happy. Of course, the perfect man doesn't exist any more than the perfect woman does. We are human beings, after all, with all of the imperfections that our humanness implies. The dream of the prince who will come save us is a myth—and a cruel one at that, since it's sold to us at an amazingly early age.

What Do Women Really Need (and Want)?

The first thing we must ask ourselves about having an intimate relationship is: Do we really need one? Many women would answer yes, but why? Most of us can live quite happily without one; we *do* have our close friends and family, after all. And relationships can be highly distracting—they take a lot of effort and can cause just as much misery as happiness.

No one wants to live in isolation, but there's certainly a good argument for choosing to stay unattached in today's world. Many of us have done very well on our own with successful careers and a busy social life. These days, single women are certainly not stigmatized as "old maids" or "spinsters," but are seen as strong, independent, successful, and glamorous individuals. It's not an accident that one of the most popular television shows of recent years is *Sex and the City,* a series about four vibrant single women.

138.

Not being in a relationship doesn't mean that we have to be celibate either. We have a choice: Some women enjoy being single and still have a full sex life, without the complications that a committed relationship entails. A recently divorced friend who's been surfing the Internet for lovers told me that her sex life has never been better (although she added that her *love* life has never been more empty). Of course, wanting to be in a relationship with someone is a natural human condition and still high on the agenda for most of us, regardless of how many times we may have been disappointed in the past. But we need to be clear with ourselves about the nature of the relationship we want. Does it involve an intimate friend who offers us sex without a commitment? Or are we looking for an emotionally available man who's open to sharing what life has in store and is ready for a long-term partnership?

If we want a relationship, then we must be clear about what we need in a partner. Identifying these qualities is very different from having fixed ideas about physical appearance, financial status, and other external issues, which can block us from being open to the right men. In other words, what we *want* can be either conscious or illusionary desires, while what we *need* are our essential requirements. There's nothing wrong with bringing both our wants *and* needs into a wish list—the difference is that we can be flexible with our wants, whereas our needs—practical or otherwise—are more fixed.

But life is not just about demanding from the universe—we have to be prepared to give, particularly in a relationship. What are we prepared to give of ourselves that will enrich the life of another? And are we prepared to trust and receive? Regardless of what our conscious mind says, are we truly ready to open ourselves up, to surrender and take the risk of unconditionally loving another in an intimate relationship?

The Relationship Wish List: A Meditation

Now is the time to check inside and ask your higher self for the clarity and wisdom to acknowledge what you truly wish to receive as well as to offer. Take some quiet time to let your conscious mind rest. Go to your special quiet place, close your eyes, and allow your active mind to relax. This is your time to ask for the answers to the questions of your heart. Give your heart permission to express its needs as well as its desires.

Ask yourself the following questions, and when you feel centered and clear, bring your attention back to the room and start writing down the answers you received.

1. *What type of relationship do I think I want? (An occasional lover? A life partner? A companion?)*

   ....

   ....

   ....

   ....

2. *What type of relationship do I need at this point in my life? (A stable, loving partnership? A casual, sexual friendship? A spiritual companion? None?)*

   ....

   ....

   ....

   ....

3. What gifts do I want a partner to give me? (Loyalty? Affection? Playfulness? Commitment? Unconditional love? Freedom? Intellectual stimulation? Communication?)

_____

_____

_____

4. What gifts am I prepared to offer a partner? (Unconditional love? Non-judgment? Support? Commitment? Space? Trust? Respect? Attention?)

_____

_____

140.

_____

5. Am I truly ready to trust and surrender to another?

_____

6. If not, why not? (Examine your reasons, and if you want to change them, make a conscious decision to do so.)

_____

_____

_____

Where Are the Men?

I never meet any available men. I know so many great single women, but where are the great single men? Men are scared of strong women. All the men I know of my age want younger women.

These are some of the urban myths that arise when single women get together nowadays. And yet, clearly there are as many available men out in the dating cosmos as there are women. There are men who *do* enjoy the company of powerful women, men who aren't looking for younger women, and younger men who are interested in connecting with experienced, older women.

Terrific, available men don't stand on street corners waiting to be found any more than terrific, available women do. I know many men who are just as anxious, if not more so, to meet a loving partner as the women I know. But keep in mind that if you have a feeling of scarcity in any area of your life, then that's what you'll tend to attract to you. If you believe that there are no quality men out there, chances are that a quality man won't appear. Yet if you believe you can manifest abundance in all the areas of your life, including relationships, then that's what you will have.

Our modern mating rituals are far different from anything that has gone before them. Roles and boundaries are much less defined these days—the only real rule is that there are no rules . . . nor should there be. Every person is unique, and every relationship grows in its own distinctive way. However, there are patterns of behavior that we should be conscious of when dealing with the opposite sex. Many professional women who use their masculine energy to help them advance in the workplace complain of the difficulty in finding a mate. Perhaps using that strongly assertive energy in social situations with men is off-putting, since many men like to feel as if they're at least participating in the chase. It's not difficult to be in your feminine energy and still remain strong *if* you allow the man to remain in his own masculine energy. Men feel threatened enough in our postfeminist society without women appearing to take over the pursuing phase of love, too.

The energy you put out is key to attracting others. If you are friendly, open, and confident in social situations, then men will be interested enough to at least try to find out more

141.

about you. But if you act desperate, try to sell yourself too much, or act standoffish, it will be a deterrent to most men. As clichéd as it might sound, the point is to relax and present yourself as you really are. A friend of mine once told me if she knew that in two years she was definitely going to meet her mate, she could just loosen up and enjoy her life without always being on the hunt for Mr. Right. I told her that if she simply enjoyed the fullness of her life right now, she most likely *would* meet someone within two years.

The most powerful way to bring someone into your life is to be open, friendly, and confident to whoever steps in. Love, more often than not, comes in a surprise package—it could happen at the bus stop, the supermarket, or at a dinner party. If you pursue your passions and hobbies, it's quite likely that you'll meet someone with common interests. There are so many ways of meeting others with the same interests—the important thing to remember is to enjoy these activities for themselves. Meeting someone while you're doing something you love is a bonus!

142. *The Tutti-Frutti MANifestation Spell*

So you've decided that you'd like to manifest a new love—perhaps *the* love—or at the very least a great new friend and lover, because you're a powerful woman and have the ability to create abundance in all areas of your life. If you wish to, ask your girlfriends over so that you can collectively put your energy together to draw some great new men into all of your lives.

This spell is a fun way to help you visualize the qualities you require in a lover—not the outward trappings, but the true essence of the man you wish to bring into your life. You're going to make a tutti-frutti smoothie that will MANifest your cutie!

Choose a powerful astrological time, perhaps that of a new or full moon or one of the sacred days listed earlier in this book. Since eye of newt and tail of bat aren't so easily available in the average supermarket, I've adapted this spell to a modern woman's lifestyle. All you'll need is a selection of exotic and everyday fruits and a blender. But don't take this spell's effectiveness lightly—the important thing in any manifestation ritual is your intention and focus.

Listed below are a number of qualities you may wish the man of your dreams would possess, and each is represented by a particular fruit. If there are qualities that you feel are missing in this list, add your own together with an appropriate fruit. From the list below and from your own additions, select the fruits that represent at least six qualities that are the most important for you to have in a partner.

QUALITY	FRUIT
Passion	Passion Fruit
Integrity	Apple
Intellect	Pear
Compassion	Peach
Strength	Pineapple
Humor	Banana
Enthusiasm	Cherries
Openness	Blueberries
Communicative	Strawberries
Creativity	Papaya
Confidence	Guava
Sensuual	Mango
Ethical	Orange
Centered	Kiwi

143.

As you pick up each fruit to prepare for your magic smoothie, repeat this sentence out loud, adding in the appropriate fruit and quality. For example: *"Magic* [apple], *add the quality of* [integrity] *to the delicious mix of my future partner . . ."*

Put the prepared fruit in the blender, and add milk, juice, or a liquid of your choice (such as soy or almond milk). Blend well, envisioning the qualities as they mix together to create the perfect partner.

When your fruity elixir is ready, recite the final part of the spell:

> *As I drink this magic potion,*
> *My manifestation I put in motion.*
> *May this spell I now create*
> *Bring to me my perfect mate.*

144.

Drink your smoothie slowly and consciously, imagining that you're in a relationship with a man who loves you deeply and contains all these qualities. Know that you love him equally and unconditionally. Experience how your mutual love feels in every cell of your body, and lock these feelings into your memory. Believe in the very deepest part of your being that you can manifest this ideal relationship in your life, either within your existing one or by attracting a new partner. Know, too, that the qualities that are important to you in a mate all exist within *you.*

Love, Romance, and Partnership.

You've found someone who seems to be the perfect partner for you—you're happy beyond belief because you're crazy in love, and you both know that this blissful state will last forever. . . . Okay, so maybe that's a bit of an exaggeration. As most of us know, even the strongest relationships go through challenging periods. While partnering with someone may be natural, merging your individuality into "coupledom"—that is, adjusting your habits and lifestyle to coincide with another person's habits and lifestyle—is a journey like no other.

According to psychologist Chuck Spezzano, Ph.D., whose work I respect immensely, relationships go through three stages: *romance,* when the bells are ringing and it's as if you're wearing rose-colored glasses; *power struggle,* when the first blush of romance has faded and control issues start to crop up; and *the dead zone,* when there's no conscious connection, either physically or emotionally. Chuck believes that honest, open communication can break through all these stages to get to true intimacy.

When you're initially in love, the world truly is perfect. Colors seem brighter, the air seems sweeter, and your lover can do no wrong. It's at this point in a relationship that expectations abound—your foremost desire is to have him fit into your life, and you're prepared to wiggle around as much as possible until he does. You don't want your illusions shattered—instead, you'd rather keep your big, pink love bubble bouncing along without reality raising its oh-so-boring head.

145.

Some of us are so addicted to falling in love that we don't even want to find out if the relationship can work in the long run. After all, the romance stage in a relationship seems to be the most exciting time. A friend of mine even said that she prefers to stay single so that she's free to keep falling in love.

But for those of us who decide to remain in a relationship with one person, we learn that the initial "love bubble" can't last forever. The time always comes when the first rush of passion starts to die down, and you begin noticing unattractive aspects of your lover that you hadn't seen before. When you fall in love, it's virtually guaranteed that you'll fall out of "being in love" sooner or later.

This doesn't mean that you'll stop loving each other. Experience teaches us that there's a love that's richer, deeper, and even more rewarding than the early, starry-eyed type of love. This is a love that results from two people supporting each other into wholeness, and it can only happen over time. It's a love that comes from overcoming obstacles; learning from mutual experiences; and creating a life based on truth, openness, and

trust. You have to work to get to this love, and it can be painful—but this type of love is the greatest balm of all. Through love with another in an intimate partnership, you can learn much about your own wounds. And by supporting another in his growth, you can learn to heal yourself.

"Are You Blinded by Love?" A Quiz

So you think you can tell the difference between real love and the shooting-stars stage of falling in love? Why not take this opportunity to find out by answering these few simple questions.

1. When you see your lover/partner, do you get nervous and flushed?

2. When your lover/partner cancels a date at the last minute because he has to work, does it make you feel insecure?

3. Do you believe that your lover/partner has no faults?

4. Do you feel sexually turned on every time you look at your lover?

5. Do you count the hours you spend apart from him and can hardly wait to see him again?

6. Do you incessantly talk about him to your friends and family?

7. Do you agree with everything he says?

8. Do you cancel dates with friends when he asks you out?

If you answered yes to each of these eight questions . . . hello, you're definitely living in the illusion of romantic love—and therefore utterly unqualified to know if this relationship is the real thing or not! If you've answered yes to between three and five of the questions, there may be some hope for you yet. And if you've said yes to less than three, you've passed through the falling-in-love stage and are probably approaching the next phase in your relationship. . . .

The Battle Zone.

It's inevitable that when two people are in a relationship, problems arise. And problems are not exclusive to any particular phase of a relationship—differing opinions are just as likely to occur in the early romantic phase as they are with a couple who have been happily married for 50 years. It's how we approach and confront the problems with our partner that differs.

In Chuck Spezzano's relationship paradigm, the power-struggle phase occurs directly after the romance period. It's as if a veil slips away, and we not only see our partners as they are, but the very things that initially attracted us now lead to conflict. If left unattended, these constant struggles will most likely lead to the real problems of the relationship. It is also in this phase that our own anxieties and inadequacies make their entrance. Most of us have experienced the toxins that can do mortal damage to a relationship: anger, jealousy, deception, resentment, blame, and a host of other poisons that crop up as our partners seem to transform from our allies into our adversaries.

The fact of the matter is that our partners probably haven't changed that much, but our most deep-seated fears have begun to surface. For example, why do we get jealous? Is it because our partners are flirting too much at parties, or is it because our own fears of rejection and feelings of inadequacy are creeping in? And when conflict disintegrates into blame and anger, isn't the cause as likely to be our own fears of losing power and control as it is the issue we're arguing about?

One of the great joys of a close relationship is that we get to know our partners incredibly well. But by doing so, we also find out their psychological weaknesses, the hot buttons that when pushed carry a direct charge to their emotional core. Who among us, fearful of losing power, hasn't pushed a button or two on our loved ones? While this temporarily gives us the upper hand in a conflict, it's ultimately destructive, weakening the bond of trust we have with our partners.

Fear is to blame here. It causes us to create harmful imaginary scenarios in our heads, it allows us to put up walls of denial when faced with real relationship problems, it pushes us apart after having reached a loving, deep connection with our partner, and it prevents us from speaking our truth when we lose that connection. We fear complete candor because "I'll say something that will lessen me in your eyes," "I'll drive you away," "I'll be rejected," or "I'll be misunderstood."

Ultimately, fear is at the root of most couple's problems. To get beyond the fear, we must confront it head on, demonstrating that we care enough for our partners to face our demons and move into closer intimacy. And the only way to do this is through open, courageous, truthful communication.

Courage and Communication—
The Keys to a Relationship Breakthrough

It's a scary proposition to give yourself and your partner permission to discuss your innermost thoughts and fears. This is particularly true if you didn't experience open communication with or between your parents in your formative years. Talking about your deepest feelings can be extremely painful, and it takes a lot of courage to deal with tough subjects such as jealousy or rejection—I know that I've experienced physical pain in the pit of my stomach when I've spoken about my most intense fears within a relationship.

149.

Like a raw nerve in your tooth, the subjects that most need to be exposed can be the ones you want desperately to keep hidden. This is when you have to trust your partner and the process the most. You each need to feel safe, knowing that neither will punish the other if things are said that you don't want to hear. When this safe environment exists, you can go where your partnership takes you, even into very rough waters. You can also be proactive in opening up as fears and sensitive issues arise—don't reject them or cover them up, but confront them together, difficult as that may be. The more you break through your darkest fears, the greater the reward of intimacy and deep love waiting for you will be.

Ask your partner tough questions while giving him space to answer. And be prepared to give honest answers to his. Don't be afraid to express your needs and desires, and encourage him to do the same. However close you are to your partner, you can't be expected to read each other's minds—so objectively examine your bond. There must not be blame in dealing with these incredibly sensitive issues. As you listen to your partner's problems and fears, stay as nonjudgmental as you can, letting him know that he's safe. Only by doing this will you peel off more layers of protection and get to a deeper place of intimacy. Little by little, you will deepen your relationship by engaging in honest and loving dialogue.

How you interact with each other on a daily basis also sets the tone for the entire relationship. If you're constantly being critical or nagging, communication will eventually break down. And keep in mind that words are only a small part of communicating—nonverbal cues (tone of voice, body language, and so on) really come into play as well. For example, if you're feeling irritated but are being careful with your words, your partner will feel it anyway. He will most likely reflect your negativity right back at you, and your connection will break down.

When two people live together, there will always be daily disagreements, but by staying conscious in all areas of your interactions, you can keep these irritations to a minimum. Take the classic case of the top being left off the tube of toothpaste or the toilet seat always being left up—by using a gentle suggestion instead of a nagging command, you can get what you want and almost make it seem as if it was his idea the whole time!

Opening the Communication Door

Finding the time to truly communicate is fundamental to every relationship. Since it's true that communication is a two-way street, *both* parties must commit to improving their connection. If your partner is unable or unwilling to open up, you may have to take it upon yourself to create a safe space where he can learn to relax and connect. But be patient—your role in this particular dance is to be sensitive to his needs and feelings.

There have been countless books written about the differences in how women and men communicate. As we've discussed, women and men's brains work differently, and we express ourselves in different ways. Women are far more open to discussing their fears and needs than men, so we need to help them understand that expressing feelings is not always about asking the other person to solve a problem. It's about taking intimacy to a new level that will help create the foundation of an even closer and healthier relationship.

Regularly checking in with your partner (or any intimate friend) to discuss any concerns he might have can dissolve potential misunderstandings before they start, as well as heal old wounds. But don't be surprised to find that what's going on in your man's brain is not what you were expecting. He's more apt to be thinking about a football game or problems at work than the misunderstanding you had this morning over breakfast, which has been nagging at you all day.

Regardless, making connecting a priority—in spite of a busy schedule of work, family, and social life—is a crucial requirement if we are to create intimacy and wise loving. For many couples, eating or lying in bed is when they take the opportunity to talk about what's going on in their inner lives. If this works for you, fine. But from my personal experience, the distraction of food or drink doesn't create the most intimate environment for opening up to our deepest emotions, so misunderstandings can occur. As far as bed is concerned, it's certainly a place for intimacy, but it's not always the space for clear discussions, as the desire for lovemaking and sleep often take priority.

I've always found that going on long walks offers a great chance to connect. Or, if you have a partner who's open to the idea, why not suggest meditating together? A bonding meditation, perhaps in front of your altar, can create the safe space and connection where, after the meditation, you can be truthful and open up to your deepest thoughts, feelings, and fears.

Create a comfortable space with your partner where you know phones, children, or any other kinds of outside distractions won't interrupt you. Sit opposite each other, either on chairs or cross-legged on the floor. This is the time when you'll be taking turns in truly expressing your feelings, and more important, *listening* to each other. Anything can come up, so trust the process and each other.

This exercise is about peeling off the layers, and it isn't always easy. The important thing is to commit to staying present—for it's in this profound space that the reflection of your truth in each other's eyes can heal wounds and deepen your ability for intimacy.

Establishing an Intimate Connection: A Meditation

Place a candle between the two of you, and close your eyes. Breathe slowly until you feel that you are in harmony with each other. Silently ask your higher self to connect with the higher self of your partner. Allow each other as much time as you need to slip into a deep, relaxed, open place. When you feel ready, slowly open your eyes— your partner may or may not have opened his eyes before you. When you both have your eyes open, gaze at each other in silent meditation as if looking into the doorway of each other's soul.

Stay in this place for as long as it feels appropriate—it could be a few minutes, it could be up to an hour. Let whatever thoughts and feelings you have come up. Hold them for a moment and let them pass. If you find your mind wandering, come back to focusing on your partner's eyes. You may wish to concentrate on the physical nature of his eyes, or, if you feel like connecting on a more intimate, energetic level, reach out and place your left hand on his heart chakra (the energy point in the middle of his chest), and allow him to do the same to you. Stay focused until one of you signifies with a loving gesture that you are ready to begin sharing your most intimate feelings. Allow the other to speak without interruption, starting with the words, "I feel . . ."

Don't be surprised about where the conversation may lead. Having been so open to each other during this meditation, you may find yourselves drawn down a path to very sensitive, and even painful, emotions and thoughts. The important thing is to stay present and be supportive and loving. Listen with all your heart, and don't take what is said as a personal attack.

When deep wounds and truths are spoken, the process may become difficult. Know that it will bring further intimacy and usher you both into an even deeper love. You will have seen your own reflection in the other's eyes, both your positive qualities and your fears, so appreciate the courage you each are demonstrating. After you both feel you have spoken sufficiently, embrace each other, feeling the other's body and breath, and let the love you have both opened engulf your entire being.

152.

Conscious Commitment.

More often or not, committed relationships seldom begin with a commitment—they just seem to happen. You start seeing more and more of each other, clothes are left at each other's homes, plans start getting made, and before you know it, you're Partners with a capital "P." And therein lies the problem. You've eased into a commitment, without necessarily thinking through the full ramifications of what you're getting into.

Deciding when the time has come to make a mutually conscious commitment and having the courage to approach the subject needs careful consideration. Broaching the subject too early can frighten off the other person, whereas if you talk about it too late, you can miss the boat. If you feel awkward about bringing up the "c-word" with your man, perhaps you're not with the right guy—after all, he shouldn't be put off by your openness or by the subject of commitment. But even if he says he's not ready yet, at least you will have had a truthful exchange, which will eventually lead either to the further blossoming of the relationship or to its rightful end.

The reasons for making a commitment to another person are many and varied—companionship, affection, regular lovemaking, mutual support, and finances are some of the obvious ones. But the most important reason to create a conscious commitment is to support each other in being complete individuals. In order to do so, you must first make a firm commitment to yourself. You, and no other, are responsible for your happiness. It's only when you've taken this responsibility that you will be truly ready to be open to another.

Many people feel that making a commitment puts constraints on them within a relationship. This doesn't have to be. A conscious commitment can be a starting point for a new kind of freedom, for you're freely giving and receiving the most wonderful gifts the world has to offer: love and support. If your commitment should ever feel like a trap or burden, you have to honestly confront these feelings, or resentment and anger will rear their ugly heads. That's why it's best to renew your commitment, even in a small way, every day. By freely reaffirming your commitment to making your relationship the absolute best it can be, you provide each other with the opportunity of growing into your full potential and creativity—individually and as a couple.

Building Trust

Trust is central to any form of conscious commitment. Begin by being trustworthy with yourself. Make a pact with yourself to stay in your center regardless of what comes up in the relationship. Commit to staying honest, open, and present. It's when trust isn't established that communication breaks down and secrets and resentments take over. When there is a sincere, conscious commitment to each other, and the relationship exists within an atmosphere where you both feel free to express your truths, trust can grow and flourish.

If you've both agreed to have a monogamous relationship, then it's essential for the future of the relationship that both partners keep to their side of their bargain. We're all human beings, and it's natural to feel desire for others besides our partner. Knowing that it's safe to express to your partner that you've had such desires (but would never act on them) means that you can let go of the sexual tension involved and actually feel closer to him. And you'll know that you're freely choosing to be with your partner, regardless of other passing attractions.

155.

Of course this doesn't mean that you need to disclose every detail of your life to each other. You are still an individual and need boundaries to preserve your sense of self. A very happily married girlfriend of mine has had some wild nights out with friends, dancing and having fun. But despite propositions from other men, she wouldn't dream of ending the evening any other way than going home to her husband. She doesn't feel the need to tell him all the details about her evenings out, even though she has nothing to hide. He trusts her and knows that she would never break the commitment they've made to each other.

In this modern world, I know many other women who choose to spend evenings without their partners. They're not looking for lovers—they just want a few hours to acknowledge their own individuality. As long as their partners are comfortable with the situation, it can only help the relationship. We don't always have the same interests or same taste in friends as our partners do, so we can appreciate each other more when we have some freedom. This type of relationship is interdependent, giving each other the opportunity to grow individually, while still building a life and partnership together.

It's when a couple does everything together and shares every detail of their lives that they move into a codependent relationship. Codependency can be more of an addiction, rather than love, for that person. Such a relationship is essentially based on fear—the fear that doing anything without each other could lead to rejection or abandonment. We all have dependency needs and feelings, often going back to childhood, but curbing a tendency to be codependent with a partner, or getting help with this if it's a serious problem, is very important if you want your commitment to be a conscious one. One of the most treasured benefits of a conscious, co-creative commitment between a man and a woman is the happy balance between togetherness and independence—where you can have joyful and expansive experiences both together and apart.

Creating a Nontraditional Contract: George and Mary's Story.

156.

Marriage is, by far, the most traditional way of making a commitment in our society. But how clear and conscious are most people who walk down the aisle?

Clarity about your commitment is what can prevent subsequent misunderstandings and provide a bedrock for your relationship. For example, my friends George and Mary decided to create a nontraditional contract when they first entered into a relationship 13 years ago (they were then in their late 40s). George had been married before and had a history of many love affairs, while Mary had a tendency to get involved with men who left her for other women, and she had no intention of going down that road again. So together, they decided to write a contract that would set out the various points that they felt were important in making their relationship work. They also agreed to renew it at certain specified intervals.

The first contract, which took them many hours to write, was for an initial three-week period and included numerous precautions about things they felt were likely to go wrong. The first thing they agreed on was monogamy—for those initial three weeks at least. Since they had their own homes, they agreed to spend a minimum of four nights together and two nights apart every week. They felt that it was as important to spend time separately as it was to spend time together, so they wouldn't "get stuck owning each other," as Mary put it.

George and Mary also agreed that there would be no unilateral breaking of the contract without discussion, that arguments were no excuse to break the contract, and that any disagreement had to be discussed in a nonconfrontational way within 24 hours. Their contract also included a promise to meditate together for an agreed period of time every week, a pledge to bring in a mediator if they couldn't agree on certain issues, a promise to check in with each other every 24 hours (as they both traveled to different countries for their work), and an agreement to spend a minimum of 15 minutes a week just appreciating each other.

"We really liked each other from the beginning," Mary told me, "but we were cautious. After the first three weeks, we extended the agreement for another short period, signing and dating the contract as we had the first. We then extended it again, this time for three months, then six months, then two years, and then three years, each time simplifying the contract. We pretty much covered all aspects of our lives, including the physical, emotional, and spiritual, although we hadn't initially planned it that way."

George told me that the hardest times he and Mary went through were when the contracts were up for renewal: "I suppose we were both worried on some level that the other wouldn't sign, but we always did. We did nearly break up at one point and went on a vacation to France to say good-bye. But as it turned out, that trip brought us closer together than ever."

After six or seven years together, Mary and George felt that they knew and trusted each other well enough to safely dispense with a formal contract. They now live together in Mary's house, where George is a paying tenant.

Creating a renewable contract, whether it's verbal or written, is a great way of fashioning a conscious commitment. Formally renewing your personal promises to each other on a regular basis keeps them fresh in your minds, reminding you of both your own and your partner's needs and expectations.

Writing Your Own Contract

Whether you're already married or in a committed partnership, at the early stages of being with someone, or single, why not write your own contract delineating your expectations for a consciously committed relationship, using the space on the following page? I've adapted some of George and Mary's points to inspire you, but please feel free to create your own. If you decide that you want to use the contract with your partner, sign and date it, making sure you both have copies, and bring it out for renewal at an agreed date.

158.

The Conscious Commitment Contract

We, _____ and _____, commit for a period of time from _____ to _____ to the following points to deepen and enhance our loving relationship:

1. We have an exclusive sexual agreement for the length of this contract.

2. We will spend a minimum of ___ nights together and a minimum of ___ nights apart a week.

3. We will never let an argument negate this agreement.

4. Neither one of us can break this agreement without the other's approval.

5. We will check in with each other at least once every 24 hours.

6. We will discuss any disagreement within 24 hours.

7. We will meditate together a minimum of ___ times per week.

8. We will appreciate each other for at least 15 minutes a week.

9. We will mutually review this contract at the end of the designated period and, if we agree, will re-sign it for an extended time period to be agreed upon by both of us.

10. _____

11. _____

12. _____

13. _____

14. _____

15. _____

Signed: _____

Signed: _____

Dated: _____

One and One = Three.

What most of us are either consciously or unconsciously yearning for is a relationship with another who will flow with our flow, mirror our dance, and, through partnership, create a more expansive energy than we can manifest individually. There is nothing more expansive than those special moments when our hearts swell almost to the bursting point for the simplest reasons—such as when you catch the eye of the man you love and you know exactly what he's thinking. Or when you spontaneously laugh at the same silly thing. When your partner is your best friend and you trust the deep connection between you, you feel both expansive and expanded by your love. It's as if you're invincible and connected with the whole universe on an energetic level.

A truly conscious, committed love is a grounded, courageous act. As author and psychiatrist M. Scott Peck, M.D., says in his wonderful book, *The Road Less Traveled:* "True love is not a feeling by which we are overwhelmed. It's a committed, thoughtful decision."

160.

Making the decision to support another person on his or her journey of emotional and spiritual growth is an empowering one. Partners empower each other with their nurturing and mutual support, and it all begins with the courageous act of simply saying yes to conscious commitment. If you stay authentically connected to each other, daring to face the issues that inevitably come up, you'll enter a place of joy, peace, and grace. And when you join with another and give of yourself wholeheartedly, holding nothing back, other areas of your life will tend to open up and flourish. You will not only connect with the person you love . . . but with your full potential, creativity, and purpose.

We all have our own journeys to take, sometimes with another as a traveling companion, sometimes on our own. Living our lives based on love—love for self, love for a partner, and love for humanity—will help us conquer our fears and create a world of light, peace, and happiness.

The GROW Commitment.

Regularly repeat this relationship affirmation when you feel ready for true partnership:

My true love and beloved partner is now entering my life.

• • • • •

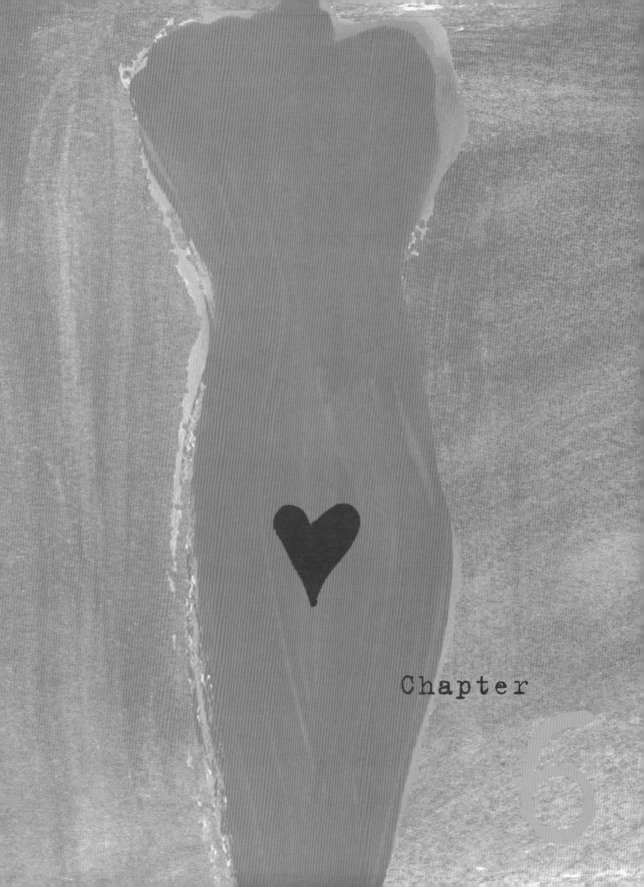

Chapter 5

Sex, Love, and Intimacy

(Where You Acknowledge Your Sexuality and Its Connection with the Divine)

What role does sex play in my life? Am I comfortable with my sexuality? How do I surrender to my lover so that even the slightest touch can result in cascades of orgasmic delight?

Let's celebrate the mystery and fullness of our sexuality: our luscious thighs, our curvy hips, the fire in our belly, the softness of our breasts, the moistness of our lips, the tenderness of our touch, the sensitivity of our skin, the flower of our scent. It's time to rejoice in the beating of our hearts, the pulsating of our blood, the quickening of our breath, the sweat on our brow, the hardening of our nipples, the wetness of our sex, and the ecstasy of our union with another person.

Being aware and proud of our sexuality brings us in touch with the beauty of being female. Our sexuality is where we hold our radiant, womanly power, which exudes from us when we're confident and fully present in our bodies. Female sexuality is not only passion unleashed during sex itself, it's an energy that we carry and can connect with at any time. We can feel it when we walk, eat, smell, touch, or dance. It's a manifestation of nature and the cosmic force; a connection of pure joy and love through connection with the self, the natural world, divine energy, and other human beings. Female sexuality is unlimited and abundant. It is the Goddess inside every woman, the ultimate yes.

My Story: The Rhythm of Life

My father informed me when I entered my teens that if I wanted to marry a nice Jewish boy, I'd better stay a virgin. The only two rules he tried to lay down were that I couldn't have sex with anyone until I was married, and I had to marry a fellow Jew. Suffice it to say, I let him down on both counts. Growing up in the '60s meant that the Pill was available from the family doctor, and I eagerly started taking it when I finally lost my virginity at 19—after a year or two of extensive foreplay with my non-Jewish boyfriend.

164.

I enjoyed sex, and from the ages of 19 to 21 (when I started living with Paul, my husband-to-be), I had a number of lovers and boyfriends whom I practiced my lovemaking skills on, even though I was much too self-conscious to express <u>my</u> needs or even be aware of them.

My initial sexual relationship with Paul was very passionate. We would make love in every possible room in our apartment and stay in bed all day on Sundays, reading the papers, eating a big break-fast, and having sex—in other words, behaving like most other young couples in the early stages of romance. But as we settled down to a life of building up our careers, buying a house, and starting a family, our sex life seemed to settle down, too. Two young toddlers and a hectic life put us on automatic pilot, where we would make love when we had the space and energy—but the heat of those early days was gone.

Without being aware of his other dalliances, I simply lost interest in making love with Paul, and through our many years in "the dead zone," I became used to weeks and even months going by with-out entering the <u>pleasure zone.</u> My husband would complain now and then, but I was just too tired. Being a career woman and mother of two young children took enough of my energy. Sex was no longer high on my priority list—periodic celibacy was a feature of my marriage, and passion had left my relationship.

After my divorce, I felt like a virgin again. I was self-conscious about my body and couldn't imagine being naked in front of another man. It took me six months and an extensive relationship workshop in Hawaii with psychologist Chuck Spezzano before I experienced sex again, with a young Japanese man who was also attending the workshop. He explained during our night of sensual lovemaking that we were both satisfying our needs and would go back to our countries the next day with sweet memories.

The experience brought me back in touch with the sexual side of my being. I appreciated how repressed I'd been, and how much I really enjoyed lovemaking. Now in my early 40s, I was ready to embark on a new journey, where I could appreciate the wonders of sexual intimacy and explore the delights that it could bring. It was around this time that I brought my love of dancing back into my life, working with teacher Gabrielle Roth and her Five Rhythms practice of ecstatic dance.

165.

I found that dancing itself could be a sexual and sensual experience, as it physically releases the body to its natural flow of oneness with the mind, emotions, and spirit. It was through my dance, vibrating with the rhythm of the music, that I was able to connect with the rhythm of my body, my heart, and my central feminine core. I started to appreciate my sexuality—as a woman in her full power and strength—in ways that I hadn't done when I was younger. Through my dancing and my sexual experiences, I began to understand who I was as a woman and how I could use my sexual energy in intercourse if I chose—but I also learned that this energy was present in other areas of my life as well, such as service, meditation, and connection with a higher spiritual realization.

Our Sexual Birthright.

Eastern philosophies and religions have traditionally celebrated sexuality: Images of the gods and goddesses engaged in erotic sexual play adorn temples throughout India; traditional Chinese and Japanese cultures celebrate the art of lovemaking; and other ancient civilizations have honored the power of sacred sex. Yet for the last 2,000 years or so, Western society, being heavily influenced by the major patriarchal religions, has considered women's sexuality and, indeed, the naked female body, as something indecent. Women were not supposed to enjoy themselves sexually or follow their desires and needs, and sexually free women were often called harlots or whores, among other slurs.

Because we still live with the vestiges of those repressive times, much of our own attitudes toward our sexuality are rife with confusion and contradiction. Sex is openly and freely talked about in all forms of the media, yet more people than ever are having unfulfilling sex lives. Supposedly secure, independent, and sexually liberated modern women are spending millions on cosmetic surgery to have their breasts inflated and their lips enhanced because they believe it makes them sexier.

Sex is sold over the Internet, the media encourages little girls to use cosmetics and wear high heels to look sexy before they're nine years old, and the advertising industry uses women's sexuality to sell everything from magazines to beer. Does all of this point to

166.

sexual liberation or another form of sexual subservience and exploitation? And then there is the "laddette" culture in Britain, where young women, often on a drunken night out, emulate the sexually aggressive attitude of the young male "lads." This confuses young men who, ironically, don't like the idea of being used as sex objects!

The truth is, we women are shackled by a male-oriented world that wants our sexuality to conform to its needs and desires. The result is that all too often we don't feel comfortable in our own sexuality or with sex in general. For us to grow into the fullness and wholeness of our female sexuality, we must consciously connect with the ecstatic energy, beauty, and joyful freedom that is our birthright as women.

Our Sexual Power

Every woman has access to her feminine sexuality, but we just don't allow ourselves to be fully in touch with it. Some of us are so engaged in using masculine energy to function at work and in our busy lives that we bring it into our attitude to sex, neglecting the feminine energy that emanates from our core sexuality. Others of us are mothers to young children and have refocused our energies to be nurturers and caregivers. And some of us, perhaps because of psychological baggage and emotional wounds, have lost our confidence as women in our full sexual power completely.

None of these reasons necessarily takes away our need for sex, love, and connection, but they can transform our relationship with sex to one of unconscious psychological need rather than one of conscious, sexual power. This neediness can impede our ability for discernment in relationships and can distract us from our life purpose, ultimately blocking us from connecting to our higher selves.

Our sexual power is like an electrical current that whips through our bodies, from the tips of our toes to the tops of our heads. When we suppress or lose contact with it, the circuit is broken and we become unable to maintain our fullness of health and energy.

Sexual Healing.

All women and men have sexual wounds—psychological scars that have developed as a consequence of growing up and living in a world that is confused about sex and sexuality. We've been conditioned from an early age to be ashamed and embarrassed regarding our sexuality, and that deeply affects our subconscious.

Many of us women were brought up with the idea that good girls don't have sex until marriage. Consequently, in our adolescence we felt mixed up and embarrassed by our body's urges. When we did lose our virginity, it was usually some awkward experience that we never felt right about. If we've been lucky, we've only had a few unpleasant sexual experiences with partners; if we've been unlucky, we may have suffered from abuse or even rape. The fact is, we all could use a little sexual healing.

For those of us who have suffered traumatic sexual experiences, the wounds are far more severe—yet healing can be accelerated with professional help. Support groups, where experiences are shared with others, have proved to be an important part of the healing process, since they help take away the feeling of isolation that so often comes with such deep trauma.

169.

Becoming comfortable with your body and your sex, ridding yourself of any fear and shame you've collected through life, and learning to trust, are first steps on the path to sexual healing. Meditation and ritual can help get to the root cause of any wounds you might carry. Listening to the stories of others can also give you insight and inspiration to face your own sexual injuries.

The Dance of Sexuality.

My friend Caroline, a strong, determined American in her mid-40s, admitted that like me, she'd lost touch with her sexuality during the last few years of her marriage. "I wasn't happy with myself or my body," she said. "The magic had gone from my relationship, and I just wasn't in touch with the sexual side of myself."

Recently divorced, Caroline decided to get fit, and took to walking for two hours every morning at the crack of dawn—but it was on a trip to Cuba that she finally rediscovered her libido. "I felt the music and started dancing again. I saw how women of all ages and sizes just seemed to ooze sexuality with such pride and confidence. They inspired me to get back in touch with my own sexuality."

Since that trip, Caroline dances regularly (right now she's learning flamenco), and she still walks every morning. She exudes health and sexuality, is attractive to both men and women, and is confident in herself as a woman. Like me, she got back in touch with her sexuality through the rhythm of dance.

171.

In cultures where people grow up dancing to the hot beat of the drum, such as in Latin America, the Caribbean, and Africa, sexuality is as natural a part of their lives as music. Take, for example, Christina, a close friend of mine originally from Brazil. Spending time with her has shown me how she naturally combines her sensuality and love of life to create a sexuality that radiates out of her, a trait she shares with her fellow Brazilians. The way they move, their music, and their general *joie de vivre* reflects an internal rhythm that's attractive to all who meet them.

We may not have grown up in countries where music and dance feature so prominently, but there's no reason why we can't make them a central part of our lives now. There's a growing popularity and availability of classes in all kinds of global dance, including salsa, belly dancing, African dancing, Hawaiian hula, and Indian temple dance.

Moving our pelvic area, hips, and breath in circular movements—be it through dance, yoga, or other exercise—releases our sexual energy. We tend to hold a lot of tension in our bodies, which can block what the Chinese call our *chi* (life force), which in turn affects our sexuality. By creating this flow of movement in our solar plexus, we can physically perceive an energy shift through our bodies, expanding and opening up our sexual consciousness.

Shake Your Tail Feather, Baby

If you feel that your body needs to release some sexual energy, you're going to have to practice some pelvic rock 'n' roll. Getting used to moving your pelvis takes a little work if you're not accustomed to it. For those of you who had a hula hoop as a kid, remember the way you moved your hips to keep it rotating? Well, that's what you have to do here.

You might want to practice the pelvic roll while danc-ing to some great music—James Brown's "Get Up (I Feel Like Being a) Sex Machine" always works for me. Or maybe get ahold of a hula hoop (yes, they're still around). The important thing to do is to create circular movements using your pelvis, concentrate on your "in" breath, and shake your tail feather. Ooh, baby—you're one hot, sexy mama!

172.

Being a Sensual Love Goddess.

Getting in touch with the sensual, erotic, desirable goddess who's comfortable in her body and with her sexuality is part of the pleasure of being a woman. Sexually attractive women come in all shapes, sizes, and ages. I've seen white-haired women of 70 radiate sexuality, just as I've seen attractive women of 25 oddly devoid of it. Being confident in our bodies and comfortable with who we are creates an energy that others instinctively react to.

When a woman with sexual confidence, whatever her size, walks in the room, we all take note. My friend Andrea Oliver, the British actress and TV presenter, is an example of a real woman who's confident in herself as a sexual being. Of Caribbean descent, Andrea is big, black, and bald, with enormous breasts and a sassy way of holding herself. She dresses in figure-hugging slinky dresses that don't hide any secrets, has enormous presence and charisma, a huge, infectious laugh, and a friendly hug. Andrea's a great cook, and her love of food is part of her larger-than-life, sensual persona. She is always a star in whatever situation she finds herself and is constantly surrounded by an entourage of men and women who adore her. When Andrea enters a room, everyone is struck!

Be they 18 or 80, sexually confident women can make sparks fly through their great posture, direct eye contact, warm laughter, open attitudes, and that certain way of dressing that proclaims: "I'm happy being who I am."

I asked various men I know what they think gives a woman sex appeal, and they responded: "It's the message in her eyes . . . her smile . . . her confidence in who she is . . . her humor . . . the way she tilts her head to one side . . . her playfulness . . . her voice . . . her openness and friendliness . . . her intelligence . . . the way she flirts . . . the way she moves. . . . "

Sexuality can be expressed in the arch of a brow, the shrug of a shoulder, or the flicker of a smile. A sexual woman can be covered from head to toe, yet the depth of her feminine mystery will nevertheless come out. Sexiness is as ancient as Eve and as modern as Catherine Zeta-Jones.

We need to relinquish the masculine masks we've put on and get back in touch with our feminine sexual essence by wearing silk lingerie; dancing with our bellies; stepping into some high-heeled shoes; donning slinky skirts with no underwear; bathing in sweet-smelling oils; sleeping on sensuous, soft sheets; swimming naked in the sea; and learning to make love to ourselves.

Welcome to the Pleasure Zone

Only *you* can discover what opens your inner flower and ensures that your sexuality reflects your whole being—so let go of your inhibitions, and don't feel guilty or self-conscious about indulging yourself. Be open to pure, unadulterated pleasure.

When you decide that it's time to give yourself a treat, make arrangements for a date with yourself. Make sure that there will be no interruptions: Send husbands, children, boyfriends, and roommates out for the night and turn off the phone. Chill some champagne or lemon water, and make sure you have some delicious chocolate and/or luscious strawberries on hand. Prepare a room that includes beautiful flowers, wafting incense, cushions scattered on the floor, a fire in the hearth, and candles emitting a golden light.

Start with a soothing bath full of healing oils and bubbles. Light some candles and play relaxing music. Let your mind melt into the sensuality of the soft bubbles and let the calming water caress you. As the water cools, step out of the bath and wrap yourself in a big fluffy towel and pat yourself dry. Put on a silky negligee, a cashmere wrap, some black silk stockings, and high heels. Dab some of your best scent between your breasts and behind your ears. You want to smell good for the person you should love most: yourself!

Walk into the room you've stocked with sensual delights and put on some up-tempo music (maybe African or Brazilian sounds). Next, go to a mirror and acknowledge the beautiful goddess that you see. Note the sparkle of her eyes, the sensual line of her mouth, and the shapely curves of her hips. Blow her a kiss and tell her aloud that you worship her passionate nature and beautiful body.

Start swaying sensually to the music, moving your pelvis as only you know how. Take a strawberry and use your senses to enjoy its every succulent aspect. First touch it, becoming aware of its feel, its small fibrous hairs, and its luscious weight in your hand. Spend time appreciating how its red color is interspersed with seeds and greenery. Smell its sweet, enticing aroma. When you're truly ready to receive its gift of taste, take a small bite, holding the fruit in your mouth as the juice slides down your throat. Continue to

eat the rest of it slowly, letting the taste of the strawberry fill your entire being with its essence. Finally, know that the appreciation you hold for that delicious piece of fruit can be a reflection of the appreciation you hold for yourself. Be aware that by loving and adoring the true essence of your being—that is, by acknowledging your beauty and sensuality—so, too, will you receive that appreciation from others.

Use the rest of the evening to indulge in your favorite delights and do what pleases you most. Feed the sexual feminine inside you, provide her with your most desired longings—nothing is forbidden in honoring the goddess that is you. Take a sip of champagne and a nibble of chocolate. If your hand wanders to your soft breasts, don't pull back; explore and enjoy their exquisiteness. Gently circle a finger around the delicate areola, notice how the skin grows taut with delight, and tenderly give your nipple a squeeze and feel the electricity start to spread through your body. And if your other hand should happen to drift south, finding itself drawn like a magnet between your now-open thighs, well then . . .

176.

Sexual Wisdom.

Sexual union between two consenting adults is potentially one of the most glorious acts we human beings can partake of. Connecting with each other in a conscious manner—skin to skin, sexual organ to sexual organ, heart to heart—can take us to a place of rapture where wise women and men can taste love and spirit in all their purity.

It's not by chance that so many of us invoke the names of the divine when we're riding the wild waves of lovemaking. It's as if, when we're at the peak of our passion, we reach out to God in prayer and gratitude. But admittedly, the sacredness of lovemaking is not always at the forefront of our consciousness when our sexual juices begin flowing. All circumstances are different—a quickie in between looking after the kids, a first night with a new friend, some letting go of tension after a heavy week's work—but we should always be aware that by engaging in the sexual act, we're creating an openness for deep human connection that has the possibility to take us into a place of divine rapture.

While a handsome face or a perfectly muscled body can be, like a peacock's tail, an enticement for sex, the keys that open the chambers to a woman's sexual bliss lie not so much with physical attributes but with more sophisticated skills. What makes a great lover of either sex is the ability to tune in to their partner—to be able to listen to the subtleties of their partner's body and dance with its rhythms. In fact, it's been said that sex is like dancing, for when you dance with another person, you communicate with your bodies through movement. The best dance is when both partners seem to be on the same wavelength—their connection is so deep and natural that they seem to move together as one. Great sex is similar: The most exquisite sexual encounter has no partner leading or following; it is a continuous flow that stems from a connection encompassing body, mind, and spirit.

Outstanding sex is never mechanical. After all, we can achieve earth-shaking orgasms through masturbation; and while that solo dance can be wonderful and rewarding, great sex with a partner, the right partner, is satisfying at another level because it brings in elements that we can't achieve alone. First and foremost is connection—that deep-seated soul bond that infuses us with such completeness when it happens. Passion is another essential element in the dance of great sex, as is creativity—the creative lover is one who never lets the act of love grow stale, but continually invents situations and nuances that keep things fresh.

177.

Humor and playfulness are also fundamental elements that add a necessary balance to the intensity that arises through sex. And while it isn't a prerequisite, love is probably the greatest gift one can bring to the sexual dance. When you love and are loved by your partner, the union of sex is that much sweeter, since it's the sharing of an open heart with the one whose body you're so intimately connected to.

Women's Sexual Mysteries.

Once we've had a certain amount of sexual experience, most of us assume that we know what we like, what turns us on, and how we like to react. But there's always room for

exploration, for discovering subtleties about our own bodies that can take us to places we've never been.

Do you really know the geography of your genitalia? Are you familiar with the shape of the exterior area of your vulva? Each of us is unique, from the color to the shapes and position of the various muscles, glands, lips, and tissues that make up our genital area. Why not take a small hand mirror and use it to examine yourself in detail. Knowing exactly where your clitoris is positioned will help you understand how to receive maximum pleasure during lovemaking. Use a little saliva or lubricant to stroke yourself, and watch the shape of your clitoris change with stimulation—the tip, which is the bit you can see, will harden like a mini-penis (in the same way your nipples do).

Your vagina, which is, of course, not visible, also changes shape and size when aroused. It's been described to me that when a man enters a woman, he feels as if he's being encompassed by a warm, moist, soft velvet glove. The vagina is where you physically receive love and where your female glory resides. Honor, love, and respect it.

179.

Despite this society's apparent sophistication with respect to sexual matters, many women I've spoken to still have questions about sex and their own sexuality. I recommend that you check out the many specialized books and videos on this subject, some of which are listed at the back of this book.

Following are some of the most frequently discussed topics concerning our sexuality.

Self-Loving

Pleasuring ourselves and being open to the different routes we can take to achieve orgasm and sexual satisfaction without a partner is of vital importance to the health and balance of any woman. Masturbation has traditionally been seen as something that's more acceptable for men, and we women have often been shy of acknowledging that we also can, and should, satisfy our own sexual needs. Even though you may feel that teaching women how to masturbate is somewhat redundant, American author and teacher Betty Dodson has inspired thousands of women (and men) to explore "sexual self-help," as she puts it.

Selfloving, her video of a sexuality seminar, shows women from 28 to 60 accepting and loving their bodies—it inspires women to discover a deeper understanding and knowledge of their own sexual path.

Touching our genitals, and even bringing ourselves to orgasm, is something many of us have done surreptitiously since childhood. It makes sense, since only *we* know how and where we need the touch to stimulate us to orgasm. Some of us need a lighter stroke, while others prefer something a little stronger—which is where vibrators come in. If and when you decide to go shopping for vibrators, there are many varieties available, from compact ones that fit in your purse to elaborate ones that come with an array of special attachments. There are sex shops aimed at women available in many cities, where you can go and investigate what's new; or you can always stay in for some home shopping with a catalog or browsing the Internet. No matter what you decide, you need to lose your shyness and take a look around at what's out there. Shop with a girlfriend if that makes it easier, and be ready to ask the salesperson for guidance.

180. A vibrator's effectiveness is about speed and texture, but it's also about how comfortable you feel using it. You may enjoy the fun of the battery-powered "Rabbit," which was made famous on *Sex and the City,* or you may prefer the electrically operated Magic Wand by Hitachi, which is a two-speed massager with a large rubber head that's available in most large drugstores across the U.S. Betty Dodson's students pleasure themselves in her videos with a similar-looking, battery-operated version.

Once women recognize what turns them on while masturbating, they can use this knowledge to make sex with a partner more satisfying. Many of the women I've spoken to said it was the experience of masturbation that made them aware of their ability to have multiple orgasms.

The True Story of "O"

Orgasms can vary in quality, quantity, and how we get them. In the '60s, when the first generation of liberated women started searching for the ultimate "O," we really didn't know too much about our sexuality. Women's magazines informed us that we should attain orgasm from vaginal intercourse, and many of us were very confused and a little ashamed that we couldn't achieve them that way.

Now we know that the majority of women need clitoral stimulation, either orally or manually, to reach full orgasm. Clitoral stimulation in tandem with penetrative sex gives the best of both worlds. It is essential for a lover to understand that we women are capable of reaching not just one orgasm, as men do, but multiple orgasms. And under the right circumstances, our female mind can easily turn the entire body into one big erogenous zone. For that to happen, we have to be in the right mood with a partner we trust, one who is sensitive and available to our needs.

G-Spot

The G-spot (named after the man who first recognized it back in the '50s, gynecologist Ernst Grafenberg) has become an acknowledged route to intensified sexual pleasure. Not visible from the outside, the G-spot is said to be located in the tissue within the vaginal wall, more or less corresponding with the external position of the clitoris.

181.

Direct stimulation of the area, either with a finger or a G-spot stimulator with a curved end, is said to cause orgasm in some women, and even create female ejaculation. The G-spot is more sensitive for some than others, so if you've never found yours, don't panic—instead, try to be more conscious of that point when aroused . . . you just may discover something new and delightful.

PC Muscle

The PC muscle controls the quality and intensity of your orgasm. It runs from the back to the front of the pelvic girdle, with three holes in it for the anus, the vagina, and the urethra. The stronger the PC muscle is, the more powerfully you'll be able to come. You can even exercise it by doing Kegel exercises, where you regularly clench and hold your PC muscle as if cutting off your urine flow. By doing this several minutes a day, you will be able to maintain the muscle's elasticity and strength. Clenching the muscle during lovemaking increases sexual pleasure for both partners, and doing so during self-loving will also increase your enjoyment.

Same-Sex Love

Although most of the information and suggestions provided in this chapter can be applied and adapted to same-sex lovemaking, most references to sexual union are aimed at heterosexual couples. This is not meant to ignore the very beautiful intimacy that can be practiced by women with women. I am no expert on same-sex love, but I do honor and rejoice in the obvious pleasure that women are able to give each other.

I've had lesbian friends tell me that making love to a woman feels much safer and more open than making love to a man does. Women enjoy each other's beauty and sexuality whether they're gay or straight, so the sensuality and playfulness of women dancing together, along with the way we communicate and understand each other, is obviously enhanced when our sexuality is engaged, too.

182.

Love Speak.

Talking before, during, or after sex is, like all things, a matter of choice. But if you can get over the hurdle of embarrassment, you may find that both playful sex talk and a mutual exchange of information can enhance your lovemaking.

Foreplay doesn't have to be limited to touch—it can be about words, too. If you're out with your lover, perhaps at a restaurant or party, talking dirty can be a real turn-on. Both of you fantasizing about what you want to do to each other when you get home will get you both so ready for lovemaking that you'll probably skip dessert.

The other crucial aspect of sex speak is being able to be open with your lover about your needs, where you like to be touched, which areas of your body are the most sensitive, and how you love to be made love to. Of course, it goes both ways—asking him how and where he likes to be touched, what positions he most enjoys, and what he wants you to do for him can only enhance your lovemaking. Although many women and men find it difficult to verbally express how they prefer to receive pleasure, with courage and trust on both sides you can overcome any shyness. Why not take the initiative to open up to him? I bet he'll love hearing how to please you.

Keep in mind that the most important thing here is not to criticize your partner during lovemaking, as men are very sensitive about that sort of thing. One friend told me that early on in her marriage she told her husband that he was rubbing her in the wrong place. He was furious and told her that he knew exactly what he was doing. After that, she never had the courage to speak up again and consequently went for years without having an orgasm when making love to him.

The most political way to inform your partner of your likes and dislikes while in the process of lovemaking is to say that what he's doing is great, but if he moved his fingers a little to the left, it would be even more pleasurable. Most men appreciate that kind of feedback.

183.

Love speak works best when you're *both* involved. When you each can express how you're feeling in the moment and how wonderful it is to give and receive pleasure, the sexual connection is amplified—and a delicious intimacy is yours.

Expressing Your Delight: A Meditation

Have you ever truly expressed to yourself, not to mention a lover, exactly how you love to be made love to? Have you ever thought through a sexual fantasy or written an erotic poem? Well, this is your opportunity to try it out. If you're already experienced in expressing your erotic thoughts, use this time to become even more creative.

Take some time and create a relaxed, sexy atmosphere with sensual music and candles. Sitting in a cozy chair, or better yet, in bed, meditate on your idea of a wild fantasy or erotic poem. Let your imagination flow into the realms of sexual delights. Indulge yourself in the pleasures of eroticism.

When you've finished, write down what you've come up with and read it aloud. You may also wish to share with your lover—who knows, perhaps he'll be inspired to create his own erotic scenarios as well.

The Truth about Men's Sexuality.

The truth about men is the same as the truth about women—their sexuality comes uniquely packaged with each individual. We all know the cliché that all men want is to get turned on, have a quick stab at lovemaking and an even quicker orgasm, then turn over and go to sleep. And while there's always some truth to clichés, for the most part, men want to please women as much as they want to receive pleasure. And deep down inside, every man wants to be a great lover. Nothing gives him a bigger ego boost than your telling him that he is . . . and if he isn't, well, girl, turn him into one by offering some gentle hints and instruction about your sexuality. But first you must know a little about *his* sexuality.

These are some things that may surprise you:

Foreplay. *The myth is that men don't like foreplay; the reality is that men don't like <u>mediocre</u> foreplay. Take the lead—he will not only follow, but will be forever appreciative. Start with kisses he'll never forget: soft butterfly caresses on his eyelids and a brush of your lips on his cheek and his open lips. Tease a little if you'd like before using your tongue. And don't confine that wonderfully sexual instrument to his mouth—a quick lick up his neck will send shivers down his spine. You may want to explore his lips and mouth once again, or you may want to take a trip around his body. Men's erogenous zones are basically the same as women's. Some are obvious (lips and nipples), while some are not (armpits, the crook of the arm, earlobes). Find the erogenous zones of your lover by exploring his body with a soft touch and a moist tongue. You'll probably hit erotically sensitive areas that he didn't even know existed!*

Control. *The myth is that men always like to be in control; the truth is that men love to surrender when they're in the hands of a talented lover. Be daring and bold: Push him down on the bed and make sure he stays there—then suck his toes, massage the back of his legs, run your fingers up his inner thighs, and put your hand gently on his belly and rub in a soft, circular motion. If your clothes are on, you can make disrobing an incredibly erotic act. Take your time, but also make sure that he's present and continues to be sexually aroused. Male attention does tend to wander, and if you ever get the feeling that your man is losing connection, then it's time to try something different (maybe turn the heat up another notch).*

The Penis. *The truth about men's penises is that they love them—the penis is the most charged and sensitive part of the male body, and it's quite literally an extension of the man himself. To love a man sexually, you must love his penis. And you <u>should</u> love it, as it gives you a lot of pleasure, too.*

If your lover's penis is flaccid, he'll love to have it awakened and aroused. Start gently . . . brush his scrotum with your fingers, using your fingernails to excite that sensuous area. Often, when the scrotum is stimulated, it will tighten, with the skin resembling a shriveled fruit. You might want to play there a little more, but also start heading up to the penis shaft.

Turn-On Techniques. *The truth is, men love when you use your mouth <u>and</u> your hands, either separately or in active collaboration. When his penis is flaccid, your lover will enjoy having your whole mouth envelope the shaft of his penis. Make an "O" with your lips—being careful not to have your teeth involved here—and gently (at first) begin sucking. You may want to play with his penis by swirling your tongue around as he's in your mouth, bringing your tongue to the underside of his penis's shaft and around its head. (If you use your hand, start by gently teasing the underside and around the head of the penis.) As he becomes more erect, more pressure can be applied.*

It always helps to keep the shaft of the penis lubricated—your saliva is the best lubricant available, but if you're using your hand exclusively, a lotion, oil, or cream specially designed for sex, such as Astroglide or Liquid Silk, will work just as well. As the penis hardens, the pressure should be increased. A wonderful variant to continually moving up and down the penis is to squeeze your hand tightly around the shaft and then release, as if squeezing a small hand pump. Be spontaneous but connected to his state of arousal.

185.

To bring a man to orgasm, steadily increase the speed and pressure of your motion along the shaft. To pull him back from climaxing, reduce the speed and pressure—but do it slowly, as a quick pullback will leave him unsettled. You can bring him to the brink several times this way, and when you do finally take him to orgasm, it will be amazingly intense . . . and he'll be thanking you for days on end.

Intercourse. For a man, this is when his manliness is in full force, as his body is undulating with yours, his hips are thrusting, and every inch of his being is filling you up. It's a glorious dance for both partners.

There are some things you can do to increase the pleasure for both of you. If he's very excited, and this is your first sexual session of the day, chances are that after a few initial thrusts he'll have the urge to ejaculate, whether he wants to or not. Slow down or even pause briefly. He'll probably experience a small mini-orgasm at that point; after it passes, he will be more fully in control of his orgasmic urges and will most likely be able to keep hard and erect long enough for your satisfaction. For the sake of your mutual pleasure, be sure that you're well lubricated, either naturally or with a lubricant.

There are many positions within intercourse, and every couple finds their own favorites. While most men like the top, "missionary" position, they equally appreciate the woman on top, especially if they've been working long and hard from the dominant position. A woman from the top can bring a man supreme pleasure by varying the thrusts of her hips, sometimes taking his penis deep within her, some-times moving it almost to the point of exit before sliding it back in—allowing him to experience the full journey along the vaginal walls. A little trick to add pleasure to both of you is to put a pillow under his buttocks as he thrusts from beneath. This raises his hips and brings his pubic bone in contact with your clitoris. Rocking back and forth in this position can bring out cascades of mutual pleasure.

Afterglow. When a man orgasms and ejaculates, a great flood of relaxation comes over him. Men have been known to float off into a wonderfully blissful and satisfied state. If you're also sexually sat-isfied, nothing is finer than cuddling up and drifting off into sweet nothingness together. However, if you're left wanting more, give him a few minutes—making sure that he doesn't nod off—and then lovingly ask him to satisfy you. Most men, if asked properly (remember, they take pride in being great lovers), have no problem in manually or orally bringing you to orgasm. If your lover does drift away or is hesitant, cuddle up, wait 20 minutes, and then rev his motor up again until he's not only agree-able, but eager for the opportunity to finish the job.

186.

The Art of Sacred Lovemaking.

Sacred lovemaking is about reaching the highest state of ecstasy possible with a lover through the combined practices of ritual, conscious breathing, meditation, and channeling energy through both partners' life forces. Sacred lovemaking is not just another method for achieving earth-shattering orgasms (although that may be a great side benefit)—rather, it's a discipline whose methods must be repeatedly practiced and refined to achieve the higher levels of sexual bliss.

Sacred lovemaking has its roots in *tantra,* an ancient form of religious sexual practice that began in India around 5000 B.C. While *tantra* has become a popular term these days, with "tantra masters" popping up to give seminars in plush resorts throughout the world, what they serve up is far from the true form. Tantra is actually a very strict and esoteric practice that takes its dedicated practitioners through complex yoga postures, the chanting of Sanskrit mantras, and various regimented sexual disciplines. Very few Westerners have actually mastered the rigors of traditional tantra. Some, like esteemed author Margo Anand, author of the international bestseller *The Art of Sexual Ecstasy,* immersed themselves in this practice and then adapted the appropriate techniques for Western use.

The basic premise of sacred lovemaking is that there's a special life energy that flows and can be channeled during sexual union to achieve not only sexual bliss, but the rapture of uniting with a higher cosmic force. To begin your exploration into new realms of sexual rapture, you'll need an open and willing partner, some free time (preferably a whole day), and a quiet, sacred space of your own creation.

How to Be a Sacred Lover

While you may not become an expert in the art of sacred lovemaking the first time you try it, if you openly let yourself partake of this practice, you'll gain new insights that will deepen your sexual pleasures and experiences.

You will need to create a sacred space that you and your partner can share. While your bedroom is a great place for sleeping, because it's so familiar it isn't always the best place to manifest the special atmosphere needed for sacred lovemaking. If possible, find a room in your home that you can transform into a magical space. Fill it with throw pillows or a mattress covered with an exotic quilt or bedspread, include vases of fresh flowers, and scatter rose petals about. A fire is always nice, but if that's not possible, light enough candles so that the room shimmers with a golden glow. Burn subtle incense and play some relaxing, sensual music. Make sure that there are juices and water to drink; and grapes, berries, and others small fruits to eat.

Keep in mind that lightness and fun are part of your sacred sexual connection. Before entering your sacred space, bathe each other in a tub of sweet-smelling water. This should be a *sensual* rather than *sexual* experience. Wash each other's hair, paying attention to and enjoying the tactile sensations of having your head massaged. After drying each other off, have some silk robes or wraps ready to put on.

188. Escort each other into your sacred place. Sit opposite each other on the floor, and invite your partner to join you in this sacred sexual journey. Drink in each other's essence with your eyes, and feel free to speak whatever words, or even prayers, that come to you. Share your fears and expectations of real intimacy with each other—by doing this, you and your partner can go to the next level, where the nakedness is not only of your body, but of your heart. When all has been said, embrace each other in an expansive, soul-to-soul, body-to-body hug, each savoring the other.

Next, delve into the sensual treats and begin feeding one another from the food that's set before you. Let the taste of the fruit fill your mouth. Exchange a kiss with the essence of the fruit's juice still lingering, offering your sweetness to him and receiving his into you.

Lie next to each other with your eyes open, and place your hands over each other's heart. Take a deep breath, then exhale, keeping your attention on his breathing and the eye contact between you. Now take some massage oil, warming some up in the palms of your hands before spreading it over his body. Continue your focus on his breathing as much as possible. Start massaging his neck and shoulders in light circular movements. Keep going down his back, his buttocks, his legs, and the soles of his feet. As his body surrenders to your touch, let your own spirit surrender to the loving energy you're now exchanging. Follow the pleasure where it leads—possibly a long massage for him and then a massage for you, or perhaps a deeper sexual dance. Wherever it goes, maintain your eye contact and breath connection as much as possible. When he finally does enter you, have him do so slowly. Fix your concentration on the sensation that union brings as you continue to breathe as one. Do not speed things up, but maintain a slow, meditative pace. If possible, bring your movements to near or complete stillness, concentrating on the powerful energy that's circulating through your bodies.

Indulge in the pleasure of giving and receiving. Take each other to ecstatic heights as you continue the dance of love. Bring your lips together in a loving kiss, breathing into each other's mouths, uniting the male and female energies as you ebb and flow in the rhythm of your lovemaking. And know that sacred sex is not necessarily about orgasm—it's about the deep connection of energy between lovers, which can continue for hours upon end, taking you both to a state of total rapture.

189.

The GROW Commitment.

Say this affirmation before lovemaking, either with yourself or a partner:

I embrace the sexual pleasure that I choose to enjoy, and I acknowledge the divine connection with my lover.

• • • • •

Part III

Connecting with Others

(Where You
Examine Your
Relationship with
Work and Business)

The Feminine
at Work

How do I ensure that I am earning my livelihood in a way that feeds my soul? What is the feminine way to create business? How do I bring my values into the workplace?

Women have always been in the workplace. And in today's society, the concept of women staying at home to look after the kids and waving the old man off to work in the morning tends to be the exception rather than the norm.

For some women, there's no choice about whether they work or not, since financial pressures make it a necessity. But for many women, whether they're married or single, work is also a way to find creative fulfillment and personal empowerment.

Throughout this chapter, we're going to look at ways in which we can work together to create value in our lives as well as in our community.

194.

My Story: A Job for a Woman

Entrepreneurship runs in both sides of my family: My great-grandparents came to England from Eastern Europe with nothing, determined to do the best for their families. On my maternal side, my great-grandmother Sophia worked as a tailor to feed her family of ten children when her husband died young. Her daughter Dora (my grandmother) took over responsibility for her mother, opening her own millinery shop at 18 in central London, supplying exotic hats to showgirls during World War I to feed her siblings.

After her husband came back sick from the war, Dora opened a seaside boardinghouse in the family home to pay the bills. And my mother, Angela, carried on the pattern by running the family business when my father became ill and was unable to work regularly. As you can tell, I grew up assuming that women worked and took responsibility for their family as a matter of course.

When I left school at 16, I was incredibly ambitious but didn't know what I wanted to do career-wise. My mother insisted that I have some preliminary training in secretarial skills, and although I had my sights set on becoming a journalist, I worked first as a typist and secretary. I got my first big break when I wrote for <u>Petticoat,</u> the first British weekly magazine for teenage girls. I worked with some incredible women, and for the first time in my life, experienced a feminine work environment. I loved it.

After <u>Petticoat,</u> I gained more writing experience as a journalist before I found a short-term position working for a small fashion PR agency. It was there that I met fashion designer Katharine Hamnett, another entrepreneurial rebel, who encouraged me to open my own PR agency. Her confidence in me gave me confidence in myself, so at age 21, with no money and little experience (but with a mass of passion and energy), I started representing Katharine and a few other young designers, supplementing my income with a secretarial job on Saturdays.

Public relations was a career made in heaven for me, since I love people, communication, and writing. By working all hours of the day and night, I learned on the job. As I began to make money, I invested my profits back into new offices and more staff. I was constantly pushing my own creative boundaries and, in the process, building up my company's reputation as a top international agency.

Without even realizing it, I became an innovator in a new style of business, in which we worked in the feminine way. My staff, which consisted mainly of young women, approached work openly and informally, and I encouraged them (and myself) to fulfill their creative potential and thrive on the constant challenges. We spent long hours together—we ate together, we played together, and in some instances during the Buddhist years, we prayed together. They became like my family, and I felt like the "mother" of the team: I nurtured my staff, and in a way, they nurtured me.

I fully understood how fortunate I was as I reached the top of my particular professional mountain. I appreciated the personal success and financial rewards I'd received, but I decided that work had to have a "contribution element" to be totally satisfying. I had been inspired to create this "give back" strategy through my deepening spiritual practices. I wanted to integrate my spiritual values with my business policy; by doing so, I learned that business can be a vehicle for positive change in society.

195.

The Feminine at Work

A policy to work for nonprofit organizations for little or no money was introduced into the agency, and the pleasure that the entire company felt when working on the promotion of environmental, human-rights, or health-awareness issues such as HIV and AIDS contributed to the positive atmosphere and enthusiasm of everyone who worked there.

What I didn't appreciate until long after I'd sold the agency was how feminine my style of management was. I saw that the intimate family atmosphere in the office created an open, lateral style of working, which stimulated creativity and enterprise in us all. I strongly believe that the way forward in creating a wise business, big or small, is to integrate feminine qualities and traits as an essential element of the core structure.

Women at Work.

196.

From ambitious young twentysomethings to baby-boomer grannies, modern women want the choice of following a career—we might even try two or three of them during our working life. The idea of women in their 50s and 60s taking care of their grand-children while their daughters work is totally old-fashioned, according to research by the British Institute of Community Studies. The grannies don't want to look after their children's babies, for they're still engaged in their own careers. And today, many of us are fortunate to have a number of choices when it comes to work: We can stay at home, putting our energies into child rearing and partnership; we can work from home using the latest technology and still be full-time mothers if we choose; we can be members of a cooperative, with shared child-care resources; we can start a business on our own or with others; or we can follow careers in the public sector; we can work for a nonprofit organization or a commercial company; we can be a massage therapist, a yoga teacher, a life coach, or a psychotherapist. The list is endless, the possibilities extensive.

The future for modern women is not about *whether* we work, but *how* we work. Although the number of working women grew enormously after the advance of the women's movement in the '60s and early '70s, many of us believed that to be truly successful,

we had to somehow outdo men. We would (and in many cases still do) work alongside men in the world of big business, earning around 80 percent of their salaries and trying to constantly prove how tough and competitive we can be.

There has been a huge change in the last few years, however, with many women waking up to the fact that both the corporate and the political worlds do not reflect our feminine values; and in any event, the top jobs still primarily go to the boys. Certainly there are inspiring female leaders in both politics and the corporate world who blend the best of feminine and masculine skills, but unfortunately, they are very much in the minority.

We first need to acknowledge our gifts and understand how we can incorporate them into our careers. By integrating who we are with what we do, we can start to become who we were born to be.

198. What Does Work Mean to You?

Have you ever taken a step back and examined what work really means to you? Are you on the right path professionally, or is it time for a change? Here are a few questions to help you focus on your professional priorities and pathway.

1. What are the reasons you work? Assign a number from 1 to 4, in order of importance, to the following list. For example, if money is your most important motivation, write down the number 1 next to the word *money* and so on.

   a) Money _____   d) To help others _____

   b) Creative fulfilment _____   e) Any other reasons _____

   c) To meet people _____

2. Describe your job.

   ....

3. Does it give you soul satisfaction? If not, why not?

   ....

4. If you're working for a company, do you know about their human-rights, environmental, and general-diversity policies?

   ....

5. Do you think your employer's values reflect your own?

   ....

6. Are your personal interests reflected in your job?

   ....

7. Do you like the people you work with?

   ....

8. When you were growing up, what did you want to do as a career?

   ....

9. Do you think you'd be happier doing something else? If so, what would you like to do?

   ....

10. Is it time for a change in your working life? If so, what kind of change?

   ....

As with all the exercises in this book, there are no right or wrong answers here. The questions are meant to be a guide to help you see your life with more clarity and consider any changes that you need to make. Now look back at your answers. Are your needs being met at work? If not, why not change the situation? It may not be as difficult as you think.

What Is the Difference Between the Feminine and Masculine Styles of Working?

Since putting my head above the parapet and writing *The SEED Handbook,* which was about the feminine way to create business, I've often been asked by journalists what the difference is between the feminine and masculine ways of working. Although our differences are important, I believe it's more important to focus on how aspects of both are necessary in running a business. After all, certain masculine traits, such as the ability to focus and take action, are essential to a business's success. Yet our feminine values have traditionally not been honored or taken seriously within the business environment.

The feminine qualities of relationship building, communication, multitasking, nurturing, intuition, compassion, and empathy offer businesses a very different perspective from the more commonly recognized masculine traits. Of course there are many women with careers in "masculine" professions such as finance, engineering, science, law, and strategic planning, but these women invariably have to work in a very male way to survive. I have met many such women at SEED events, and they're either desperate to change careers and move out of such male environments, or they want to know how to bring a more feminine approach into their workplaces. I've worked with these women to identify ways that they can get in touch with their "feminine core" so that their work reflects who they are. Sometimes they haven't been able to actually feminize their current workplaces, but they *did* bring their skills into a different arena. Many decided to create partnerships in their chosen fields with other women, start their own businesses from home, or join companies whose values are more "people-based." Others chose to

201.

discuss the changes they wanted to make with their management—including more flex-time, healthier workplace environments with access to fresh air, the availability of lots of pure drinking water, more nurturing atmospheres for the staff, and some form of community integration.

Once we've made the shift to a more feminine way of doing business, we women blossom as human beings, our health invariably improves, we change our hair and the way we dress, and we sometimes even speak in a softer manner. Even more important, because we're back in balance with ourselves, our attitude and outlook to both work and life improves.

How Do You Bring Feminine Values into the Workplace?

When you head off to work each day, do you find yourself putting on a "masculine mask"? Some women have told me that they do just that, to the point of dressing more manly and even adopting a lower tone of voice at work. So perhaps the first step you need to take in bringing your feminine values to work is to strengthen the sense of what you, as a woman, embody. Being confident and proud of your feminine qualities makes expressing them at work that much easier. Rather than putting on a different personality when you leave in the morning, your workaday persona can simply be a natural extension of yourself.

The feminine characteristics that many of us try to hide while we're at work are actually some of our greatest assets. And they contribute not only to our personal success but to the success of the businesses and communities we're part of—and to the world as a whole. For example, the ability to communicate well and build strong relationships enables most women to excel at networking, a skill that is invaluable in the working world, yet is usually far more difficult for men. And a woman's intuition comes in handy on the job, too—men prefer to work from a linear and logical perspective, but working intuitively can produce creative solutions that often elude pure logical thinking.

While the feminine values of compassion and nurturing may seem to be in direct opposition to the work environment, they can further a business's objectives by creating supportive relationships between colleagues. Helping and supporting our co-workers through problems and crises is the womanly way, as is giving each other the time to share specific working concerns—all of which make for a deeper sense of empathy and connection. In all of my companies, we've always tried to take a few minutes to meditate together before starting our work, which has helped to create a harmony that lasted throughout the day.

As business leaders, it's important for us women to be role models by fostering openness with our staff and colleagues. Keeping unnecessary secrets as part of the power game is not the feminine way, although it's often the norm in the world of big business. On the other hand, good communication is a two-way deal: Encouraging and appreciating positive suggestions and opinions from other team members is key to creating a healthy, positive workplace.

203.

Caring for others adds a different outlook to external business relationships as well. The principles of ethical business practices, such as contribution back to community and sustainability, are by no means exclusive to women—but our basic feminine need to be concerned for others makes us more sensitive about taking responsibility for Mother Earth and her occupants. As women, we can bring sustainable values into our working life in a variety of ways, depending on our job or business. Even simple things like recycling paper, conserving energy, and purchasing environmentally friendly stationery can make enormous contributions to the world we all share.

Here's a final suggestion for bringing your feminine values into the workplace: Offer your experience to those who can benefit from your guidance. While mentoring is certainly not an exclusively female pursuit (many of us have been mentored by wise, generous men who were willing to share their expertise with us), it is one that fits our natural feminine role as teacher. When we use it in the workplace to encourage and teach others, we become the beneficiaries as well—we get to enjoy the tremendous satisfaction that comes from showing others the way.

Creating a Feminine Environment at Work.

Wherever you work—be it a spacious office or a tiny cubicle—you should have a little corner of your own where you can introduce your own sense of feminine style. So many work spaces are cold, linear, and institutionalized, yet it only takes a little effort to soften and feminize your space.

If you work in an office, it's easy to bring in fresh flowers, which not only give you, but also your colleagues, great pleasure. (You could also keep a green plant to be watered and nurtured near your desk.) Where there's space, add photographs of your loved ones, images of nature, some favorite crystals or colored stones, and even, perhaps, a small desk fountain. A goldfish or two swimming in a bowl is considered relaxing by adherents of Feng Shui, the Chinese art of interior harmony and positivity, and I totally agree. Chinese lucky bamboo, which hardly needs any care, represents good luck and always looks attractive. In addition, nature-themed stickers on your notebook, floral stationery, and an aromatic candle to light at the beginning of the workday and blow out when you're ready to leave will also add a more feminine touch.

204.

How you dress will, of course, add to the femininity of your workplace. If your job requires you to dress in more formal corporate attire, you can soften your look with a colored silk scarf, a sexy shirt, or bold earrings. If you have freedom in how you dress, then be yourself: If you enjoy vibrant colors and soft shapes, then wear them; if you prefer to dress in fashions that show a shapely silhouette, then go for it. You are a woman in your full glory, so you should celebrate your beauty every day in the reflection of your choice of feminine, sensual clothes.

Creating a Feminine Workplace

There are always ways you can feminize your workplace, whether you use some of the suggestions above or create your own ideas. It's as much about how you go about your work as it is about the space in which you work.

Use this space to come up with at least five new ways in which you can bring the feminine into your working day.

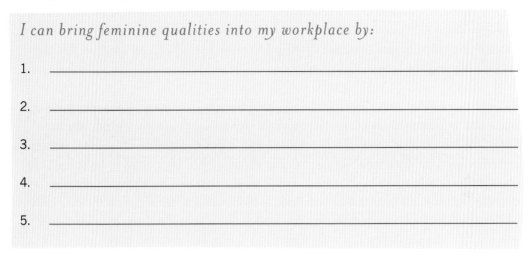

I can bring feminine qualities into my workplace by:

1. _____

2. _____

3. _____

4. _____

5. _____

205.

Finding a Balance Between Life and Work.

Like plants, human beings blossom with fresh air and water. However, for at least eight hours a day, five days a week, most of us are sitting in one place with little of both. We get headaches from working on computers all day and clamping cell phones to our ears much of the rest of our waking hours. We often work under a tremendous amount of stress—today's biggest health hazard—and then we fill our bodies with junk food and too much coffee. In addition, we take too few bathroom breaks, don't get enough exercise, experience uncomfortable journeys to and from work, and often turn to unhealthy personal habits in the evenings just to relax. And then we have to squeeze our personal life and responsibilities into the small space that's left over after work. No wonder we're not well.

With so many people taking time off work with back pain and other stress-related illnesses, governments as well as employers are investigating the subject of work/life balance. Many large companies are considering a flextime system, which is aimed particularly at working mothers. Others allow lengthy time off for sabbaticals, while still others are developing job-share situations. But even with these positive reforms, many people continue to suffer from work-related stress and poor health. Not enough thought goes into the nutritional value of cafeteria food, there often isn't any purified drinking water in the office, and fluorescent lighting and permanently closed windows are hard on the eyes and the lungs.

So what can we do? We've already talked about bringing feminine values into the work-place with our own initiatives. And of course if we work for ourselves, especially from home, we can create a working environment that is positive and healthy, but it isn't quite as easy when you work for other people. Regardless, there are bound to be some simple changes you could make in your routine that would ensure a healthier, more balanced day. For instance, make sure that you have bottled water to drink during the day instead of stocking up on coffees or teas. You can walk at least some of the way to work, even if you drive or use public transportation. And you could walk through parks and other green areas to meetings or during your breaks. Take "air breaks" as often as you can, bring your own nourishing food to eat, and save some carrots or nuts for that afternoon "sugar break." Try not to use your cell phone unless you have to, and move away from your computer when you can, massaging and exercising your hands and fingers as much as possible.

You can also do some simple exercises during the day to relieve tension in your neck and shoulders. Following are three simple stretches that will keep your muscles from tightening up.

206.

The Office Stretch

Neck Roll: *Slowly and gently roll your head 360 degrees in a circular motion from shoulder to shoulder—first one way, then the other—consciously breathing in and out. Do this at least twice. (This first exercise could even be done while sitting at your desk.)*

Side Bend: *Stand with your feet together. Keeping your arms as straight as possible, raise them above your head and press your palms together. Bend from your waist—slowly to one side, and then to the other—keeping your navel connected to your spine. Tighten your bottom and breathe normally. Repeat three times.*

Forward Bend: *Stand against the wall with your feet shoulder-width apart, hands on thighs. Put your weight on the balls of your feet and slide your hands down your legs, keeping your back flat. Go as far as you can, then release your arms and back, letting everything hang. Relax and keep breathing. If you can, grip your ankles to give yourself that extra stretch. When you're ready to come up, bend your knees, put your hands on your thighs, and slowly unwind vertebrae by vertebrae until you're upright. Keep breathing all the way through. You'll grow a couple of inches by the time you're straight again!*

208.

Just Breathe.

It's important that you keep remembering to breathe fully, no matter how stressed you get. It's amazing how often we tend to hold our breath without even noticing. Meditation breaks and quiet times are always calming and give us a clearer perspective when we refocus. If you can't find any quiet space at your office, just go to the restroom and close the door. At least you won't get disturbed there.

In addition, it's essential to take vacations. And if you live in the inner city, do try to get away for weekends whenever you can. Go for hikes in the country as much as possible, and be sure to stay physically active.

If you feel that your employers would be open to it, why not suggest some changes that you feel could help the health and stress levels for you and your co-workers? Perhaps there are some ideas that would be easy to implement but simply haven't been thought of yet. After all, it's in their best interest to keep their staff happy and healthy. And if you work for yourself, there are bound to be some improvements you can make to help alleviate stress and keep you more balanced through the busy workday.

Improving the Quality of Your Workday

Only you know which simple changes you could make that would create an enormous difference in the level of stress and pressure you feel each day. So, based on some of the previous suggestions, along with your own ideas, list five things you could immediately do to improve the quality of your workday.

1. _____ 209.

2. _____

3. _____

4. _____

5. _____

Sustainable Enterprise and Empowerment Dynamics: The Feminine Way to Create Business.

the *feminine* way to create business

Starting your own business, whether you plan to build a large company or just remain a one-woman show, is a liberating, empowering experience . . . but no one ever claimed that being an entrepreneur is easy. It means that you never really clock out, that you're responsible for your decisions (whether they're right or wrong), and that you're the one who will ultimately be dealing with any problems arising from them. But having your own business also offers you a fulfilling way of living and working, where you can stand by your values, explore your creativity, and follow your dreams. Being financially independent and passionate about what you do, as well as having the opportunity to contribute to your community, are wonderful goals, which are often much easier to achieve when you're working for yourself.

In my book *The SEED Handbook,* there are many practical exercises to help you integrate your gifts, your experience, and your passion into creating a sustainable enterprise. Of course, you don't have to start a business to apply these aspects to your work—these same exercises apply to whatever type of job you do and give you the opportunity to determine if you're really following a professional direction that empowers and enriches your life. I don't want to repeat that entire book in this one, but I do think that it would be irresponsible of me not to give you the opportunity to explore several of SEED's most effective exercises. They will guide you into acknowledging your passions and talents, while determining if they can be used in creating a sustainable business or incorporated in other ways into a fulfilling career.

212.

What Puts the Sunshine into Your Soul?

Whether it's working with animals, taking photographs, being a Reiki healer, or helping those less fortunate than yourself, doing work that ignites your enthusiasm and lights up your soul is what every woman seeks.

After some inner reflective time, use this opportunity to list what truly excites and inspires you.

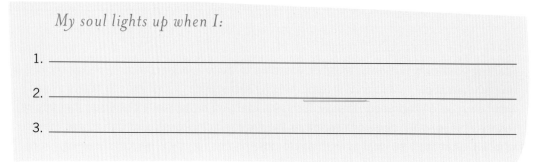

My soul lights up when I:

1. _____

2. _____

3. _____

4. _____

5. _____

6. _____

7. _____

8. _____

9. _____

10. _____

What Did You Love to Do When You Were Young?

Now think back to the hobbies and activities you enjoyed when you were younger. Even though you may have forgotten and left behind some of your "favorite things" as you got older, these things can offer clues as to how you might incorporate what brings you joy into your work.

For example, if you loved designing clothes for your doll when you were a child, that passion could easily translate to working in fashion. If you enjoyed writing stories as a teenager, maybe you have a real talent as a writer. Perhaps you were the one always coming up with ingenious ways to raise money for charity when you were at school—that piece of your personal history could mean that you'd be great at fund-raising for the nonprofit sector.

Use this opportunity to get back in touch with the passions of your youth.

When I was a child, I always played:

1. _____

2. _____

3. _____

4. _____

5. _____

When I was a teenager, I spent my time:

1. _____

2. _____

3. _____

4. _____

5. _____

Starting Your Own Business.

Now that you've got some clarification on your passions, you can decide if you'd like to use them to create your own business or at least do what you love when working for others. If starting a business is what you really want to do, it's important to consider how doing so would fit in with the rest of your life's vision: Do you have young children whom you want to be available for? Do you want to live in a city or the country? Would you prefer to work from home? Do you want to make lots of money, or would you settle for less if it meant an easier, less pressure-filled life? Are there other aspects of your life to take into consideration before deciding to create your own business?

Once you're clear about the practicalities of tying in your dream career with the other parts of your life, you can begin to make the pieces of your life/career puzzle fit together. In the SEED program, we talk about creating a garden where ideas can bloom like flowers. By incorporating your passions and talents with the practical needs of your life, you can start getting a sense of the seeds you need to plant.

Coming up with a general idea for your new enterprise is just the beginning. To make your "business garden" bloom, you'll need to do some practical research, budgeting, and basic legal groundwork. You'll also need to devise a business strategy, using your intuition as well as more traditional routes. As an actual start date for your business approaches, you'll have to get involved in marketing so that your message gets out to the right people. Only then will you be ready to rock 'n' roll!

For the complete program on growing a business the feminine way, including guidance on all of the above elements, see *The SEED Handbook*. Also check out my Website, **www.seedfusion.com**, for information regarding any local or online SEED groups where you can network, mutually mentor, and train. Good luck, and as we say at SEED: See you in the garden!

Money Matters.

As we've discussed, making lots of money is often not the main focus for many working women. However, valuing ourselves sufficiently to earn what we're worth in the professional marketplace is crucial. There's nothing wrong with making or having money, and any such notion should be banished from our thinking.

Sometimes it's our own lack of self-esteem that allows our employers to financially exploit us. As we know all too well, we women are seldom paid the same as men, even when we're quite high up on the job ladder, but it's up to *us* to ensure that we ask for what we want and deserve. If we're doing a job we love, with people we trust and admire, and we're learning a skill or making a positive difference in the lives of others, then fine, working for a lower salary than we're worth could be acceptable. After all, helping someone we believe in build up a small, entrepreneurial business that reflects our values is often more rewarding than earning twice the amount in an anonymous, uncaring corporation. But even so, we need appreciation. If our employer can't afford to pay us a high wage, there are other ways to show gratitude. We all need a pat on the back, so other considerations such as free lunches, flexible hours, bonuses, profit sharing, and perhaps, most of all, being listened to, count for much.

However, even if you make the choice to earn less money because of other more fulfilling considerations, it's important to be clear about what money means to you. Have you ever examined your relationship to money? Does it bring up your fears of self-worth? Are you afraid to ask for repayment of a loan or the raise that you believe you're entitled to?

Knowing Your Worth

Whatever your occupation—including if you're a homemaker—there's a price tag on what you do. So let's take the time to acknowledge your true market value.

First, make a list of all the different things you achieve in the course of an average working day. These all have a particular value, and you need to know what it is. You can see what the open market pays for someone with your skills by reading business magazines, making phone calls to colleagues, and visiting Internet sites such as **www.salary.com.** Put a price next to each of the different jobs you do, whether it's doing the laundry or writing a press release, and add up the final amount. I think you'll be shocked to see just how valuable your skills are.

On an average working day, I do the following:	Which is worth:
1. _____	_____
2. _____	_____
3. _____	_____
4. _____	_____
5. _____	_____

My total weekly rate is: _____

Total: _____

Multiply your total by five
(or however many days you work)

_____

218.

Once you've tallied up the monetary value of your skills and expertise, present your findings in a strong, positive manner to a friend or partner, or to your women's friendship circle. Do this practice presentation in a way that convinces them (and you) of your actual monetary value. Now you'll be well prepared to make the same presentation to those who are in the position to pay you what you're truly worth!

Funny Money.

At the end of the day, money is just energy, a means to an end. It has no intrinsic value other than what we put on it. And there are certainly other ways to obtain goods and services, as direct-barter or community-money systems prove. The massive fluctuation of the major stock markets in the last few years—along with the billions of dollars that constantly flow in and out of major corporations and even countries—have enabled us to see how fragile the concept of money really is.

As my friend Hazel Henderson, the internationally respected futurist and economist, has said on many occasions, the international monetary system is a global casino that can collapse any time. Hazel is a great advocate of bartering, or exchanging one object or service for another. Hazel calls bartering the "love economy," and believes that the Internet is a great tool for it. Together with her husband, Alan Kaye, Hazel has invested a lot of time and money in developing international barter Websites and other visionary vehicles dedicated to creating social change through the advancement of an alternative economy.

Women are natural leaders in the barter economy, as we saw recently in Russia and Argentina when their traditional monetary systems broke down. Bartering is the most basic means of acquiring what you need, and it's becoming more relevant in today's volatile global economy—but it can also be used in a positive way to create community. I have traditionally used an exchange of expertise in my various businesses, offering PR skills or public speaking in return for specialist input from others. It's a win-win situation. A great organization that promotes this concept is Womanshare, which was created in New York City in the early '90s as a cooperative-skills bank. Members exchange a wide variety of skills, from baking cakes to giving massages, based on their principles of "joyful living." The concept has been copied and adapted in many cities all over the world.

"Community money," which is often based on the Local Exchange and Trading System, or LETS, is what's used when a group of people, usually linked geographically, agree to trade in a particular way by exchanging goods or local currency. There are many LETSystems being used all over the world, and they can be tracked on the Internet if you wish to find one near you.

Cooperatives, Collectives, Networks, and Partnerships.

Colorful piles of vegetables fill the market stalls in the small African town, while the village women who grew them haggle with their customers, knowing that the profit they make will not only feed their families but finance their next crop. . . .

These women work as a collective with their neighbors, pooling their seeds and jointly growing produce before bringing it to market. As they create a small surplus, they invest in more seeds so that the younger women from their tribe can be financed to join them. The ways for women to earn an income in developing countries—where poverty, disease, war, and corporate exploitation are rife—are limited. They can become part of the great army of humanity who work for very little money growing food, while risking their health from toxic pesticides; or, particularly in Asia or Latin America, they can become exploited factory workers in the garment and textile industries; or, as in so many sad cases, they can become sex workers.

But alongside all the sad stories are ones of great hope. Women are survivors—they fight like tigers to feed their children, they bond and work together with other women to get their families' needs met, and they're natural entrepreneurs who create clever initiatives to earn their living. The African women at the United Nations' Fourth World Conference on Women that I attended in China in 1995 were by far the most inspiring of the delegates . . . and they were probably the poorest. Many had walked a fair way across their countries to make connections to China, determined to attend this milestone event, and yet they were still vibrant in their brightly colored robes and headdresses. They would sit there on the sidewalks of Beijing, selling the different wares that they'd made to pay for their trip. They were taking control of their lives in every way they could.

221.

I've heard many encouraging stories from around the world of women taking creative action to ensure that their families overcame the poverty they were confronted with. After the tragedy of war, women can be found selling food or other commodities by the side of the road. Or, in countries with collapsed economies, they will barter with their neighbors to exchange six eggs from their chickens for milk and cheese.

Village women from less-industrialized societies than ours have much to teach us in the West about traditional styles of cooperative working. When these methods are combined with our modern resources, we can create new and exciting designs for a more feminine way of working together. This sense of sharing in the context of the workplace is as much a philosophy as it is a practice, and can be integrated into the corporate world as well as the entrepreneurial sector. It's about supporting each other and being open to collaboration rather than following the established system of competition and confrontation.

Of the many inspiring stories I've heard of women working together in a new, cooperative way, there are two that I find particularly powerful. They originate in very different societies on opposite sides of the world, but they both demonstrate how women who have nothing can work together to empower their lives.

SEWA, the Self-Employed Woman's Association, was started almost 40 years ago in Northern India by a powerful and determined woman named Ela Bhatt. A Gandhi follower, lawyer, and union activist, Ela is one of the world's great unsung heroes, who has quietly changed the lives of hundreds of thousands of women as well as initiating ideas that have influenced the world.

Ela Bhatt formed SEWA at a time when women in India were still considered the possessions of their fathers and husbands. These women were the poorest of the poor, married very young, were completely uneducated and mostly lived on the streets. Corrupt police officers would take money from those who had any kind of employment, and their husbands would take the rest of their earnings at the end of the week.

222.

Ela and her team devised a way for the women to create their own bank, where the SEWA members could save their money in accounts identified by their thumbprints. Their savings would then be loaned out in small amounts to other members to expand their businesses. Repayments were almost always met in short periods of time, and SEWA became a model for one of the first modern microenterprise banks, lending women small amounts of money to start or expand a business.

As the SEWA members' businesses grew, they became leaders in their communities, showing other women how to financially empower themselves. They taught each other how to read and write, put roofs over their families' heads, and sent their daughters to college—all in just one generation.

Another extraordinary group of women started working as a cooperative after the terrible ethnic wars in the former Yugoslavia. I was brought in by the United Nations Educational, Scientific, and Cultural Organization (UNESCO), who was partnering with the World Bank to help promote handmade knitwear produced by the group, under the name "Knitting Together Nations." Hand knitting is one of the cultural pastimes of most women from that region, regardless of their religion, and this initiative was seen as a healing process for poor women from Sarajevo who had suffered terribly in the war. Some had lost their husbands, sons, and other members of their families; some had lost their homes; some had been sexually abused; and all of them had lost their self-esteem.

The women were encouraged to come together to knit, and a limited-liability company was set up, which was owned by the women themselves. I was told that the standard of knitting was high, but the group's management didn't have the contacts to sell their products. So fashion agent Gaby Schneider and I got in touch with our friends in the fashion business, and we were able to interest a number of fashion designers—including Betty Jackson, Edina Ronay, Sophia Swire, and Christina Kim of Dosa—to produce items for the cause. These community-minded designers spent a considerable amount of time personally training the women, and were all very patient with the group's lack of commercial expertise. It was a life-changing experience for these women in Bosnia. They started feeling good about themselves, gained confidence, earned money to feed their children, and started to heal many of their postwar wounds by working and talking together.

223.

● ● ●

As more and more women decide that they want to work in a feminine way and help each other enjoy a fulfilling work life, they create some exciting new kinds of networks. As we know, women like to spend time together, sharing information and supporting each other, so why not in business? But big business lunches, playing golf, or hanging out in bars tend to be the masculine way of bonding with colleagues—and these don't really reflect a woman's style.

We do like to network, though, which is why a profusion of professional women's networks have sprung up in countries all over the world in the last few years. I've spoken at many of these professional women's associations and have found women's openness and eagerness to share information with others extremely exhilarating. When we get together to discuss professional concerns, we tend to talk as much about our relationships, our children, and our hormonal concerns as we do about our businesses or jobs. We get to know each other by first sharing personal information and problems—then we move on to business and see how we can help or work with each other.

Networks are especially useful for women running small businesses. There are so many ways we can work together—promoting our businesses, getting advice, and even saving money on collective purchasing—that we can help each other while helping ourselves. My vision has always been for SEED to grow into a global network for sustainable women entrepreneurs, who can exchange local and global information, barter goods and services, and mentor and support each other. I have put my vision out to the universe and am delighted to watch the SEED garden grow as the Website and local groups develop. Since I also believe in networks working together, wherever possible I link and promote other women's business networks. We can do so much more as a group to help each other and create positive social change than we can ever do individually.

Sharing offices and resources is another way in which working women can help one another. And they're increasingly doing so: Collectives and cooperatives with child-care centers, accessible stores, and community-education facilities are springing up across the world. WeiberWirtschaft in Berlin is one such group, which I visited when launching SEED in Germany. It's become a model cooperative for professional women around the world, showing how an idea that originates from a few can become a major catalyst for change. The large building, owned by the cooperative in East Berlin, includes low-cost housing for some of its members, artists' studios, adult-learning facilities, and even a bookstore. The co-op offers different levels of membership, depending on whether each one is an associate member or is based in the building.

As this is a very ambitious building plan, WeiberWirtschaft has certainly experienced some financial pressures—but by holding on to their vision, they have created an inspiring example of women working together for the collective whole in the new feminine way. Their success should inspire some canny property developers across the globe to see the potential in converting old factories or warehouses into collectives aimed at women entrepreneurs—after all, we're great tenants, we're happy to share resources, and we pay our rent on time.

Starting businesses together, either as partners or collectives, is another way in which women can share their talents—but like any business initiative, it's important to get the legalities clear when working with others. If you're thinking about creating a new project

224.

or enterprise with some friends, colleagues, or family members, make sure that your relationships can survive the problems that may crop up with the business. As with any relationship, a business partnership has to be based on open, honest communication—all parties must be prepared to invest the time into expressing their feelings. And where money is concerned, it's always important to have clarity, particularly with partners. You'll want to be certain that your vision and values are truly along the same lines and that there is an easy, painless exit if things don't work out.

One of the ways that women are becoming entrepreneurs is by joining network-marketing businesses and selling products from their home. There are a number of successful enterprises that market their products in this way, and many of the female sales agents who work for them attest to feeling very empowered by their role. Some companies that market their products in this "pyramid selling" method have proven to be somewhat less forward thinking, and indeed some have fallen by the wayside. But network marketing is still an enormous business, with millions of women gathering friends and neighbors together in someone's living room to sell them everything from vitamin pills to sex aids.

I believe that network marketing isn't taken nearly seriously enough by the conventional business world, even though it's a rapidly growing arena, particularly in the area of holistic health care. Mail-order catalogs have traditionally used women selling from home as representatives, which works particularly well in rural areas. Avon is the most successful global brand of this type of personalized sales, and they have a vast international network of female sales agents. With many women on their senior management staff, Avon has a reputation as a caring, ethical company. They put a lot of effort and funds into charities and programs that support women, such as breast-cancer research and encouragement of women entrepreneurs, and they continue to be innovative in their products and marketing.

This phenomenon of small-scale, personalized selling in people's homes in an era of high-tech depersonalized commerce shows how successful businesses can be when they consider women's needs and attributes. Women like to spend time together, and by turning selling and buying into a social experience in each other's homes, a sense of community is created. Naturally, such enterprises also give many women an independent income, which can turn out to be quite considerable.

There are lots of opportunities if you want to join a women's business network, be part of a cooperative, or become a network marketer. To find the group that's right for you, do research on the Internet, look through specialized business or women's magazines, or visit trade exhibitions. And word of mouth is always so powerful—just ask your friends or colleagues if they know anything about your particular area of interest, and you'll soon get networked in.

Working to Make a Difference.

There are many ways in which we can contribute to society and our planet through our work. We all have gifts and skills that would be appreciated by others in need: Volunteering some spare time to a local group, such as a hospital or children's home, would be so rewarding; spending a couple of weeks in a rural crafts collective in a developing country helping them understand design, technology, or marketing could be the best trip we ever take; and giving old office equipment to the local youth center will always be appreciated.

I know of two charitable initiatives in the U.S. and U.K. aimed at women that are particularly inspiring and innovative. One involves hairstylists and makeup artists donating their time to give makeovers to homeless and low-income women. Initiated by beauty writer Jo Fairley and the beauty industry organization Cosmetic Executive Women (CEW), more than 100 young women living at the Centrepoint Shelter in central London have been given a new look and their confidence back. Similarly, Dress for Success outfits low-income women in donated suits appropriate for job interviews and gives them interview and career advice. These organizations' contributions to women's self-esteem is hard to measure in dollars or pounds. So it's not always the grandest schemes that mean the most to an individual in need—giving someone a new hairdo or a slightly used suit can help change her life in a small but meaningful way.

You may choose to contribute your time by mentoring a young person, particularly one from an impoverished background; or you might want to organize a group of work colleagues (or perhaps your women's friendship circle) to go clean up a local playground or redecorate a senior citizen's home. However you choose to give back, you can be sure that you'll end up *getting* back more than you could ever imagine.

How Can You Contribute?

Take this opportunity to see what you could comfortably contribute in either expertise or practical donations to some deserving cause in either your local or global community. Think about which of your skills and experience would most benefit a specific venture that you know needs help—or perhaps you could initiate a new project in your community that your friends would be happy to join in with.

Give yourself a time line to clarify what you'd like to do, researching the most appropriate beneficiaries. Then schedule in a date to put your thoughts into action. See how much you enjoy it and how incredibly rewarding it is!

227.

The GROW Commitment.

Repeat this affirmation before starting work in the morning:

My work creates value in both my life and in the lives of others.

• ■ ■ • •

Chapter 8

Finding Your Community

(Where You Examine
the Importance of the
Extended Family
and Look at Your
Tribal Roots)

Do I feel connected with my neighbors, co-workers, and friends? Where do I belong? Where is my community?

There is a call, the call of the desert woman, that once heard is never forgotten. It's the high-pitched yowl of female tongues that sweeps like wildfire throughout old villages in North Africa and the Middle East. It's a call based in antiquity, commemorating marriages and births, celebrating successes of the clan, and expressing mourning for the dead. That this chorus continues to exist is evidence of the vital role women have played and continue to play in weaving together the tapestry of community.

My Story: Finding My Tribe

I must confess: I'm a community junkie. I've always belonged to a myriad of different tribes of friends and like-minded souls, while still staying open to finding others.

Being born a Jew gave me a great sense of community as a child. Like many ethnic groups, we Jews enjoy belonging; and take great care of our young, our poor, and our old. Through my local synagogue (as in any church, temple, or mosque), I met other young people growing up in my community whom I'd hang out with and with whom I experienced the first pangs of teenage love.

Being in London in the '60s gave me access to larger tribes. I was fortunate enough to experience the excitement of the Mods and the Rockers, the British street gangs who were easily identified by their taste in music, fashion, and hairstyles. I'd see another Mod, and with the subtlest of nods, we'd acknowledge each other. With my girlfriends, I'd go to the coast on public holidays and hang out with the other Mods, while our enemies, the Rockers, would glare at us. Primitive? Yes, extremely. Fun? Of course! We were hip, we were cool, and we knew it.

After graduating to pseudo-hippiedom in my early 20s, I appreciated that a certain philosophy or common perspective on life was also part of belonging to a tribe. Being a hippie in London in the early '70s was about being political: We went on marches to free Angela Davis, we wore Marxist

230.

badges, and we all protested against nuclear war at the U.S. Embassy. We also bought our clothes from flea markets, wore our hair long, and were known to wear bells around our ankles and wrists.

I found that since working and engaging with people was my hobby, it was a delight to make it my career. Public relations was a natural for me, and I became part of the fashion industry—the young designers I promoted and the media I worked with became my new community.

In my mid-30s, stressed out from working all hours with two small children, I came across another tribe. I joined the Soka Gakkai, a lay Japanese Buddhist organization that offered me the secrets to a balanced, joyful life. We regularly prayed together, chanting our mantra, <u>Nam-myoho-renge-kyo,</u> which means "I devote myself to the mystic law of cause and effect."

One of the great joys in my life has been to bring my various tribes together. As I got more involved with my Buddhist friends, I enthusiastically told my fashion community that I had found the secret to manifesting what I wanted in my life. I invited them to come to meetings, and although some thought I was crazy, a good many started chanting with me. It was the early '80s, and before we knew what was happening, our little group was dubbed "Designer Buddhists" in <u>The Face,</u> one of the trendiest magazines around.

After that article, Buddhism became the hottest religion in London. When the next Fashion Week rolled around (which I organized), I suggested that a few of us get together to chant for the success of the event. And so, right before the event, a large crowd of designers, PR people, fashion-show producers, models, and makeup artists gathered together and collectively let rip with a cascade of spirited chanting. Our "good vibrations" could be felt the length and breadth of London's Kings Road, and I'm sure it was no coincidence that after such a powerful communal effort, the week was greeted with particular enthusiasm from the press and the international fashion buyers.

Since then, other communities have played extremely important roles in my life. I learned to communicate through my dance with Gabrielle Roth's Tantric Warriors, and I became a regular meditator with the Brahma Kumaris, who developed into my new spiritual family as they worked toward social change and divine global consciousness. The organic growth of my SEED community—whose global network of female entrepreneurs have met either through the SEED Website or the live events and training sessions—has filled my heart with joy, as I see them connect, barter with, and support each other. And finally, I found Deià, a community in the true sense of the word. I greet and am greeted by many of the locals I pass on the road during my early-morning walks, we care for each other in times of sadness, and we celebrate together in times of joy.

One community leads to another, as one individual leads to another. We spin our thread, we weave our cloth, we connect our lives together . . . and communities develop. By keeping myself open to giving and receiving, I continue to be blessed by new introductions and new friends. What seems to be by chance becomes a synergetic experience as my life continues to grow through community and connection.

Our Tribal Roots.

232.

Human beings are naturally tribal. For the most part, our ancestors were born into close-knit communities where they grew up, got married, had children of their own, grew old, and died, surrounded and supported by people they'd known their entire lives. Community was the glue that held societies together, and women in particular were (and still are) its linchpins. When our nomadic ancestors first settled in one place, it was the women who fetched the water from the wells, gathered the food, cared for each other's children, and created the structure of the extended family.

The grandmothers held much of the tribe's wisdom, stories, and memories. These female elders kept the spiritual rituals and beliefs alive in their communities (as they still do among many native peoples), preserving the social fabric of the community as they taught the younger tribal members their heritage and the legends on which to base their lives. The grandmothers also taught natural healing—which herbs would cure and which would kill. They imparted their knowledge, their advice, and their warnings, are today, sadly, denigrated as "old wives' tales."

Within native and rural tribes, women still maintain the spirit of the community, while men, deprived of being hunters and warriors—with nothing to hunt and no one to fight—have often turned to alcohol and violence.

Modern Times.

In Western society, rural women stitch together the threads of local community through their churches, school associations, local branches of national women's organizations, or town councils. But that sense of community is often missing from the lives of busy women working and living in big cities. Sure, we have our associates at work, our families at home, and our friends whom we meet for dinner or a quick drink at the end of the day—we may even have a nodding acquaintance with our neighbors and occasionally greet the guy who sells the newspapers—but where is the community for the modern woman? Where is the group of people we want to grow old with? Where are the folks we cry with over our losses and celebrate with over our joys?

We women need daily connection with others who are on a similar journey, with whom we have a communal sense of history and vision. We need to share our lives with others, to discuss our problems, to nurture each other, and to give and receive touch in order to stay healthy as well as happy. Yet we live in a world where, for the first time in history, the majority of people are living in large cities, separated from their families, roots, and cultures. Nevertheless, all members of the human race need a sense of belonging—we need our tribes, our communities, and our extended families so that we can fully develop a sense of self. We need to know where we come from to know where we're going.

There is an urgent need for women to take a leadership role in creating a new kind of community in society, one that integrates the best of the old with the needs of today. It is time to find our tribes, whether geographical or virtual, with whom we can create unity out of individual diversity. Modern society offers us many different ways in which we can do this, and in the pages that follow, you'll find a sampling of different types of communities, each with their strengths and weaknesses. By combining what resonates from each, together with the exercises in this chapter, we can integrate the principles of community that we choose to have in our lives, wherever we may live.

Life in a Small Town.

While modern-day villages vary tremendously throughout the world, there are similarities that are consistent everywhere. For example, when you're born into a small community, the likelihood of knowing everyone who lives in the surrounding area (as well as the details of their lives) is high; you'll all probably follow the same religion, eat the same food, and attend the same schools; you're most likely related to a good portion of the village; and you may very well marry someone from your locale. Growing up in a small town, you'll have a clear sense of roots—that is, where you came from and where you fit in. And it's comforting to know that you have the safety and support of the other members of your village "tribe" with whom you'll stay connected your entire life.

Yes, there are clearly positive aspects to living in a small village, but there are drawbacks, too—such as the fact that you live your life in a fishbowl. Gossip and falling-outs are inevitable within a small community, and young people may not find the greatest economic or professional opportunities.

Nevertheless, the attraction of becoming part of a small village community is still tempting to many of us. I bought my home in Deià in the early '90s to get away from the frantic pace of urban life. I needed somewhere that I could enjoy quiet time in a natural and beautiful environment, but once ensconced, I found that I was living in a unique place with a truly eclectic mix of people, and I couldn't help but be drawn into the community. The inhabitants are probably some of the most diverse of any small village in the world—there are the central group of Mallorcan households, descendants of families who have lived in the area for hundreds of years and who have grown up with their roots fully planted in the beautiful region; mixed in with them are the foreigners who fell in love with the artistic and bohemian tradition of Deià, as well as the natural splendor of its setting.

The unique mixture of Deià inhabitants is wonderfully described by California-born social anthropologist Jacqueline Waldren (herself a Deià resident) in her book *Insiders and Outsiders: Paradise and Reality in Mallorca (New Directions in Anthropology)*. In many ways, Deià is an example of a new type of 21st-century community, a melange that blends people and traditions into a new cohesiveness. It was from this perspective that Jacky told me that community is something that holds different meanings for different people. The cohesiveness inhabitants feel comes from the basic sharing of space and activities, from a mutual interest in making their environment a better place to live, and from a general feeling of being part of other people's lives. She said that the type of community that exists in Deià allows for different cultures and nationalities: "Relationships are not just about blood kinship. They are about extended families who help each other when needed."

The citizens of Deià are consciously trying to create an integrated community of people who care about their environment, along with quality education for their children and a safe, sustainable setting to live with their families. This blend is especially evident on Spanish "Saint Day" holidays, when one can often find a modern mix of children and adults of all ages, races, and nationalities eating the traditional Mallorcan dish of *pa amb oli* (olive oil and tomatoes spread on local bread) while dancing around a giant open fire to James Brown one minute and traditional Mallorcan folk music the next, all played by local DJ Juan Graves.

To ensure that the values of the village are sustained, a core group of concerned residents formed the Deià Community Association in 2000. Along with uniting the village to try to protect the land and the beach from overdevelopment and environmental degradation, the association has initiated cultural, educational, and sports activities to bring the various strands of the community together. In its first two years, the group created such diverse activities and educational courses as building traditional stone-walled terraces, olive-tree pruning, Mallorcan cooking, climbing and walking trips across the local mountain range, and neighborhood fitness and ballroom-dancing classes. They applied for faster Internet connections for the area, actively promoted the village's craftspeople, and sponsored events such as "open community," with food provided by the local restaurants. The association also introduced environmental programs, such as distributing

236.

cotton shopping bags to cut down the use of plastic bags, and encouraging locals to use their organic waste to make garden compost.

As far as a global contribution, our Deià Community Association has raised a significant amount of money for distribution to developing-world charities that are connected in some way with the village or island. All of this was done by a small group of individuals with different talents and limited resources, acting collectively with purpose, passion, and commitment to bring a community together and effect positive change.

Practical Steps in Getting to Know Your Neighborhood.

238.

Do you feel involved with your neighborhood, or is it just somewhere you live? Do you know your neighbors? Would you like to walk out your front door first thing in the morning knowing that friendly faces will greet you?

There are many lessons in community building that we can learn from a small village such as Deià, where good neighborhood practices come with the territory. However difficult you feel it would be to initiate such practices in your area—particularly if you live in a large city—remember that most people around you would welcome the opportunity to be part of a friendly, united community.

Why not take the initiative and use the following ten practical steps to bring small community customs into your daily life?

Ten Friendly Neighborhood Practices

1. Introduce yourself to at least five neighbors whom you see regularly.

2. Ask your postman his name and make a point of greeting him.

3. Familiarize yourself with local community events by reading neighborhood flyers, papers, and bulletin boards. Find at least two events that you would enjoy, and commit to going to them.

4. Introduce yourself to your neighborhood bank manager and staff, greeting them by name whenever you visit.

5. Get to know your local shopkeepers by asking them their names and introducing yourself.

6. Familiarize yourself with any future plans your local city council or governing body has for your area.

7. Go to the local library or newspaper office and research the history of your neighborhood.

8. Become familiar with your local doctor, dentist, and other health-care centers.

9. Visit the local churches, temples, mosques, and other spiritual centers in your area and introduce yourself to any of the clerics you meet.

10. Join your local community association and attend some meetings.

You may not do all of these things immediately, but as we say in Mallorca, *a poc a poc,* or little by little, your community, your neighbors, and the very streets that you walk on will become your friends.

Life in the Big City.

Cities can be wonderful—with the air of excitement, the sense of adventure, the rich tapestry of people of all colors and backgrounds—but what makes them so wonderful can also make them exceedingly challenging. The bustle of energy can become overwhelming, city adventure can easily turn into an urban nightmare, and the diverse assortment of people may well become a mass of anonymous humanity in which a person can become lost and lonely. The curse of the modern city is that it's so large and impersonal that people end up experiencing feelings of isolation and separateness. For many, the television is their best friend, and within the walls of their small apartment is where they feel most safe. Sadly, as city dwellers, many of us seem to have lost the most primal aspect of human society: connection.

While there are urban communities in which residents feel an authentic connection to one another, they are the exception, not the rule. This was not always the case. Cities were originally a collection of communities—neighborhoods were usually religious or ethnic enclaves that mirrored the countries or villages from which their inhabitants came. Even when I was growing up in London's suburbs in the '50s and '60s, I experienced a friendly neighborhood community where everyone was acquainted with each other. My own father was the local butcher who, like most of the local shopkeepers, knew his customers personally and greeted them all by name. The neighbors all kept an eye on each other's children, and the local parks were safe for us to play in.

Yet change is inevitable, and that sense of community has disappeared from most neighborhoods. Urban growth and large-scale immigration, together with the profusion of bland shopping malls and chain stores, seem to have brought a more impersonal perspective to municipal life. What has been lost is the most valuable aspect of community—a sense of belonging, of knowing who we are and where we come from—in other words, the roots that define us as human beings. And it's this lack of belonging that has left many of us feeling unsettled.

In the central London area where I live, Arabs live, work, and pray next to Jews; Eastern Europeans of all nationalities and ethnic backgrounds reside alongside each other; and

240.

Indians own all the local food shops. Irish-Catholic *and* Protestant people drink in the same pubs, and the local restaurants offer the best of Asian cuisine. Afro-Caribbean and mixed-blood families live in the nearby estates alongside working-class Cockney Brits, wealthy media yuppies, and rock stars. Everyone gets along fine, although the crime rate from local youths, as in many cities, is higher than it should be.

Unfortunately, young people are particularly affected by the lack of belonging. They need their tribes, and if society doesn't supply them, they create their own. It's ironic that in today's urban communities, the tribes that have evolved most organically are adolescent street gangs, which bring together young people who are looking for somewhere to fit in and people to connect with. The problem is that without any wisdom from their elders, a sense of history, a code of ethics, or any values except what they get from rap music and MTV, the street gang becomes an insular community that offers no growth for its members and no place for a person to mature into a responsible adult. This can be changed with the right attitude and positive energy. If progressive alternatives are made available to these kids—that is, alternatives that fulfill their natural human need to belong—then the attractiveness of gangs would diminish.

241.

In London I heard about an exceptional community-youth initiative, Kids Company, which was founded and run by Camila Batmanghelidjh. Camila has amazing energy and enthusiasm, and is a wonderful example of grass-roots leadership: She raised the funds to create the center in a desolate, impoverished inner-city area—and it's become a beacon of hope to minority children, who mostly come from underprivileged, one-parent families. Kids' Company provides these young people with a positive environment in which to grow and express themselves.

Likewise, when I was living in Los Angeles, I came into contact with several grass-roots programs that encourage young people from some of the poorest communities to live their lives to their fullest potential. Several schools in East L.A. created programs that had the students plant and grow organic gardens in their schoolyards. For example, students from Crenshaw High School sold their produce and products derived from their garden as sauces and dressings, branded "Food from the 'Hood," to bring in funds for computers and other basic tools that were in short supply. And I met other students who had organized a mentoring system after school, where they helped each other gain communication and presentation skills that would help them find employment. Many of these kids were the children of immigrants and were desperately hungry for adult mentors who could advise them on how to get jobs and get into colleges rather than turn to street crime.

Talkin' 'bout My Generation

I believe that by initiating intergenerational dialogue we can help create community wherever we live. As we remember to listen to and learn from each other—from children to elders—we'll once more open our hearts so that true community can begin to take root and flourish. One way to do this is to arrange a dinner party for about 12 people from your neighborhood. Invite a cross-section of guests who aren't related to each other, who wouldn't normally hang out with one another, and who encompass all generations. Perhaps include a leader from a local spiritual community; several elders with open attitudes; some young people who don't usually have access to switched-on seniors; a young single mother; a married, middle-aged couple; and a local shopkeeper.

Once your guests arrive, create an atmosphere of ease and openness in the room with your positive, welcoming energy. Before you eat, let everyone take turns introducing themselves, and ask each guest to briefly explain the biggest passion in their life. If appropriate, say a small blessing for the meal, perhaps incorporating the theme of peace and abundance in your neighborhood as well as throughout the world. Make sure that you encourage everyone to take a turn. Have them change seats around the table between courses so that they can have a one-on-one exchange with everyone there. The goal of the dinner is for everyone to break down the barriers that prevent communication, and to move past the stereotypes of age, background, and ethnicity so that real connections and insights can be made.

As the dinner draws to a close, encourage everyone to swap phone numbers with the other guests they particularly connected with. Suggest that they might want to get together again, either in your home or in the home of one of the other guests, with a specific theme they all might want to discuss, anything from music to community relations. Finally, provide a closing ritual, which could be something as simple as everyone formally bidding each other farewell by name. As you clean up, think back on the enthusiastic conversations around the table and the connections that were made within such a diverse crowd, and know that you planted a seed for your community.

Life in the Magic Garden.

Almost everyone I know has a dream of his or her ideal community—and you probably do, too. Since the beginning of civilization, humankind has attempted to create a blueprint for the perfect one. In 360 B.C., Plato outlined his vision of the perfect state in *The Republic,* designing a society where its citizens could live in harmony politically, spiritually, and philosophically. And in 1516, the Catholic martyr Sir Thomas More published his forward-thinking, detailed description of the perfect community in his treatise *Utopia,* which is said to have inspired Anabaptism, Mormonism, and even Communism.

243.

Jesus talked about loving our neighbors as ourselves, and from the apostles onwards, many of the early Christians lived in fraternal communities where they developed the concept of unconditional love and service to others. Religious communities such as Christian monasteries, convents, and Indian ashrams offer their devotees the opportunity to separate themselves from the mainstream of life and live together as one single unit. In the 19th and 20th centuries, the Quakers, Shakers, and Mormons created communal villages in which their lives were governed by the same, often rigid, set of religious and societal rules.

Since the 1960s, there has been a growth in another kind of intentional community, where like-minded baby boomers have chosen to live together, collectively incorporating their beliefs and values into daily life. Many of these communities were initially structured as mutually supportive communes in which possessions and responsibilities were shared.

One of the best-known intentional communities of our time is Findhorn. Situated outside Inverness on the east coast of Scotland, Findhorn was founded in 1962 by three determined and dedicated people: Eileen and Peter Caddy, and their friend Dorothy Maclean. Over its 40 years of existence, Findhorn's reputation has grown to where it's recognized internationally as a leading center for spiritual growth and sustainable innovation. Today, the Findhorn Foundation's aim, according to their recent annual report, is "to practice conscious and sustainable living as citizens of the earth, while recognizing the essential divinity of all life, and to provide inspiration and education that helps others do the same."

Findhorn initially started as one small mobile home with an annex on a windblown, litter-covered site, which was shared by the Caddys, their three small children, and Dorothy Maclean. They all strongly believed in living their lives based on God's guidance and based their practical decisions on the messages Eileen received in silent meditation. (She actually received this guidance when she was sitting in the public restroom in the early hours of the morning, which was the only place she could get any peace.)

Many myths and legends surround the early days of Findhorn, such as the giant vegetables that the group managed to grow to feed themselves. They originally created their tiny garden from a mostly inhospitable terrain with the use of compost made partly of seaweed from the nearby beach and horse manure from the neighboring fields. It's been said that through the guidance received by Dorothy from the "devas," or nature spirits of the plants and the vegetables, they were able to develop the garden and produce truly extraordinary results. Eileen Caddy wrote in her autobiography, *Flight into Freedom and Beyond,* how exciting it was to grow vegetables under the direct guidance of the angels in charge of them. Stories of fantastic and magical experiences are not unusual in communities that are open to the unexpected. When nature combines with faith and the human spirit, events or synergistic coincidences can happen that cannot be analyzed by logic.

Although very different characters, Eileen, Peter, and Dorothy were unified by their common sense of purpose. They became a solid trinity by combining their different gifts: Eileen's commitment to communicating with God produced the messages that guided their lives; Peter's strength of purpose and action made their dreams materialize; and Dorothy's connection with the spirits of the plants and minerals connected them with the land itself.

Inevitably the story of the "magic garden" and the Findhorn community's determination to create a center of spiritual light through meditation started to spread. Gradually, people of different ages and from many different countries came to join them. A community started to develop that was committed to the common purpose of building a center, which could both transform individuals and indeed the world. In fact, one of the early messages Eileen received for the community stated that "one garden can save the world."

Findhorn's influence in teaching people how to live in harmony and love with each other and the planet has grown from that small caravan to encircle the earth. Members of the community travel constantly, telling their story and giving workshops, as well as holding important international conferences and educational events in Findhorn itself, such as the "Experience Weeks," during which newcomers find out what it's like to live a life of service in a spiritual community.

246.

With their growth, the Findhorn Foundation has initiated several member-run businesses, including the manufacture of solar panels, a thriving publishing business, the production of natural aromatherapy oils, and perhaps the most successful of all, *Angel Cards,* which sell by the thousands all over the world every year. These affirmation cards feature small drawings of angels illustrating a quality such as *abundance, obedience, creativity, joy, love,* and *compassion.* Certainly inspired by the angels of Findhorn, many people (including me) start their days by selecting one or two of these cards.

Findhorn continues to blossom and grow, and today it includes a large communal dining room and kitchen; meditation sanctuaries; individual eco-homes, (some of which are made from old whiskey barrels); the impressive Universal Meeting Hall; and, of course, the stunning gardens, which offer visual as well as nutritional sustenance to Findhorn's many thousands of visitors, who, more often than not, leave with some form of life transformation. I know I certainly did.

Lighten Up Your Neighborhood: A Meditation

The Findhorn community believes that consciously manifesting love for specific people or places through meditation can change energy for the better. Whether the focus of the meditation is a garbage-strewn trailer park, inner-city streets, or a suburban neighborhood, negative energy can be replaced by positive. Using the Findhorn story as inspiration, take this opportunity to reflect upon your local neighborhood. Through this simple meditation, you can visualize creating harmony between your inner self and the area where you live.

Go to a quiet place, perhaps in front of your altar or in nature. Give yourself the space and time to be in touch with your feelings and to hear your inner voice, which directs you to your truth. As you sit in quiet meditation, feel your heart fill with love, a gift that honors the splendid being of light that you are.

Visualize the love as golden light, which radiates out of you, expanding throughout the room, house, or garden where you're sitting. Offer this light of love and peace to your community. Imagine it bathing your street, your neighborhood, and your town with its positive glow, creating a feeling of friendship and harmony in its path. Let this golden light fill empty spaces, streets, parks, and buildings, bringing sensations of love and safety to all who live there or pass by.

As you enjoy the warm feeling of neighborhood harmony, think of the faces of the people you see every day. Think of your postman, your neighbors, and the people working in your local shops. Surround them with your positive energy, and see the golden light unite them into a group of people with common interests and concerns.

Know that your light, the expanded prayer that is the love you have for yourself, has the power to transform anger and fear into love and peace. Hold the intention for it to fuse with all the other prayers of light being offered across the world so that you co-create a conscious network of energy that heals this planet, bringing all neighborhood communities everywhere together as cities of light.

Finding Your Community.

Do you ever count how many other human beings' paths cross yours during the course of a single day, especially if you live or work in a city? Every 24 hours you probably pass by hundreds, if not thousands, of people. How many of them do you connect with? Would you recognize any of them again?

Have you ever thought about how many of these strangers could actually be part of your tribe? Some could hold similar spiritual beliefs, others may have the same leisure interests, and still others may dream of social change like you do. In other words, people who could be true kindred spirits may live right under your nose, yet they merely swirl past you in the flurry of your busy life. No matter—there are ways to find each other if you're open enough. You might start a conversation while standing in line at the health-food store, remark to a fellow bus rider that you really enjoyed that book she's reading, or share a joke with someone you regularly see at your yoga class.

248.

If you're the mother of young children, the other parents waving their precious little ones off to school in the mornings will clearly have the same interests and concerns, but there are many other ways to connect with people who share your interests. They, in turn, will likely have other friends you could meet, and before you know it, you will have found an entire community that you've become a valued member of.

Networking like this, in a natural, spontaneous way, is clearly easier for some than others. Knowing who you are, being friendly, and feeling good about yourself is a magnet for other people. If you prefer a more scientific approach to finding a community that appeals to you, the Internet is a good starting point, for it can help you identify specific organizations and groups. Chat rooms and community bulletin boards provide information and links to others who are looking to meet people with similar interests.

Keep in mind that it's quite common to belong to several communities at once—the people on your block, your co-workers, your friends, and members of your spiritual or religious group. Some of these communities will be very different from others you're connected with—some will become permanent features in your life, while others will be more transient. If you wish to find a community or communities that you can share your interests and passions with, it's important to first identify what you're actually looking for. What does *community* mean to you? Which aspects of community life would you like to enjoy? What types of communities would you like to be part of?

What Does Community Mean to You?

Take this opportunity to answer a few simple questions that will help you identify your beliefs about your needs for community. And remember that there are no right or wrong answers.

1. Do you believe that you are part of one or more communities? If so, what are they?

   _____

2. Do these groups of people currently serve your needs? If not, what elements are missing? (For example, social, spiritual, professional . . .)

   _____

3. Do the communities to which you belong represent your true values? If not, why not?

   _____

4. Do you think that there's a difference between social friends and community? If so, what is it?

   _____

5. Do you think that there's a difference between family and community? If so, what is it?

   _____

6. Do you know your neighbors? If not, how might you get to know them?

   _____

7. How many local shopkeepers do you know?

   _____

249.

8. How do you think that belonging to a community improves your life?

_____

9. How do you see your role in your community?

_____

10. What do you give to your community?

_____

11. What does *community* mean to you?

_____

Creating Your Community.

251.

As the traditional family unit grows increasingly rare, single parents become the norm, and countless people over the age of 40 stay unmarried by choice as well as circumstances, so many of us are searching for a new model of community. We want to live in our own space, alongside others with similar values and vision.

Many forward-thinking individuals believe that if you can't find the community you want to live in, you can create one with other similarly minded people. For example, a number of single people and couples are now following a collective style of purchasing—they turn large properties that they couldn't have afforded on their own into individual units run on a communal basis. Others are looking to small rural villages in beautiful countries where land is cheap and they can more feasibly create their particular community. Still others are favoring a large farm environment, where they can work and live in eco-harmony. And in the U.S. and the U.K., adult-only villages for the over-45 crowd are being built, where residents can share leisure and sports activities, medical and health care, and peaceful environments where they can grow older.

These new versions of the ideal community often incorporate forms of cooperative living without the rigid rules that inevitably hamper personal and economic freedom.

Enterprising Communities.

Local communities are taking responsibility for the development of their own neighborhoods more and more. In the U.K., for example, there are a growing number of development trusts that are set up to regenerate neglected areas where there has been a downturn in the economy. With funding from regional, national, and European governments and support from banks, these nonprofit associations are taking dying neighborhoods and, with a whole assortment of different initiatives, creating exciting new developments. Artists' studios, hip restaurants, centers for entrepreneurs, nursery schools, community newspapers, and sustainable-energy centers are springing up that are run by locals, where previously falling-down buildings, litter-ridden streets, and crime were the norm. These enterprising communities aren't sitting back in despair and worrying about unemployment—instead, they're taking their collective power and creating social enterprise opportunities that will assist them all in raising their standard of living.

252.

City planners and architects are also taking into account the need for a new kind of communal habitat. They've observed that certain common elements have proven key to a modern community's success, including cultural diversity; input from all age groups in forming community policy; a relatively small population; a friendly, open design; communal leisure and meeting areas; affordable, high-quality eco-housing; a garden area for growing vegetables as well as plants and flowers; shared child-care resources; and the modern technology necessary to run businesses from home.

One such new community has been co-created by environmental architect Bill Dunster in Southwest London. The Beddington Zero Energy Development, or BedZED, has the look of a giant Lego construction, yet this eco-friendly, carbon-neutral development of housing and workspace has incorporated low-technology solutions such as harnessing wind power for ventilation and solar energy for heat. With backing from the Peabody

Trust, one of London's oldest housing associations, BedZED is a unique mix of social and private housing, with a residential blend of retired couples, young families, and singles.

BedZED exemplifies the communal ideals that I feel are so important. I believe it's time to move back to tribal living and the sense of extended family, where different generations can support and learn from each other. There is a demand for open, vibrant communities where members celebrate each other's successes, console each other's losses, and dance, pray, and grow together.

Our society is going through a major shift, and the human need to share and belong to a community is already manifesting throughout the Western world. When we help create or become part of such communities, we not only enrich our own lives, we enhance our society as a whole.

The GROW Commitment.

Repeat this affirmation when you feel a need for connection with your community:

I am committed to my community and will contribute to it in every way I can.

• • • • •

(Where You Look at
Women's Natural
Roles As Leaders in a
New Type of Society,
Based on Peace,
Love, and Cooperation)

The Future Is Feminine

How can we collectively, as well as individually, create change in our modern world? Can we create unity out of diversity? How can we shape a cooperative future?

A Mayan Indian woman from Guatemala born into a poor peasant family becomes a leading international advocate of Indian rights; a Burmese woman lives under house arrest as a result of her peaceful protest against the unjust leaders of her country, while her beloved husband dies of cancer in a faraway country; a Muslim lawyer uses her country's Islamic law to fight for the rights of victims of government repression—and all three women are subsequently awarded the Nobel Peace Prize for their efforts. Elsewhere, small groups of Protestant and Catholic women from Northern Ireland who are committed to creating peace in their country open community centers where young people from both sides can learn to live alongside each other; Israeli and Palestinian women work side by side in children's nurseries and women's refuges; female Afghani teachers continue to hold classes for young girls, despite the fact that Taliban soldiers are threatening their lives. . . .

256.

There are so many stories of women who have courageously lived by their feminine principles to bring social change and justice into their communities. These women are so often unsung heroes who fearlessly risk their lives to bring about conflict resolution and unity for their people. But what can we learn from the actions of Guatemala's Rigoberta Menchú Tum, Burma's Aung San Suu Kyi, Iran's Shirin Ebadi, the Northern Ireland Women's Coalition, or the brave women from the Middle East? Are women the leaders of a new way of creating social change based on cooperation and understanding? Can we work in our own communities with others from different backgrounds and ethnicities to create a better future for our children? We will explore these questions and more in this chapter.

My Story: What Women Want

Although I was always a strong woman, I had been too locked into my family and career to understand the importance of the women's movement. It wasn't until I left my PR agency in the early '90s that I started to appreciate how important it was for women to work together if we wanted to create change in today's society. I was asked to chair a new women's radio station, and although its owners were more interested in creating a commercial concern than a vehicle for community building, it brought me into contact with many different women's organizations and high-profile female leaders from different disciplines. The station also gave me the opportunity to present my own show, Frankly Speaking, where I was fortunate enough to interview leaders and feminists such as Gloria Steinem, Body Shop founder and environmental activist Anita Roddick, singer Sinéad O'Connor, and British politician Claire Short.

It was as if I'd found a major missing link in my life. My eyes opened as I learned of the difficulties that so many women face all over the world. I started connecting with nonprofit groups and grass-roots associations, working together to bring awareness of women's issues to the front of the public agenda. Inspired, I decided to put on an event in London that would attract public and media attention to women's roles in today's society. After talking with several like-minded friends, I was determined to put on a celebratory conference and concert called "What Women Want," just prior to the United Nations' Fourth World Conference on Women in Beijing in August 1995.

With hardly any resources, financial or otherwise, I embarked on creating an event that would not only affect the lives of many women, but would change my life in ways I hadn't even dreamed of. I was about to embark on the rest of my journey.

With the help of an assistant; my then-teenage daughter, Jessica; and some great friends, including Anita Roddick and a couple of commercial sponsors, we pulled together the first major women's event ever held in Britain. We featured workshops and discussions on a wide range of topics from technology, natural health, and domestic violence to consumer power and sexuality; and we had women from many different communities and nationalities representing their individual interests in a dialogue with each other. There were exhibitions by female artists, actors, musicians, and massage therapists inside London's South Bank Centre, with enormous banners and street performers outside the Royal Festival Hall, alongside the river Thames. Women learned how to use the Internet, what herbs to take if they had PMS, and how to dance the Five Rhythms. We talked at length about the power of female consumers and how we're portrayed in the media by other women, and we took an extensive look at violence against women in our society.

Spirituality was introduced by the Brigidine Sisters, an order of Irish nuns, who started off the evening concert of female artists with a prayer. Germaine Greer read her speech, stating that "the opposite of patriarchy is not matriarchy, but fraternity." Sinéad O'Connor performed her first full London set in several years; other wonderful performers included Chrissie Hynde, Zap Mama, Angélique Kidjo, and Sarah Jane Morris; and comedian Jo Brand linked the whole thing together with her raunchy humor. The evening ran over by more than an hour and finished with a tribal chant by all of the artists onstage, including me.

I thanked the audience, as well as the artists, for their incredible contribution and support, and I acknowledged the power of the Goddess that I believed had brought this event together. I felt empowered and inspired, realizing that it was time for me to commit to using my skills and experience to create and support initiatives that would bring value to women's lives, including my own.

I was about to become part of a local and global web of individuals and organizations that worked together to bring about social change. I left the concert knowing that "What Women Want" was just the beginning of my new life.

Post-Feminism.

The feminist movement of the '60s and '70s certainly paved the way for change for women in society: These days, at least in many countries, we have a larger number of female politicians, business leaders, and academics; we have control over our own bodies and can chose birth control, abortion, or even artificial insemination to determine our reproductive process; it's easier for us to borrow money from banks; and politicians pay a lot of lip service to get our votes. But there is, nonetheless, a glass ceiling: A considerable pay gap between women's and men's wages still exists, and there are still relatively few women in places of true national and international power. In addition, horrifying acts of violence continue to be perpetuated on women in countries all around the world.

Many of the women who managed to move into the world of politics and business since the '60s and '70s found it necessary to use their masculine energies if they wanted to succeed. The male qualities of competition, confrontation, and conquest are clearly not natural for most women, but it seemed as if they were necessary to get to the top. But now there's a new type of female leader coming from the grass-roots level, who's showing us that there's a more feminine, inclusive way of living and working together, from which we can create a new style of holistic society.

Each and every one of us can move into our own leadership role as we individually contribute to creating a better world—this will then create the new paradigm, when the quality of life for every inhabitant of planet Earth will become respected and honored.

Tipping the Balance.

Have you ever wondered how trends and attitudes catch on in society? As a PR consultant for many years, it was my job to observe what influenced people to buy certain products. When I was creating a campaign for a client, perhaps marketing a new beauty product or fashion line, I always judged the optimal moment when enough media stories would have appeared to stimulate word of mouth, which would in turn create demand.

Certain types of people are "influencers" as well. For example, high-profile celebrities such as movie stars and musicians can wear new fashions that are then taken up by millions. (By the same token, celebrities can create a huge awareness for their favorite cause or charity.) But it's not just entertainers who influence the public's thinking—journalists, sports stars, filmmakers, TV producers, politicians, designers, and even authors all have tremendous power over our attitudes and belief systems. And, of course, the marketing industry itself—with its glossy advertising, billboards, and millions of dollars to spend—can determine consumer trends.

Influencing the way people think doesn't always have to be about new ways of getting

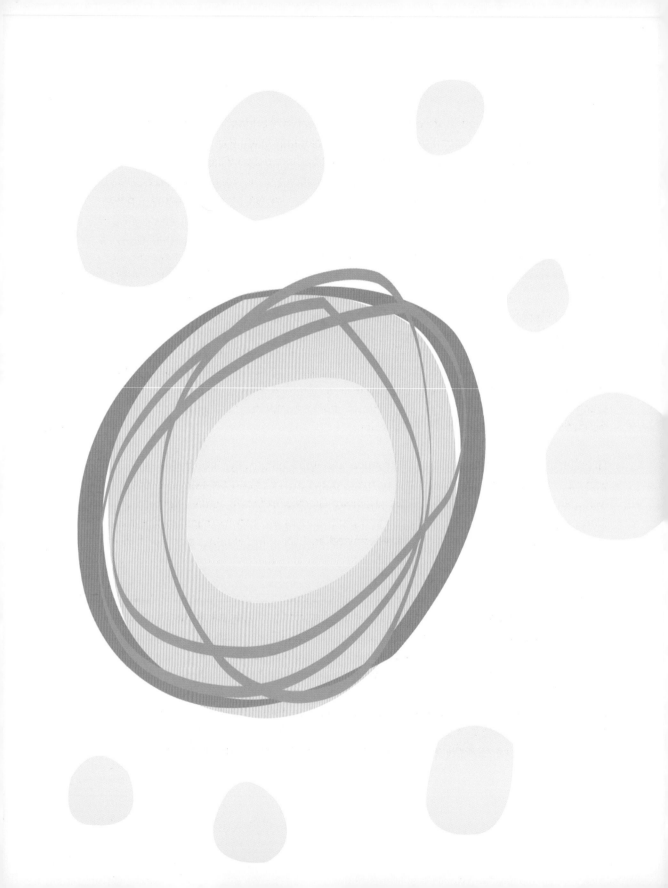

them to spend their money. It could instead be about disseminating information on different ways in which we can take action, which can improve the quality of our lives and those of others. In this new age of technology and the global village, we can use organic, grass-roots techniques to shift public opinion. Any one of us can spread a message when we feel strongly about something—and when we feel enthusiastic, our passion will spread to others.

This reminds me of British biologist Rupert Sheldrake's theory on morphic resonance, which is based on universal collective memory and instincts, which affects every aspect of nature, including human beings' behavior. He quotes the 100th-monkey principle (said to be a metaphor rather than based on science), which tells the story of a breed of monkey that lives on two islands. One day, one of the monkeys found out that if he dipped his fruit in the sea, the skin would soften and he could peel it easily. The other monkeys copied him; once 100 monkeys were doing it, *all* the other monkeys automatically knew how to do it, including the monkeys on the other island. We humans work much the same way: Once a number of us are doing things in a certain way, others instinctively know how to do the same thing.

These days, we're able to spread information and opinions quickly through the Internet or by word of mouth—when enough people become aware of and are talking about a new idea or belief, there is what author Malcolm Gladwell refers to as *the tipping point*. When this point occurs, a critical mass of the population will become significantly influenced, and the idea or belief will be recognized and accepted within a significant part of society.

For example, genetically modified (GM) food lost its market in the U.K. when enough individuals protested to the supermarkets and other retailers. This particular campaign was backed by action from various organizations such as Greenpeace, which would take customers around to supermarkets, pointing out what food contained GM ingredients and how harmful they were, not only to the human body, but to agriculture.

On the other hand, organic food became a multibillion dollar industry when enough people became aware that it was a healthier way to eat. Green & Black's, the British organic-chocolate company, pay the Belize Indians who grow the raw ingredients for their Mayan Gold chocolate bar a guaranteed fair price for their produce. Green & Black's are registered with Fairtrade (a foundation set up to ensure "a better deal for third-world producers"), who made sure that the public knew about the chocolate through their affiliations with churches and other grass-roots networks. In fact, it was churchgoers who initially helped the company become successful by complaining to their local supermarkets that the product wasn't on their shelves. And on a larger scale, forty million people, influenced by their religious leaders, recently registered their concern regarding the Kyoto Protocol and emissions into the atmosphere on the World Council of Churches' Website.

When momentum builds, there's a moment when the balance of opinion shifts to a position that cannot be stopped. It coalesces, taking an idea from possibility to actuality. And new ideas move fast—whether related to fashionable consumer goods or different types of social issues, when influencers get behind them, the message spreads.

What's *Your* Tipping Point?

It's time to look at the social influences that have affected different decisions you've made in your life. We are going to look at certain tipping points that have affected *you*—that is, how you were influenced to buy a new product or start a new way of thinking. By tracking back through your habits, beliefs, or patterns, you can become aware of what influences your behavior.

Let's take a look at one or more relatively recent changes to your life, where you made a decision to do things differently than before. Choose a course (or courses) of action you decided to take because it was healing for you or the planet—it could be what led to you to begin eating a more healthy diet or why you decided to recycle your garbage. Do you remember what influenced you to you start a regular exercise regime or how you began your spiritual journey?

Once you've settled on a thought or lifestyle pattern, think back to when it or they began. What did you hear or read that changed your belief system? Where did the influences come from? Media will always have a strong presence in how we think, but we women get our information from many sources. Use this opportunity to examine what influences you.

I decided to _____

because _____

_____

_____

_____

I came to this realization/lifestyle change through influences such as

_____ *, and my tipping point was*

_____

Knowing what information to trust and where to find it gives you the power and focus to expand your areas of knowledge and wisdom. A new idea may begin with one person, but once it collectively resonates and gathers steam, it can influence millions—and that is the starting point for personal as well as societal transformation.

Making a Difference.

It does seem impossible—after all, how can a single voice or an individual act of con-science make a difference? It rarely seems that it does. But a cascade of drops makes a stream, streams make rivers, and rivers pour into oceans. Even the very smallest action, which may seem inconsequential at the time, creates an environment for change. Yet without the individual action first, the large mass effect could never occur. Every one of us can make a difference in some way that contributes to society. Yours could be the signature on a petition that qualifies it for the ballot, or you could travel to a peace march to join millions of others and your single voice raised with other voices could unleash a loud chorus of protest that could be heard all over the world. It is the individual action, the single "drop of water," that collectively starts the tidal wave.

It's when these activities start to build, both locally and globally, that we create a new kind of world consciousness. In the demonstrations against the Iraq War in 2003, we saw for the first time how protests brought millions of people from many different backgrounds peacefully together. In hundreds of cities around the world, small and large groups of the rich and the poor, the urban and the rural, and the young and old turned up. The atmosphere at all of the protests was peaceful, using street theater, humor, and music as well as raised voices to deliver the message.

The huge numbers of women of all ages who were at these demonstrations, many of whom had never joined in a protest before, held hands in their pursuit of a common goal: peace. Women don't create war, but it's always women and children who are the innocent victims of terror and violence. At the London demonstration, the crowd went wild when politician and former actress Glenda Jackson read a message from Yoko Ono that said: "A dream we dream alone is only a dream, but a dream we dream together is reality. Speak up, shout loud, and stand for peace."

We may not have stopped the machineries of war that time around, but for the first time, many of us realized that if we could all work together, we could create long-term peace. With the combined efforts of similarly minded people working together at the grass-roots level, changes can happen in local communities as well as globally. We have collective power in how we vote, how we spend our money, where we choose to work, and how we engage with other groups. When people are united into a community by positive attitudes and a common focus, the energy created is a powerful force.

There are so many ways in which we can make a difference to the future of this planet—it's when we believe we can't change anything that we become apathetic and hopeless. By taking a stand on how we want to live our lives and contribute back to the world, we become empowered. Personal action creates an energy of hope, which not only expands us as individuals but deepens our bonds with the rest of humanity.

What Can You Do?

Taking positive action for social change can come in many different forms, so incorporating even small adjustments in your life could have considerable long-term effects. Perhaps you're already living a consciously sustainable lifestyle, where you try to create a balance between your consumption, reduction of waste material, and use of energy and water. If not, know that there are very simple ways of incorporating these principles into your life: Turn the light off to save electricity when you don't need it, recycle as much as possible, and when you can, walk or cycle to get to your destination.

Take an honest look at your lifestyle. Are there ways in which you could incorporate more sustainable and environmentally friendly habits into your day? Perhaps you could buy food that doesn't come wrapped in plastic or, if you have a garden, create compost with your biodegradable waste. How about using an environmentally friendly laundry detergent or investigating the possibility of using solar instead of electrical power? Change starts at home with your own daily living habits.

265.

There are so many little things we're each able do that, when added up, make a huge contribution. Why not take this opportunity to write down some changes that you could incorporate into your daily life that will make a difference to the planet as well as yourself.

Five Ways to Save the Planet

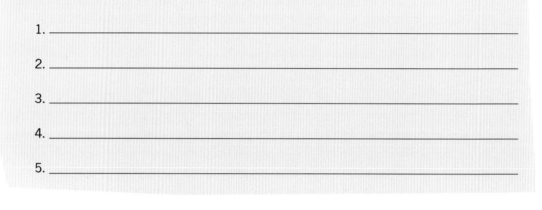

Write down at least five small actions you can regularly take, based on the sustainable principles of saving energy, reducing consumer consumption, and recycling.

1. _____

2. _____

3. _____

4. _____

5. _____

266.

Putting on the Pressure.

To create change in a democratic society, it's crucial for members of the public to make their point of view known. This can be done in a number of ways—for example, if you're not happy about something in your community, you could attend local meetings or write to those who have power. Find out who your legislative representatives are and pressure them with letters, e-mails, and calls about your concerns. I'm not suggesting that you become a nuisance for the sake of it; however, they *are* public servants, and since you're one of their constituents, it's your right to let them know exactly how you feel about issues that concern you. At the end of the day, you aren't powerless: You have a vote to keep them in office or not. You may also find that there are organizations that are just as concerned about the issues that you are—research them in your local library or on the Internet and determine if you can be more effective by joining them than you can be on your own. You'd be surprised to find out how many people share your views. Together, your voices can create change.

If you feel passionate about an issue, you may even want to start your own action group. There are always new issues that need addressing, such as protesting the closing of a local hospital to make way for a new factory, or the turning of a children's playground into a shopping mall. Similarly, there's always a need for proactive action as well, such as creating a community garden on some wasteland or getting a traffic light erected on a busy street corner.

If you're inspired to create positive change, it's easy to begin—all it takes is your commitment. And this applies to local, national, and even international issues. Once you get involved, the rewards you'll reap from being at the center of progressive action are enormous.

Speak up. Speak loudly. It works.

268. From Local to Global.

Some years ago, an American friend complained to me that finding a good hamburger in England, much less Europe, was practically impossible. Our European version of that American speciality was either too dry or too tasteless, not seasoned right, not cooked right, not in the right bun, or didn't feature the right condiments. Fast-forward to the present—that Amcrican fricnd has no complaints now, as she can get her beloved American-style hamburger at any one of the thousands of McDonald's that have sprung up like mushrooms in every major European city and all over the globe. The same can be said for any American jeans she might want, or shoes, or music—or almost any other consumer good, for that matter.

Like it or not, the world is getting smaller. We're being bound closer than ever before, both economically and culturally. Civilizations that have evolved for thousands of years are now being swept up into a homogenous global culture. The messenger of this culture is satellite TV, and the values that it spreads are ones of cash and consumption.

The word *globalization* is bandied about quite a bit these days. Its basic premise is to create an integrated, no-border economic and trading system where every country is on equal footing to compete on the open market in goods, labor, and services. The theory is that over time, poorer countries will become richer because of the influx of capital. This creates a higher standard of living, allowing those who are gaining more money to spend more of it, thus setting up an ever-increasing demand for goods and a continual upward spiral of economies. It all sounds fine in theory, but in practice, it's another matter.

The mechanism of globalization today sees the more advanced governments and large multinational corporations taking advantage of the poorer countries and their people. Loans, which come from global institutions such as the International Monetary Fund (IMF) and the World Bank to supposedly right the economies of poor countries, are instead sending them deeper in debt. In dictating the terms for poorer nations to receive economic aid or loans, the West has essentially stacked the deck in its favor. The monetary gap between the West and developing nations has risen, not fallen, while poverty in these countries has increased, not diminished.

269.

Groups such as the World Trade Organization (WTO), whose influential members all come from the Western world, have created international trade laws that mostly benefit themselves and the businesses they represent. The WTO has also made it easy for multinational corporations to exploit poor countries' labor and resources. In fact, much of the hip, trendy clothes we wear are actually made by people in developing nations who work for long hours at very low wages.

Another unfortunate aspect of globalization can be seen in the agricultural sector. Large businesses wielding their economic might try to control how and what farmers plant. One way this has been done is by patenting new types of seeds (many of which are created through genetic engineering) and then introducing them into local areas. For example, several years ago in India, farmers were encouraged to plant crops of a single type, such as cotton or rice, rather than to produce a diversity of crops as they had traditionally done. Unfortunately, when the market for the single crop plunged, the farmers were sent into bankruptcy. The crisis grew worse because other foods had not been planted. This miscalculation not only destroyed the diversity of local food cultures, but entire local food economies as well.

Globalization has been equally devastating to the environment. By throwing open access to the natural resources of developing nations, companies have come in to exploit natural resources for profit. More forests are being cut down, more land is being torn apart and mined for minerals and precious stones, more air is being polluted, more water is being rendered undrinkable, and more species of plants and animals are disappearing. While there has been some minimal profit made by countries—mostly going to their corrupt governments rather than to the citizens of the country—resources are being plundered and destroyed forever . . . while the people in these countries continue to suffer.

Celebrated eco-feminist Vandana Shiva, who has written a dozen influential books on global ecology, believes that a new feminine perspective holds the solutions to the world's age-old problems. I attended a conference in Spain where she stated, "The paradigms that are being accepted combine military power with power in the economic domain through globalization and the deployment of irresponsible technological power in an unrealistic manner which becomes reality only through the use of force. Reality is a feminist and ecological vision that is so real, it doesn't need power to find its place."

270.

Concerned Consumer.

One way in which we women can do our part in trying to prevent this exploitation of people and land by large corporate entities is to become conscientious consumers. With at least 80 percent of all consumer decisions made by women, it means we have power and influence, if we choose to use it.

We must start asking questions: First and foremost, we need to know about the food we buy, which we can do by checking a product's ingredients. Does it have any real nutritional value? Was it made with any genetically modified ingredients or harmful pesticides or chemicals? Obviously, buying organic is usually the wiser choice. That's not always possible, though, which makes it all the more important to be as vigilant as possible about ingredients and production methods.

There are other simple things we can do as a conscientious consumer. We can check on our household cleaning products to find out if the ingredients are harmful to the environment. We can buy products with the least packaging and tell our retailers why. We can support the manufacturers and retailers who *do* ensure the sustainability of their products—for example, small local businesses who make an effort to contribute to our communities deserve our loyalty. We may sometimes pay a little more for doing business with them, but the more support they get, the sooner they can bring their prices down.

We also need to check the ethical policies of companies we buy from to ensure that their business practices reflect our own values. And we should consider staying away from advertisers whose ads don't support a positive image of women. If we see an ad that we feel falsely represents or exploits women, then we should let the heads of these companies know by writing them or complaining to the magazines where we saw the ads featured.

Another place to be a conscientious consumer is with the clothes we wear. I'm as quick to buy the new seasons' fashion as the next person, but some of today's clothing is made with unhealthy materials and is manufactured using child labor and inhumane conditions. We can put questions to the retailers we buy from about the clothing they sell. Chances are that they're uninformed, so we can suggest that in order to keep our business, they get informed. We can also write directly to the manufacturers, who may answer, and perhaps will even start taking responsibility for exploitive labor practices or using harmful chemicals in the fabrics. However, there *are* manufacturers who use organic fibers, genetically modified-free cotton, and natural dyes. There are also businesses who use community or fair-trade labor as much as possible. These are the good guys who are taking responsibility for the planet, and they deserve our full support.

271.

One area of manufacturing that is notorious for labor exploitation and horrific working conditions is the furniture and carpet industries. Again, we need to be knowledgeable about the products we buy—the last thing any of us wants is to be curled up in a chair or bed knowing that it was made under inhumane conditions. If we have concerns or are just curious about the ethical practices of any company, we can do research. It isn't that difficult—through human rights and environmental organizations, the Internet and the media, information is now freely available to us about how major brands and large international corporations produce their goods.

The only way we can stop these inhumane practices is to demand that companies change their policies or else we won't buy their products. If we decide not to buy a company's products because we don't approve of their ethics, we need to let them know by writing to their CEO and telling him or her why we reached that decision. If we're really concerned about a corporation's values, and we can afford it, we could even buy a few shares in their business—which gives us the right to go to a shareholders' meeting and ask challenging questions in front of other investors. Becoming a shareholder of a company, however small the investment is, gives us a tremendous amount of power—they *have* to listen to us.

If we wish to invest more than a token amount of money in a company, we can do so in companies that reflect our values. There are many profitable businesses that not only make good investments, but who are also socially conscious and progressive.

Again, collectively we can achieve so much. Organizations such as the Women's Institute in the U.K., with their thousands of regionally based members, have enormous collective spending power. If we use our power in groups, we can put real pressure on companies to appreciate that ethics and values are good for business.

Spending Wisely

Try to make this week's big shopping trip a more interesting experience. Using some of the examples we've talked about in this section, together with your own ideas, examine everything you pick off the shelves for content and point of origin. Where you can, ask to see the manager and question him or her as to the background of the products you wish to buy. Ask if he or she knows how the people who grew or manufactured the products were treated and if there is anything in the goods or the packaging that may damage the environment. Also, check that the contents of the products are healthy—which might be a little difficult because so many products *claim* to be healthy when they're not. But at least check for added artificial ingredients or chemical additives.

Tell the manager how much you regularly spend in the store and explain that although you don't want to be difficult, you're a concerned consumer who wants to know that your money isn't going to unethical companies. Finally, ask what the general trading ethics and principles of the store's parent company are. The manager probably won't have the answers to most of your questions, so ask for the details of the head office and readdress your questions in a letter to the CEO of the company.

I'm not suggesting that you do this exercise every time you shop, but by doing it at least once, you will instinctively use a more discerning eye next time you're pushing your cart down the supermarket aisle.

Networks for Change.

The reality of a "perfect" world may seem unattainable at times, but if we hold and share the vision, then we have a future to work toward. There are currently networks of progressive individuals and organizations who collectively are creating the blueprint for global transformation. They include powerful international nongovernmental organizations (NGOs) with high-profile public memberships, such as Greenpeace, Friends of the Earth, Oxfam, Amnesty International, the World Wildlife Fund, and Human Rights Watch, which are able to continue their crucial work through our support. Alongside the NGOs are the international agencies of the United Nations, such as UNESCO, UNICEF, and UNIFEM, which work primarily in developing nations on social issues relating to children, women, culture, and education.

In addition, there are tens of thousands of other, far smaller, nonprofit organizations that work at the grass-roots level, initiating projects to bring practical aid to society and the environment, and that are also working toward building a better future. And business networks for social change, such as Business for Social Responsibility, Social Venture Network, and Spirituality in Business, continue to thrive. There are also committed "for profit" companies who use their success as a platform for social change. Businesses such as Anita Roddick's Body Shop, Ben & Jerry's ice cream, and the Mallorcan-based Camper shoes, plus fashion designers Katharine Hamnett, Sybilla, and Christina Kim of Dosa, are inspiring examples of how those in private enterprise can contribute to global transformation.

Above: *Speaking in 1998, Monica McWilliams of the Northern Ireland Women's Peace Coalition, surrounded by other members at the multiparty talks on the future of Northern Ireland*

Below: *Hazel Henderson, internationally respected futurist and economist*

Above: *Rigoberta Menchú Tum—1992 Nobel Peace Prize Winner*

The Brahma Kumaris women, Top: *Dadi Janki* Left: *Sister Jayanti*

Above: *Aung San Suu Kyi—1991 Nobel Peace Prize Winner*

Spiritual organizations such as the Brahma Kumaris, Soka Gokkai, and the Bahá'í Faith are constantly joining with other global change makers such as His Holiness the Dalai Lama, Nelson Mandela, and Hazel Henderson to exchange ideas for a more compassionate, loving world.

There are hundreds of brilliant think tanks such as Rocky Mountain Institute, which looks for alternative energy sources; The Natural Step, an international organization that advises businesses on practical ways to be kind to the environment; the New York-based youth-culture catalysts Pop Sustainability, and Britain's New Economics Foundation. In addition, there are thousands of local churches, synagogues, mosques, colleges, universities, foundations, charities, environmental groups, women's networks, community land trusts, and professional organizations that *care!*

As this web of the wise, the young, the old, and the optimistic continues to grow stronger, innovative ideas and initiatives are inspiring a new generation of concerned women and men. There is strength in unity, and as more of us have the courage to stand up and express our beliefs and values, then change can happen. I see a new, incredibly powerful force coming together that crosses economic, racial, national, cultural, and political boundaries. It's exciting to see that voice grow stronger and be heard all over the world. There is reason for optimism.

275.

ABOVE: *Shirin Ebadi—*
2003 Nobel Peace Prize Winner

BELOW: *Eco-feminist Vandana Shiva*

Basic Principles for a Sustainable Society

- Respect and care for the community of life:
  — Care for and respect the earth's diversity
  — Protect human rights and the environment
  — Build a democratic society
  — Preserve nature for present and future generations

- Ecological integrity:
  —Conserve natural resources
  —Preserve biodiversity
  —Produce, consume, and reproduce within the earth's carrying capacity
  —Advance ecological sustainability education

276.

- Social and economic justice:
  —Eradicate poverty
  —Promote fair human development
  —Secure gender equality and equal access
  —Uphold the universal right to dignity, health, and spirituality

- Democracy, nonviolence, and peace:
  —Support transparent and accountable democracies
  —Respect all living beings
  —Develop and integrate sustainability education
  —Promote tolerance, nonviolence, and peace

(One of the blueprints for a new future was created for the Earth Charter Project in March 2000 by some of the architects in the global network of NGOs, including the International Union for the Conservation of Nature, the United Nations Environment Programme, and the World Wildlife Fund.)

Shaping the Future.

As women, we are traditionally the caretakers of our culture. Our responsibility is to understand and somehow make sure that the changes that are happening in our world preserve the basic humanity in us all. By connecting with the principles of the sacred feminine, such as those found in ancient matriarchal civilizations, a more nurturing society can evolve—one that abhors violence; advocates such values as justice, compassion, and love; and raises its children to reach their full potential as human beings.

When people talk with such idealism they are often accused of being naïve. How can we change a world that's solidly entrenched in the way of competition, domination, and violence? My answer is that without creating the vision, nothing can be achieved. And without having the intention for that change in our hearts, we will find ourselves living in a world that perpetuates everything that goes against our feminine sensibilities. Brahma Kumari leader Sister Jayanti addressed this point at a conference on conflict resolution in Sweden in 2001. She said, "It would only take a relatively small group of committed individuals to initiate the transformation of human consciousness to a more positive, caring society. The beliefs of the minority reaching the point of critical mass will shift the majority and create a culture of peace."

277.

If we're talking about getting rid of the old, outdated patriarchal ways of running the world, it's essential to present a pragmatic vision of what we want to replace it with. We need an overall blueprint of what a new world, based on principles of the sacred feminine, would look like and how it would work. The primary foundation for such a world is *cooperation.* First and foremost, it's cooperation between male and female. As women, we know that the best and most efficient way to get things done is to work together, and that means living and working with men in harmonious coexistence, valuing the perspectives and strengths of both sexes, and creating a higher quality of life for all. It must also be a world of cooperation between business and community, human beings and the planet, national governments and nongovernmental organizations, young and old, spirituality and science, and our inner and outer selves.

The opportunity to create this world *does* exist now. It *is* possible to create a society where we can bring people together and heal our families, our communities, and our world. To do so would take a new breed of leaders, ones who aren't tied to the old way of doing things. Rather than money or power, these leaders must have spiritual values to guide them. And since spiritual values are at our core, it is vitally important for women to step up and take the lead in this transformation of society.

A cooperative society is an organic, evolutionary step away from the world we presently live in. When the power of national governments diminish, that power will naturally transfer into specific small and large networks that transcend national boundaries and link with one another. Consequently, a new economic order could be created that truly rewards effort, including the caring of others. Distribution of land and natural resources would be fairly shared among the people who live on it, and the need to conquer and repress others in the name of power would not be a consideration.

Cooperative ways of working together, whether in agriculture or small enterprise networks that encourage individual creativity instead of exploiting workers, would develop gradually as this new feminine paradigm took hold. And in a cooperative society based on a feminine perspective, training in technology skills would be open for all, and education in understanding and respecting the differences between cultures and beliefs of others would become an intrinsic element of society. Traditional and holistic medicine would integrate, creating a new science that treats and cures disease based in part on sensible nutrition, exercise, and meditation. Our senior citizens would be revered and respected, keeping our history, both personal and societal, alive. Men and women would create new kinds of relationships—sexual *and* platonic—based on mutual respect and love, rather than selfish needs and society's expectations. We would have freedom of choice in how we wished to live every aspect of our lives.

Yes, it *is* a somewhat utopian vision—but we must believe that it is also possible to achieve it. Our personal responsibility in making all this come about is to first bring ourselves into the same sort of harmonious balance we wish to see the world in. By finding a state of peace within us, where we stay calm and balanced, we can project a sense of love and creativity to those we engage with. Through our feminine principles, we can achieve a natural state of being that is connected with others. It is then up to us to live within our own cooperative world. Only when we achieve this personally can we begin to create a true, feminine future.

Praying for Peace.

Alongside powerful action is always the need to reconnect to the foundation of our spiritual strength. By generating thoughts of peace and an attitude of compassion, we can strengthen the ties that bind us to our human family, embracing them with our prayers of love.

We can find power in moments of stillness and silent reflection. Either on your own, or together with your women's circle, go into deep silence and visualize a positive outcome to your concerns about this planet. By connecting with the divine, we are in touch with our source of truth and can spread our prayers throughout the world.

The GROW Commitment.

Include this affirmation for world peace in your daily prayers:

I am committed to the feminine principle of cooperation
to create a world of harmony and peace for all beings.

● ● ● ● ●

Part Iv
Tying It All Together

Chapter

10

The Destination

(Where You Learn
to Be All That You
Were Born to Be)

How do I integrate the different aspects of my being into the whole? What are the essential tools for my life's journey? How do I manifest my dreams?

In this final chapter, you're going to learn how to integrate all the aspects of being a modern woman in today's society into a vision for your entire life—in other words, you're going to start to live your life to your full potential.

My Story: The Whole Picture

The journey of my own life continues to take me to myriad places, both emotionally and geographically. As I've gotten older, I've become more conscious of my patterns—I now see how I continue to repeat self-defeating actions. The difference these days is that I can rapidly spot my negative ways and change my state of being into a more positive direction. I'm able to laugh at my most powerful fears and allow myself to feel them, integrate them, and let them go. I've learned that life truly is a journey—nothing stays static, so by allowing change to happen without fear, I can grow and develop along the way.

Now that I'm in my mid-50s, with my children grown, I'm at the point where I'm seriously considering how I want to spend the rest of my life. Like a butterfly emerging from a cocoon, I feel as if I'm evolving to a new stage that promises even greater rewards, as I'm now far more appreciative of life itself.

I know that I want to spend the next 30 years or so using my gifts and talents, in harmony with other like-minded souls, to build a better world for my grandchildren to grow up in. Therefore, my life plan is to spend one-third of my time working on creative projects that I believe in and that will bring me an income to allow me to live the way I wish; one-third of my time on projects that will serve others but that I don't necessarily earn from; and one-third of my time on me so that I can restore my energy, be with the people I love, and spend time in nature.

I've learned that relationships and connection are my priority, and that after so many years living in my "male-achiever" energy, I'm ready to learn to stay in my feminine center, flowing with my life while staying clear about my dreams and my vision. I intend to continue to learn how to love myself and show it by nurturing and caring for my body, while still allowing myself to have fun and play. I know that my personal growth will continue until the day I die, and if I can create change in myself, then I will be able to show others some of the things I've learned on the way.

I've learned that my life's purpose is to be a teacher and communicator, a woman who's dedicated to healing, love, and the divine. I believe that my life so far has been some kind of training for fulfilling this goal, and I'm ready to surrender to wherever my journey will take me.

Tying It All Together.

We've gone on quite a journey together in this book, which has given us opportunities and tools for reflection and examination of various aspects of our lives.

We started by acknowledging the real you, the modern woman who, by getting in touch with her feminine values, can live her life in her truth. We followed this by recognizing the need to attend to your physical well-being, discovering the connection between mind and body, and learning how self-care is so connected with self-love. We then celebrated the return of the sacred feminine, in ourselves and in society. We examined the history of the Goddess in both the ancient world and the modern, and how we can bring divine power into our daily life through ritual and prayer.

We observed the complexities of parenting in our modern society, with the breakdown of the traditional family and its democratization. We discussed how we relate as mothers as well as daughters, and brought up opportunities to heal old family patterns as well as embrace the new. Intimate relationships, whether with our families or with our partners, are our greatest teachers in life. We examined what we truly want from our relationships, along with how we can co-create loving, interdependent partnerships.

Our sexuality is where we hold much of our power, yet so many of us are scared to acknowledge it. By letting go of our shame and embarrassment, and embracing the fullness of our being, we saw how we can radiate the purity of our sexual energy to empower us in so many areas of our lives.

Examining our relationship with work, and how work can work for *us*, gave us the opportunity to find out if we're earning our income and creating professional success in a way that reflects our core values—or whether there's another way to use our skills and gifts to create economic independence. We've noted the importance of community in modern society, and how a return to a more tribal, mutually beneficial lifestyle could improve the quality of our lives.

And finally, we learned how our collective power as women can truly create unity out of diversity. By empowering ourselves, we discovered that we can create a new paradigm, one in which feminine energy can guide the world into a more loving, cooperative society.

286.

Your Story.

Every one of us has a unique story that has contributed toward the patterns and beliefs that make up our lives—and just like the rest of us, you have the power to change your story, take control of your life, and live to your fullest potential. By having read this book and done its exercises, you're now able to use its practices and tools to take a good look at the various aspects of your life, adjust them where needed, and move ahead in your full power as a modern woman. But where do you move ahead to? How do you incorporate the variety of information in this book into a life plan that will bring you both day-to-day and long-term fulfilment?

To begin, it will help to take one more look inside—by analyzing yourself, you'll see how you can use your strengths to your advantage while being aware of the patterns that create your weaknesses. Again, it's most important to be absolutely honest with yourself when answering these questions.

So with pen in hand, steal a few moments of quiet time, take in a few relaxing breaths, and prepare to go deep into your truth. You're going to chart some of the highs and lows of your life's journey, so hold on to your life jacket and get ready for the voyage.

Strengths

1. What were the high points in your life—when you were at your most powerful or felt the best about yourself? (They could have been at work, in your social life, with your family, or in some personal-growth area.) When did they happen? What were the specific incidents? How did they make you feel emotionally? Was there a positive physical feeling as well? What specific talents did you tap in to at that time to create the success?

_____

_____

287.

_____

_____

_____

_____

2. What are some of the positive behavioral patterns of your life that create winning results? For example, do you respond well under pressure? Do you always consider decisions carefully before committing? Are you always friendly to other people?

_____

_____

_____

_____

_____

_____

3. What are the personal characteristics you can use to help build the future you
   desire? (For example: *tenacity, integrity, analytical mind,* or *passion.*)

_____

_____

_____

288.

_____

_____

Weaknesses

1. What were the low point(s) in your life, when you experienced personal failure?

_____

_____

_____

_____

_____

2. What are your specific weaknesses that have been constantly associated with past failure? (For example, *insecurity, impatience,* or *poor judgment of people.*)

_____

_____

_____

_____

_____

_____

3. What weakness or negative pattern, if removed, would have the most positive impact on your life?

289.

_____

_____

_____

_____

_____

_____

Now that you've answered these questions, it should be very clear which personal tools you already use to create positive solutions in your life . . . and how you can sabotage yourself when old patterns take hold. Of course it would be unrealistic to say that from this moment on you're only going to live by exhibiting positive behavior patterns. Old, self-defeating ways have a habit of insidiously popping up when you least expect it—but like any old foes, they can be your best teachers once they've been exposed. By becoming aware of them, you'll start to take away their power.

By taking this detached look at your past, you can learn so much about what to take into your future. And remember, nothing in your life has been a mistake: We need losses and failures to learn and grow from, as much as successes. But now it's time to move on.

Creating Your Vision.

It makes sense that to create the life you want, you first need to have a clear vision of the entire picture. You're now building the foundation for your future, step by step, so you need to integrate *all* aspects of your dream. You may not believe that you have your vision yet, but rest assured, deep inside your unconscious mind there's a very clear picture of how you want to live the rest of your life.

This is the time to tap in to your intuition—that is, your inner vision and/or inner voice that instinctively knows how you can reach life fulfillment. At this point in the book, try to take a day to consciously do nothing except to take note of who you truly are and how you want to create the rest of your life. Think about which chapters of the book most resonated with you, and which aspects of your life you wish to consciously focus on.

I believe that we can manifest what we want in our lives when we clearly know what it is that we do want—and *GROW* has been designed to bring you to that very place. Projecting into the future—say 5, 10, and 20 years—is an interesting exercise in creating the whole picture of our lives, because we so often make short-term plans without considering how they affect us in the long term. Meditating will help us attain that clarity for our long-term vision.

Catching a Train to the Future: A Meditation

Now is the time to envision what your life will look like in the future. Close your eyes and imagine that you are on a fast train to the rest of your life. See the train stop at the first station, where you dismount and walk down the platform to a door that you step through. On the other side is your life in five years' time. You can see what you look like, where you are living, who you are living with, and what job you are doing. Everything is clear and bright.

Step into the "you" that is there, and feel what it's like to be living your ideal life. Remember this feeling and how good it is, while noticing all the details. When you feel you have absorbed the sense of who you are going to be, say good-bye to this future "you" and leave that world to get back on the train.

Step out at the next two stations, imagining yourself 10 years, and then 20 years, in the future. See the people you are surrounded with, the environment you are in, and feel the sense of pleasure in being who you are going to be.

292.

Practical Vision Tools.

It's often helpful to make something physically concrete to go back to when you need to be reminded of what your vision is and how it looks. One easy and fun tool is to make a GROW poster, which you can display as a daily reminder of your dreams. Get a large piece of white cardboard, approximately 3´x 4´. Find a favorite picture of yourself, one that embodies the joy inside your soul, and paste it right in the center of your poster.

Next, fill in the details of the vision that you want to create. You can now use the work you've done throughout this book as a guide for this poster. So, extending out from your picture, create nine separate areas that correspond to the nine chapters of this book: Self, Health, Spirit (the Goddess), Family, Relationships, Sexuality, Job, Community, and

Global Citizen. Use the exercises you've already completed to help you create the details for your poster. For instance, if you're single and want a husband and family, take what you wrote about the traits you wish for in a man and incorporate that. Similarly, if you want to find a new job or start a business, use what you discovered about your career goals and weave them into the details of your vision for a job.

You can create your images any way you'd like—a collage of magazine pictures, painting, drawing, even words—the only rule in creating this vision poster is that it must be an accurate reflection of what you want your life to be. Have fun. Be creative. And make it as beautiful as you are.

When you finish, admire your life to come. Doesn't it look great?!

Manifestation—Making It Happen.

293.

Manifestation is very powerful, for when the will is set, it can move mountains. Yet manifestation isn't about just wishing and hoping that your dreams come true. Rather, it's about creating the right circumstance, then using that power you have to tap in to the universal force to bring what you desire.

You might tap in by prayer, chanting, ritual, or meditation. Sometimes you may know exactly what you're trying to manifest, such as a new job; while sometimes you may simply wish to open a channel to bring a new relationship into your life, even though you're not exactly sure what kind of person or relationship you want. When you feel the passion of your dreams throughout your whole body—that is, when your intention is focused clearly on achieving your dreams—you're ready.

How to Manifest

Once you've decided to manifest something into existence, you must create an atmosphere to make it as real as possible for you. If you have objects that represent what you're trying to manifest, you may want to put them on your altar. Or perhaps you want to manifest something that's pictured on your GROW poster—if that's the case, bring the poster into your meditation area so that when you begin your manifestation practice, you'll have the object to be manifested before you, and you can focus on it.

The most important aspect of bringing something into your life is to actually believe that it already exists for you, and you're just opening the door so it can present itself. A good way to start this process is by meditating.

> Go to where you regularly take your meditation time, close your eyes, and begin to draw your attention to your breath. As you become more relaxed and sink into a meditative state, start summoning up in your mind's eye the image of what you wish to manifest.

> If it's represented on your GROW poster, bring that image to mind. If you just have a mental picture of it, fill in all the details—see it as a reality. Visualize it already happening. How big is it? What color is it? How does it smell? Taste? Sound? Feel? How are you interacting with it? Linger with this image, bringing it to life. And as you gently bring yourself out of the meditative state, don't let go of the image, keep it in your memory as you return to full consciousness.

Repeat this meditation every day you wish to manifest. And when you go out into the world, believe that your manifestation has already happened, that what you're bringing into this world is already a part of your life, which indeed it is.

One of the paradoxes of manifestation is that in creating the vision of what you desire, you also, in a sense, must let go of that absolute vision and be prepared to accept what the universe gives you. When you set an intention, let go of the need. In other words, when you expect nothing and are open to everything is when the universe delivers its greatest gifts.

Plan for Action.

The next crucial stage in making your vision for personal fulfillment a reality is to create a plan of action. A realistic and carefully conceived plan of action is like a good road map, containing the practical aspects of how to grow into the full life you've envisioned for yourself.

You can use the space provided in this book to create your plan, or you can use your computer or even a big piece of paper, similar to the GROW poster. To help you focus on the areas of your life you'd like to change, you may want to revisit the subjects in this book that most resonated with you. For example, do you wish to focus on career, health, and relationships, or are you more interested in social action, spirituality, and community? Once you've made that determination, read the corresponding chapters again and, if you haven't done the exercises, now would be a good time to do so.

In creating this plan, remember that it's important to set goals that are lofty, but also realistic. Don't set yourself up for failure—instead, create a plan that you'll enjoy doing. While it may seem as if you're creating a lot of work for yourself, it's so important to keep up a daily and disciplined routine if you wish to see results. Even if you doubt your abilities or the worth of the work you're putting in, know that as a cathedral can only be built brick by brick, so, too, can you only change yourself one step at a time.

GROW Action Plan

- Key result areas (such as health, relationships, work):

_____

_____

_____

- Vision (what I wish to see in these areas of my life):

  _____

  _____

  _____

- Barriers (what is presently blocking me from achieving this):

  _____

  _____

  _____

- Strategic action (what specific actions I intend to take in order to deal with the barriers):

  _____

  _____

  _____

297.

- Milestones (the small victories I'll achieve along the way):

  _____

  _____

  _____

- When (will I have achieved this)?

_____

_____

_____

- What small action can I take every day that will move me toward my destination?

_____

_____

_____

- What small actions can I take every week that will move me toward my goals?

_____

_____

_____

- What are my four goals for the next 12 months?

_____

_____

_____

If you refer back to your action plan on a daily basis, keep an activity diary, stay passionate about your intention, and practice daily meditation, you will create the energy to manifest your vision.

Support from Others.

I believe that in our hearts, we all basically want the same thing—to live life to its fullest while staying true to our core values. And I also believe that we're all here to learn from each other.

It's so important to surround yourself with others who have the same values, who can mentor, coach, or be models for you. Modeling yourself on someone who has the qualities you're striving to attain is a highly effective tool when manifesting your preferred future. This person may be someone you know or someone you've read about in the newspapers—no matter whom you choose, observe as much as you can every aspect of the way they live their lives: See how they handle others and make their decisions. In addition, learn from your peers and your elders—note their mistakes and their vulnerabilities while also keeping in mind how they achieve their goals despite setbacks.

300. We women strengthen each other by sharing our visions and telling our stories, so why not work with your women's circle in creating and manifesting the vision of your lives? As part of your regular group activities, each of you could take turns being in the center of your circle, allowing the other members to visualize a different aspect of an individual's dream. Let the group tell that person how they see her future—that is, where she's going to live, what she'll be doing, and whom she'll be doing it with. Show the others the way to do an action plan, and support each other with your progress. Check in with each other often, and acknowledge each other as the incredible, passionate women you all are.

The Final Surrender.

As you move into the truly powerful being who is the real you, accept that you're going to be tested. So love and forgive those who hurt you, and apologize for hurting them. Appreciate that by forgiving them, you'll be forgiving yourself as well. Show your generosity of spirit not only to others, but most of all to yourself. Stay focused, spoil yourself, appreciate the magic in the moment, and stay flexible while still holding your vision.

Always remain open to the universe, see the beauty in the stars, and value your every moment. Even when you're in the depths of despair and sadness, see the joy and abundance in every area of your life and feel gratitude. Above all: *Trust the process.*

You've worked hard to get to this place, so use the tools you've acquired through the course of reading *GROW* and join me in celebrating this incredible experience we call life!

The GROW Commitment.

Finally, create your concluding affirmation—the definition of your life purpose. Meditate deeply, asking your higher self to tell you what, in the simplest terms, is your main purpose in this lifetime:

I am committed and dedicated to living my life's purpose by

_____

[please fill in the blank].

No more time to waste, no more excuses
Gotta reach out your arms and embrace the sun
No more time for self-pitying abuses
Gotta stand up and shout and say
"I am the one"
'Cause there's been too much crying and talk of being free
Gotta jump off that cliff and be who you were born to be

(This is the first verse of "Be Who You Were Born to Be," written and performed by Lucinda Drayton and Andrew Blissett of Bliss, from the album *Bliss*.)

• • • • •

Conclusion

I decided to share my story because in some way we all reflect each other. I certainly don't believe that I have all the answers—but I'm learning all the time. I so passionately believe that now is the time for women to *grow* into our full, powerful selves, and by having the courage to live our lives according to our values, we can bring love into a world that's crying out for it.

I believe that together with the many beautiful, conscious men who are our contemporaries, we can create a new world, a "golden age," where human beings can respect all living things, as well as the planet that feeds and nurtures us. And by getting back to our intuitive selves, we can remember what it is to be a woman and be connected to our true essence. It's time for the sacred feminine once more to lead humankind into the future.

Thank you for having the courage to come on this journey with me. I, for one, know that it's not an easy one, but I'm so grateful for the incredible rewards that are here for us all along the way.

God bless you,

Lynne .....

References

Chapter 1

At the Root of This Longing: *Reconciling a Spiritual Hunger and a Feminist Thirst,* by Carol Lee Flinders (Harper San Francisco, 1998)

The Four Agreements, by DON Miguel Ruiz (Amber-Allen Publishing, Inc., 1997)

Gabrielle Roth: The Power Wave—*A High Velocity Ecstatic Dance Workout (Videotape),* (Sounds True, 1992)

God's Healing Power: *How Meditation Can Help Transform Your Life,* by B.K. Jayanti (Michael Joseph/Penguin Group, 2002)

In Search of Women's Passionate Soul, by Caitlin Matthews (Element Books, Ltd., 1997)

The Invitation, by Oriah Mountain Dreamer (Thorsons/HarperCollins Publishers, 1999)

Maps to Ecstasy: *Teachings of an Urban Shaman,* by Gabrielle Roth (Mandala/HarperCollins Publishers, 1989)

Meditation Made Easy, by Lorin Roche, Ph.D. (HarperCollins, 1998)

Meditation Secrets for Women, by Camille Maurine and Lorin Roche, Ph.D. (HarperCollins, 2001)

The Power Is Within You, by Louise L. Hay (Hay House, Inc., 1991)

Revolution from Within: *A Book of Self-Esteem,* by Gloria Steinem (Corgi Books, 1993)

A Woman's Worth, by Marianne Williamson (Random House, 1993)

Women's Tao Wisdom: *Ten Ways to Personal Power and Peace,* by Diane Dreher (Thorsons, 1998)

Chapter 2

Age Power: *The Revolutionary Path to Natural High-Tech Rejuvenation,* by Leslie Kenton (Vermilion/Random House, 2002)

Alternative Health Care for Women, by Patsy Westcott (Grapevine/Thorsons Publishing Group, 1987)

The Best of Everything (Videotape), by The Optimum Health Institute

Digestion with Dr. Andrew Tutino (Videotape), by The Optimum Health Institute

Earth Magic: A Wisewoman's Guide to Herbal, Astrological, and Other Folk Remedies, by Claire Nahmad (Rider/Random House, 1993)

Eating for Beauty, by David Wolfe (Maul Brothers Publishing, 2002)

Eating Well for Optimum Health, by Andrew Weil, M.D. (Alfred A. Knopf, 2000)

8 Weeks to Optimum Health with Andrew Weil, M.D. (Videotape), (Inner Dimension Video, 1999)

The Endorphin Effect: A Breakthrough Strategy for Holistic Health and Spiritual Well-Being, by William Bloom (Piatkus Publishing, Ltd., 2001)

Flushed with Success: The Bottom Line on Colonic Irrigation, by David R. Newman (Cedar Publishing, Ltd., 2002)

Healing and the Mind, by Bill Moyers (Doubleday, 1993)

Hormonal Health, Nutritional & Hormonal Strategies for Emotional Well-Being & Intellectual Longevity, by Dr. Michael Colgan (Apple Publishing, 1996)

Natural Healing for Women: Caring for Yourself with Herbs, Homoeopathy & Essential Oils, by Susan Curtis and Romy Fraser (Pandora/HarperCollins, 1991)

The Natural Health Bible, by Lisha Simester (Quadril Publishing, Ltd., 2001)

Natural Woman, Natural Menopause, by Marcus Laux and Christine Conrad (HarperCollins, 1997)

The Okinawa Way: How to Improve Your Health and Longevity Dramatically, by Bradley Willcox, M.D., Craig Willcox, Ph.D., and Makoto Suzuki, M.D. (Mermaid Books, 2001)

Raw Energy, by Leslie and Susannah Kenton (Vermilion/Random House 1994)

Red Moon Passage: The Power and Wisdom of Menopause, by Bonnie J. Horrigan (Thorsons/Harper Collins, 1996)

Secrets & Mysteries: The Glory and Pleasure of Being a Woman, by Denise Linn (Hay House, Inc., 2002)

Self-Nurture: Learning to Care for Yourself As Effectively As You Care for Everyone Else, by Alice D. Domar, Ph.D., and Henry Dreher (Penguin Books, 2000)

Sick and Tired? Reclaim Your Inner Terrain, by Robert O. Young, Ph.D., with Shelley Redford Young, L.M.T. (Woodland Publishing, 2001)

305.

Smart Medicine for Healthier Living, by Janet Zand, Allan N. Spreen, and James B. LaValle (Avery Publishing Group, Inc., 1999)

Spontaneous Healing *(Videotape),* Andrew Weil, M.D. (Inner Dimension Video, 1996)

Sweat Your Prayers: *Movement As Spiritual Practice,* by Gabrielle Roth (Most Tarcher/ Putnam Books, 1997)

Ten Steps to a Younger You, by Leslie Kenton (Vermillion/Random House, 2000)

What Your Doctor May Not Tell You about Premenopause, by John R. Lee, M.D., Jesse Hanley, M.D., and Virginia Hopkins (Warner Books, 1999)

The Wheatgrass Book, by Ann Wigmore (Avery Publishing Group, Inc., 1985)

Women's Bodies, Women's Wisdom, by Christiane Northrup, M.D. (Bantam Books, 1994, 1998)

The Wrinkle Cure: *Unlock the Power of Cosmeceuticals for Supple, Youthful Skin,* by Nicholas Perricone, M.D. (Warner Books, 2000)

Yoga for People Who Can't Be Bothered to Do It, by Geoff Dyer (Abacus, 2003)

You Can Heal Your Life, by Louise L. Hay (Hay House, Inc., 1999)

306.

Chapter 3

Answers, by Mother Meera (Rider/Meeramma Publications, 1991)

Beautiful Necessity: *The Art and Meaning of Women's Altars,* by Kay Turner (Thames & Hudson, 1999)

Buffalo Woman Comes Singing, by Brooke Medicine Eagle (Ballantine Books/Random House, 1991)

Companion of God, by Dadi Janki (Hodder & Stoughton, 2003)

The Complete Book of Women's Wisdom, by Cassandra Eason (Piatkus Publishers, 2001)

The Dancing Goddess: *Principles of a Matriarchal Aesthetic,* by Heide Gottner-Abendroth (Beacon Press, 1991)

Daughter of the Goddess: *The Sacred Priestess,* by Naomi Ozaniec (The Aquarian Press/ HarperCollins, 1993)

Ecstatica: *Woman's Realms of Power,* by Rivka Leah (Sacred Vision Press, 1994)

The Feminine Face of God: *The Unfolding of the Sacred in Women,* by Sherry Ruth Anderson and Patricia Hopkins (Bantam Books, 1992)

The Fifth Sacred Thing, by Starhawk (Bantam Books, 1993)

Goddess: *Mother of Living Nature,* by Adele Getty (Thames and Hudson, 1990)

The Goddess Path: *Myths, Invocations & Rituals,* by Patricia Monaghan (Llewellyn Publications, 2000)

Goddess Remembered, The Burning Times, Full Circle *(Videotapes),* Direct Cinema, Ltd.

Grandmother Moon: *Lunar Magic in Our Lives—Spells, Rituals, Goddesses, Legends & Emotions Under the Moon,* by Zsuzanna E. Budapest (HarperSanFrancisco, 1991)

The Language of the Goddess, by Marija Gimbutas (Harper & Row, 1989)

Loving the Goddess Within: *Sex Magick for Women,* by Nan Hawthorne (Delphi Press, Inc., 1991)

Medicine Woman, by Lynn V. Andrews (Arkana/Penguin Group, 1988)

Mists of Avalon and ***The Avalon Series,*** by Marion Zimmer Bradley (Penguin Books)

The New Book of Goddesses & Heroines, by Patricia Monaghan (Llewellyn Publications, 2000)

Peace and Purity: *The Story of the Brahma Kumaris—A Spiritual Revolution,* by Liz Hodgkinson (RiderBooks, 1999)

The Power of Myth, by Joseph Campbell, with Bill Moyers (Doubleday, 1988)

Sophia: *Aspects of the Divine Feminine, Past & Present,* by Susanne Schaup (Nicolas-Hays, Inc., 1997)

The Spiral Dance: *A Rebirth of the Ancient Religion of the Great Goddess,* by Starhawk (HarperCollins, 1979, 1989)

Truth or Dare: *Encounters with Power, Authority, and Mystery,* by Starhawk (HarperSanFrancisco, 1987)

Weavers of Wisdom: *Women Mystics of the Twentieth Century,* by Anne Bancroft (Arkana/Penguin Group, 1989)

When God Was a Woman, by Merlin Stone (Harcourt Brace Jovanovich, 1976)

The White Goddess, by Robert Graves (Faber and Faber Ltd., 1948, 1997)

The Woman's Encyclopedia of Myths and Secrets, by Barbara G. Walker (HarperSanFrancisco, 1983)

The Women's History of the World, by Rosalind Miles (HarperCollins, 1993)

Women Who Run with the Wolves: *Myths and Stories of the Wild Woman Archetype,* by Clarissa Pinkola Estes, Ph.D. (Ballantine, 1992)

Chapter 4

The Courage to Heal: A Guide for Women Survivors of Childhood Sexual Abuse,
by Ellen Bass and Laura Davis (Harper & Row, 1988)

How to Talk So Kids Will Listen and Listen So Kids Will Talk, by Adele Faber and Elaine Mazlish
(Avon Books, 1999)

Liberated Parents, Liberated Children: *Your Guide to a Happier Family,* by Adele Faber and Elaine
Mazlish (Picadilly Press, 2002)

Miranda Castro's Homeopathic Guides: *Mother and Baby,* by Miranda Castro (Pan, 1996)

The New Contented Little Baby Book, by Gina Ford (Vermillion, 2002)

Parenting with Love and Logic: *Teaching Children Responsibility,* by Foster W. Cline and Jim Fay
(Navpress, 1990)

Positive Parenting: *Raising Children with Self-Esteem,* by Elizabeth Hartley-Brewer (Vermillion, 1994)

Raising Boys: *Why Boys Are Different and How to Help Them Become Happy and Well-Balanced Men,*
by Stephen Biddulph (HarperCollins, 2003)

Sisters Unlimited: *Every Girl's Guide to Life, Love, Bodies, and Being You,* by Jessica Howie
(Vermilion/Random House 2002)

The Working Mother's Guide to Life, by Linda Mason (Random House, 2002)

Chapter 5

Conscious Loving: *The Journey to Co-Commitment,* by Gay Hendricks, Ph.D., and Kathlyn Henricks,
Ph.D. (Bantam, 1990)

Do You Feel Loved by Me? *Practical Suggestions for More Caring Relationships,* by Philip Rogers
(Living Well Publications,1998)

The Maiden King: *The Reunion of Masculine and Feminine,* by Robert Bly and Marion Woodman
(Henry Holt and Company, 1998)

Men Are from Mars, Women Are from Venus, by John Gray, Ph.D. (HarperCollins, 1992)

Recycled People: *Forming New Relationships in Mid-Life,* by Coral Atkinson and Paula Wagemaker
(Shoal Bay Press Ltd., 2000)

The Road Less Traveled, by M. Scott Peck (Simon and Shuster, 1978 [U.S.]; Hutchinson & Co,
1983 [UK])

Soul Mates: *Honoring the Mysteries of Love and Relationship,* by Thomas Moore (HarperCollins, 1994)

The Surrendered Single, by Laura Doyle (Simon and Schuster UK, Ltd., 2002)

What Women & Men Really Want, by Aaron Kipnis, Ph.D., and Elizabeth Herron, M.A. (Nataraj Publishing, 1995)

When Women Choose to Be Single, by Rita Robinson (Newcastle Publishing Co., 1991)

Whole Heartedness: Healing Our Heartbreaks, by Chuck Spezzano, Ph.D. (Hodder & Stoughton, 2000)

Why Men Don't Listen & Women Can't Read Maps, by Allan & Barbara Pease (Orion Books, Ltd., 2001)

Venus in Spurs: *The Secret Female Fear of Commitment,* by Sheila Gillooly (Hodder & Stoughton, 1994)

You Just Don't Understand: *Women and Men in Conversation,* by Deborh Tannen, Ph.D. (Ballantine Books, 1990)

Chapter 6

The Art of Everyday Ecstasy, by Margot Anand (Broadway Books, 1998)

The Art of Sexual Ecstasy, by Margot Anand (J.P. Tarcher, 1989)

Erotic Massage: *The Tantric Touch of Love,* by Kenneth Ray Stubbs, Ph.D., with Louise-Andree Saulnier (J.P. Tarcher, 1999)

Finding God Through Sex, by David Deida (Plexus, 2000)

How to Give Her Absolute Pleasure, by Lou Paget (Judy Piatkus, Ltd., 2000)

Intimate Communication: *Awakening Your Sexual Essence,* by David Deida (Health Communications, Inc., 1995)

Multi-Orgasmic Response Ecstasy Training for Women and Their Lovers *(Videotape),* (Margot Anand Presents Higher Love Video Series)

Selfloving: Portrait of a Women's Sexuality Seminar *(Videotape),* by Betty Dodson, Ph.D. (Pacific Media Entertainment, 2000)

Sexual Energy Ecstasy: *A Practical Guide to Lovemaking Secrets of the East and the West,* by David and Ellen Ramsdale (Bantam, 1993)

Chapter 7

Business Capital for Women: *An Essential Handbook for Entrepreneurs,* by Emily Card and Adam Miller (MacMillan, 1996)

The Ecology of Commerce: *A Declaration of Sustainability,* by Paul Hawken (HarperBusiness, 1993)

Funny Money: *In Search of Alternative Cash,* by David Boyle (HarperCollins, 1999)

The Goddess in the Office, by Zsuzanna E. Budapest (HarperSanFrancisco, 1992)

Hey You! *Pitch to Win in an Ideas Economy,* by Will Murray (Momentum, 2001)

In the Spirit of Business, by Robert Roskind (Celestial Arts Publishing, 1992)

The Nine Secrets of Women Who Get What They Want, by Kate White (Random House, 1998)

The Nine Steps to Financial Freedom: *Practical and Spiritual Steps So You Can Stop Worrying,* by Suze Orman (Crown Publishers, 1997)

No More Frogs to Kiss: *99 Ways to Give Economic Power to Girls,* by Jolene Godfrey (St. Martins Press, 2000)

Our Wildest Dreams: *Women Entrepreneurs, Making Money, Having Fun, Doing Good,* by Joline Godfrey (HarperBusiness, 1992)

The Secrets of Self-Employment, by Sarah and Paul Edwards (J.P. Tarcher/Putnum Books, 1997)

The SEED Handbook: *The Feminine Way to Create Business,* by Lynne Franks (Thorsons/HarperCollins, 2000)

Unlimited Power, by Anthony Robbins (Fireside/Simon and Schuster, 1986)

The Web of Inclusion, by Sally Helgesen (Currency/Doubleday, 1995)

When the Canary Stops Singing: *Women's Perspectives on Transforming Business,* edited by Pat Barrentine (Berret-Koehler Publishers, 1993)

Women's Ventures, Women's Vision: *29 Inspiring Stories from Women Who Started Their Own Businesses,* by Shoshana Alexander (The Crossing Press, 1997)

Chapter 8

Beloved Majorcans, by Guy De Forestier (La Foradada, 1997)

Bread & Oil: *Majorcan Culture's Last Stand,* by Tomas Graves (Prospect Books, 2000)

Flight Into Freedom: *The Autobiography of the Co-founder of the Findhorn Community,* by Eileen Caddy (Element/Findhorn Press, 1988)

Generation to Generation: *Reflections on Friendships Between Young and Old,* by Sandra Martz and Shirley Coe (Paper-Mache Press, 1998)

In Search of the Magic of Findhorn, by Karin Bogliolo and Carly Newfeld (Findhorn Press, 2002)

Insiders and Outsiders: *Paradise and Reality in Mallorca,* by Jacqueline Waldren (Berghaha Books, 1996)

Utopia, by Sir Thomas More (Penguin Books, 1965)

Chapter 9

The Age of Unreason, by Charles Handy (Arrow Books, Ltd., 1989, 1991)

Building a Win-Win World: *Life Beyond Global Economic Warfare,* by Hazel Henderson (Berrett-Koehler, 1991)

The Caring Economy: *Business Principles from the New Digital Age,* by Gerry McGovern (BlackHall Publishing, 1999)

The Chalice and the Blade, by Riane Eisler (Pandora/HarperCollins, 1987, 1990)

The Changing Culture of Leadership: *Women Leaders' Voices,* by Elizabeth Coffey (Partnership Limited, 1999)

Compassion or Competition: *A Discussion on Human Values in Business and Economics,* by H.H. the Dalai Lama (Spirit in Business, 2002)

Connexity: *How to Live in a Connected World,* by Geoff Mulgan (Chatto & Windus, Ltd., 1997)

Creating Alternative Futures: *The End of Economics,* by Hazel Henderson (Kumarian Press, Inc., 1996)

Factor Four: *Doubling Wealth, Halving Resource Use,* by Ernst Von Weizsacker, Amory B. Lovins, L. Hunter Lovins (Earthscan Publications, Ltd., 1997)

The Female Eunuch, by Germaine Greer (Paladin, 1971; HarperCollins, 1999)

Fire with Fire: *The New Female Power and How It Will Change the 21st Century,* by Naomi Wolf (Random House, 1993)

Funky Business: *Talent Makes Capital Dance,* by Jonas Ridderstrale and Kjell Nordstrom (Pearson Education, Ltd., 2000)

Localization: A Global Manifesto, by Colin Hines (Earthscan Publications, Ltd., 2000)

Natural Capitalism: *Creating the Next Industrial Revolution,* by Paul Hawken, Amory Lovins, and L. Hunter Lovins (Little, Brown & Company, 1999)

The New Rulers of the World, by John Pilger (Verso, 2002)

No Logo, by Naomi Klein (Flamingo/Harper Collins, 2001)

Our Global Neighbourhood: *The Report of The Commission on Global Governance* (Oxford University Press, 1995)

Paradigms in Progress: *Life Beyond Economics,* by Hazel Henderson (Berrett-Koehler, 1991, 1995)

The Planetary Bargain: *Corporate Social Responsibility Comes of Age,* by Michael Hopkins (Macmillan Press Ltd., [UK]; St. Martin's Press, Inc. [USA], 1999)

Sex and Power, by Susan Estrich (Riverhead Books /Penguin Putnam, Inc., 2000, 2001)

Sex, Economy, Freedom & Community, by Wendell Berry (Pantheon Books, 1992,1993)

Take It Personally: *How Globalization Affects You and Powerful Ways to Challenge It,* by Anita Roddick (Thorsons/HarperCollins Publishers. 2001)

The Tipping Point: *How Little Things Can Make a Big Difference,* by Malcolm Gladwell (Little, Brown & Company, 2000)

Tomorrow's Biodiversity, by Vandana Shiva (Thames & Hudson, Ltd., 2000)

Visionary Voices: *Women on Power Interviews,* by Penny Rosenwasser (Aunt Lute Books, 1992)

Women and Power: *How Far Can We Go?* by Nancy Kline (BBC Books, 1993)

The World We're In, by Will Hutton (Little, Brown & Company, 2002)

Chapter 10

The Bodacious Book of Succulence, by SARK (Fireside, 1998)

Cultivating Sacred Space: *Gardening for the Soul,* by Elizabeth Murray (Pomegranate, 1997)

Feminism in Our Time: *The Essential Writings, World War II to the Present,* edited by Miriam Schneir (Vintage Books, 1994)

The Highly Sensitive Person: *How to Thrive When the World Overwhelms You,* by Elaine N. Aron (Thorsons/Harper Collins, 1999)

No Boundary: *Eastern and Western Approaches to Personal Growth,* by Ken Wilber (Shambhala, 1985)

A Passion for the Possible: *A Guide to Realizing Your True Potential,* by Jean Houston (HarperCollins, 1997)

A Return to Love: *Reflections on the Principles of <u>A Course in Miracles,</u>* by Marianne Williamson (The Aquarian Press/HarperCollins, 1992)

Sixth Sense: *Unlock Your Inner Powers for Success and Happiness,* by Susie Johns (Headline Book Publishing, 1998)

Succulent Wild Woman: *Dancing with Your Wonder-full Self,* by SARK (Fireside, 1997)

Using Your Brain—for a CHANGE: *Neuro-Linguistic Programming,* by Richard Bandler (Real People Press, 1985)

Visioning: *Ten Steps to Designing the Life of Your Dreams,* by Lucia Capacchione, Ph.D. (J.P. Tarcher/Putnam, 2000)

When God Winks: *How the Power of Coincidence Guides Your Life,* by Squire Rushnell (Atria Books, 2001)

The White Hole in Time: *Our Future Evolution and the Meaning of Now,* by Peter Russell (The Aquarian Press/HarperCollins,1992)

313.

• • • • •

Useful Resources

Chapter 1

You are the resource.

Chapter 2

Australia

Aphrodite Women's Health
www.aphroditewomenshealth.com
E-mail:**diana@aphroditewomenshealth.com**

Brisbane Holistic Health Centre
www.holistic.co.au
E-mail: **hands@holistic.com.au**

Camp Eden Health Retreat
www.campeden.com.au
E-mail: **health@campeden.com.au**

Canada

Canadian Health Network
www.canadian-health-network.ca
E-mail: **chn-writeus@hc-sc.gc.ca**

International

Pilates Studio
www.pilates-studio.com

The Yoga Directory
www.yogadirectory.com
E-mail: **info@yogadirectory.com**

Ireland

The Women's Health Council
www.whc.ie
E-mail: **Info@whc.ie**

New Zealand

Everybody
www.everybody.co.nz
E-mail: **content@everybody.co.nz**

The New Zealand AIDS Foundation
www.nzaf.org.nz
E-mail: **contact@nzaf.org.nz**

Soil and Health Association of New Zealand
www.soil-health.org.nz
E-mail: **s.browne@organicnz.pl.net**

United Kingdom

The Association & Register of Colonic
Hydrotherapists
www.colonic-association.com

Breakthrough Breast Cancer
www.breakthrough.org.uk
E-mail: **info@breakthrough.org.uk**

British Holistic Medical Association
www.bhma.org
E-mail: **Bhma@bhma.org**

The Moving Centre School UK
www.mcauk.com
E-mail: **roland@5RhythmsUK.com**

Natural Healing
www.natural-healing.co.uk
E-mail: **gsolomon@netcomuk.co.uk**

The Natural Menopause Advice Service
www.nmas.org.uk
E-mail: **info@nmas.org.uk**

Neal's Yard Remedies
www.nealsyardremedies.com
E-mail: **mail@nealsyardremedies.com**

Positively Women
www.positivelywomen.org.uk
E-mail: **info@positivelywomen.org.uk**

Raw Network
www.rawnetwork.com

The Soil Association
www.soilassociation.org
E-mail: **info@soilassociation.org**

STAT: The Society of Teachers of the Alexander
Technique
www.stat.org.uk
E-mail: **office@stat.org.uk**

Therapy World
www.therapy-world.co.uk
E-mail: **admin@therapy-world.co.uk**

The Vegan Society
www.vegansociety.com
E-mail: **info@vegansociety.com**

<u>United States</u>

Andrew Weil
www.drweilselfhealing.com or
www.drweil.com

Colon Health Network
www.colonhealth.net

Dr. Robert Young—Innerlight
www.thephmiracle.us
E-mail: **stevedom@rcn.com**

Gabrielle Roth
www.ravenrecording.com
E-mail: **ravenrec@panix.com**

Hippocrates Health Institute
www.hippocratesinst.com
E-mail: **info@hippocratesinst.com**

Living and Raw Foods
www.living-foods.com

National Breast Cancer Coalition (USA)
www.natlbcc.org

National Women's Health Resource Center
www.healthywomen.org
E-mail: **nwhrc02@erols.com**

The North American Menopause Society
www.menopause.org
E-mail: **info@menopause.org**

Optimum Health Institute
www.optimumhealth.org
E-mail: **optimum@optimumhealth.org**

Rawfood.com
www.rawfood.com

Women to Women
www.womentowomen.com
E-mail:
personalprogram@womentowomen.com

315.

Chapter 3

<u>International</u>

Brahma Kumaris—World Spiritual
Organisation
www.bkwsu.com

H.H. Dalai Lama
www.dalailama.com or **www.tibet.com**
E-mail: **info@tibet.com**

Soka Gakkai International
www.sgi.org

The Bahá'í World
www.bahai.org

<u>UK</u>

Avalonia
www.avalonia.co.uk

Alternatives
www.alternatives.org.uk
E-mail: **alternatives@ukonline.co.uk**

Brahma Kumaris UK
www.brahmakumaris.org.uk

Hallow Quest
www.hallowquest.org.uk

The Druid Grove
www.druidry.org
E-mail: **OBOD@druidry.org**

<u>USA</u>

Center of the Sacred Feminine
www.sacred-feminine.org
E-mail: **amalyagoddess@aol.com**

Interfaith
www.interfaith.org

New Moon Visions
www.newmoonvisions.com

Starhawk
www.starhawk.org
E-mail: **mer@starhawk.org**

The Kabbalah Center
www.kabbalah.com
E-mail: **kabbalist@kabbalah.com**

Chapter 4

<u>New Zealand</u>

Mothers Network New Zealand
www.newmother.org.nz
E-mail: **auckland@mothersnetwork.co.nz**

<u>South Africa</u>

Growing Child
http://www.eparent.co.za
E-mail: **eparent@mweb.co.za**

<u>UK</u>

Fathers Direct
www.fathersdirect.com

Home Start
www.home-start.org.uk
E-mail: **info@home-start.org.uk**

National Family and Parenting Institute
www.nfpi.org or **www.e-parents.org**
E-mail: **info@nfpi.org**

316.

Parentline Plus
www.parentlineplus.org.uk
E-mail: **centraloffice@parentlineplus.org.uk**

Single Parents Action network
www.spanuk.org.uk
E-mail: **info@spanuk.org.uk**

<u>USA</u>

Parenthood
www.parenthood.com

Chapter 5

<u>Australia</u>

Relate Australia
www.relate.gov.au

<u>UK</u>
Relate
www.relate.org.uk
E-mail: **enquiries@relate.org.uk**

<u>USA</u>
Chuck Spezzano
www.psychologyofvision.com

David Deida
www.deida.com
E-mail: **info@deida.com**

John Gray
www.marsvenus.com

M. Scott Peck
www.mscottpeck.com

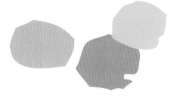

Chapter 6

<u>Australia</u>

Bliss Sensuality Boutique for Women
www.bliss4women.com
E-mail: **info@bliss4women.com.au**

<u>New Zealand</u>

Sexual NZ
www.sexual.co.nz
E-mail: **info@sexual.co.nz**

317.

<u>UK</u>
Ann Summers
www.annsummers.com

Emotional Bliss
www.emotionalbliss.com
E-mail: **info@emotionalbliss.com**

Sh! Women's Erotic Emporium
www.sh-womenstore.com

<u>USA</u>

Betty Dodson
www.bettydodson.com

Good Vibrations Catalog
www.goodvibes.com

Pleasure Chest
www.thepleasurechest.com

Tantra.com
www.tantra.com
E-mail: **contact@tantra.com**

Chapter 7

Australia

Australian Council of Businesswomen
www.acob.org.au
E-mail: **acob@bigpond.com**

Bartercard
www.bartercard.com

Women in Business (Australia)
www.womeninbusiness.com.au
E-mail: **info@womeninbusiness.com.au**

Canada

Canadian Women's Business Network
www.cdnbizwomen.com
E-mail: **admin@cdnbizwomen.com**

Ireland

Network Ireland
www.networkireland.ie

India

Self Employed Women's Association (SEWA)
www.sewa.org
E-mail: **mail@sewa.org**

New Zealand

Business and Professional Woman
New Zealand
www.bpwnz.org.nz

South Africa

Women'sNet
www.womensnet.org.za
E-mail: **women@wn.apc.org**

UK

Aurora Women's Network
www.busygirl.com
E-mail: **admin@auroravoice.com**

The Bag Lady
www.bagladyit.com
E-mail: **info@bagladyit.com**

Prowess
www.prowess.org.uk
E-mail: **admin@prowess.org.uk**

SEED
www.seedfusion.com
E-mail: **info@seednetwork.com**

Social Venture Network Europe
www.svneurope.com
E-mail: **info@svneurope.com**

Via3.com
www.via3.com

Women in Business International
www.forwomeninbusiness.com
E-mail:**info@forwomeninbusiness.com**

USA

Black Career Women
www.bcw.org

318.

Business for Social Responsibility
www.bsr.org
E-mail: **advisoryservices@bsr.org**

Center for Women's Business Research
www.womensbusinessresearch.org
E-mail: **info@womensbusinessresearch.org**

Cosmetic Executive Women (CEW)
www.cew.com
E-mai: **krieg@cew.com**

Dress for Success
www.dressforsuccess.org

NAWBO (National Association of Women Business Owners)
www.nawbo.org
E-mail: **national@nawbo.org**

Social Venture Network
www.svn.org
E-mail: **svn@svn.org**

Spirit in Business
www.spiritinbusiness.org

Chapter 8

<u>Australia</u>

Aboriginal and Islander Women's Congress of Western Australia
www.aboriginalwomen.org.au
E-mail: **enquiries@aboriginalwomen.org.au**

Australian National Committee on Refugee Women
E-mail: **ancorw@ozemail.com.au**

Community Info
www.communityinfo.com.au
E-mail: **info@communityinfo.com.au**

<u>New Zealand</u>

Minitatanga mo nga Wahine (Ministry of Women's Affairs)
www.mwa.govt.nz
E-mail: **mwa@mwa.govt.nz**

Otautahi—Maori Women's Welfare League
www.poutokomanawa.co.nz/otautahi/default.asp
E-mail: **mwwl@xtra.co.nz**

<u>UK</u>

BedZED
www.bedzed.org.uk

Development Trusts Association
www.dta.org.uk
E-mail: **info@dta.org.uk**

Fawcett
www.fawcetsociety.org.uk
E-mail: **info@fawcettsociety.org.uk**

Findhorn
www.findhorn.org
E-mail: **enquiries@findhorn.org**

Girl Guides
www.girlguiding.org.uk
E-mail: **join.us@girlguiding.org.uk**

Kids Company
www.kidscomp.org.uk
E-mail: **info@kidsco.org.uk**

Northern Ireland Women's Coalition
www.niwc.org
E-mail: **info@niwc.org**

The Prince's Trust
www.princes-trust.org
E-mail: **info@princes-trust.org.uk**

The Women's Institute
www.womens-institute.co.uk
E-mail: **hq@nfwi.org.uk**

The Women's Resource Centre
www.wrc.org.uk
E-mail: **info@wrc.org.uk**

<u>USA</u>

Asian Women's Resource Exchange
www.aworc.org
E-mail: **aworcweb@jca.ax.apc.org**

Aviva Center
www.avivacenter.org

Big Brothers Big Sisters of Los Angeles
www.bigbrothersbigsisterslaie.org
E-mail:
ContactUs@bigbrothersbigsisterslaie.org

Esalen Institute Retreat Center
www.esalen.org

Hispanic Women's Corporation
www.hispanicwomen.org

Jewish Women's Caucus
www.nwsa.org/jwc.htm
E-mail: **jodi@jodiandLarry.com**

MANA—A National Latina Organisation
www.hermana.org
E-mail: **hermana2@aol.com**

Ms. Foundation
www.ms.foundation.org
E-mail: **info@ms.foundation.org**

Chapter 9

<u>Canada</u>

Adbusters
www.adbusters.org
E-mail: **info@adbusters.org**

<u>International</u>

Ecofeminism
www.ecofeminism.net

Greenpeace
www.greenpeace.org
E-mail:
supporter.services@ams.greenpeace.org

Human Rights Watch
www.hrw.org
E-mail: **hrwnyc@hrw.org**

International Union for the
Conservation of Nature
www.iucn.org

Mother Earth
www.motherearth.org
E-mail: **international@motherearth.org**

UNESCO
www.unesco.org

UNIFEM
www.unifem.org
E-mail: **unifem@undp.org**

Vandana Shiva
www.vshiva.net
E-mail: **vshiva@vsnl.com**

Womankind Worldwide
www.womankind.org.uk
E-mail**: info@womankind.org.uk**

World Wildlife Fund
www.wwf.org

Europe

Pop Catalunya
E-mail:
popbarcelona@popsustainability.org

South Africa

ANC Women's League
www.anc.org.za/wl

UK

Amnesty International
www.amnesty.org

Ethical Trading Initiative
www.ethicaltrade.org
E-mail: **eti@eti.org.uk**

Friends of the Earth
www.foe.co.uk

Human Rights Watch London
www.hrw.org
E-mail: **hrwuk@hrw.org**

New Economics Foundation
www.neweconomics.org
E-mail: **info@neweconomics.org**

Oxfam
www.oxfam.org.uk
E-mail: **webteam@oxfam.org.uk**

Traidcraft
www.traidcraft.co.uk
E-mail: **comms@Traidcraft.co.uk**

USA

Mothers Against Guns
www.mothersagainstguns.org

Pop Sustainability
www.popsustainability.org or
www.thinkpop.org

Rocky Mountain Institute
www.rmi.org

Riane Eisler
www.partnershipway.org
E-mail: **center@partnershipway.org**

Sierra Club
www.sierraclub.org
E-mail: **information@sierraclub.org**

Women's Edge
www.womensedge.org
E-mail: **edge@womensedge.org**

321.

Chapter 10

You are the resource.

Bliss
www.blissfulmusic.com

• • • • •

Acknowledgments

Thank You . . .

Every modern woman needs a good man as a friend whom she can cry with, laugh with, pray with, and create with. Sometimes that man is a life partner, while other times he's a beloved friend and collaborator. Michael Bockman is in the latter category—he's a beautiful soul whose versatile mind and generosity of being have supported and stimulated me throughout the birthing process of this book. This isn't the first time we've worked together, nor will it be the last. I would like to thank him from the depths of my soul for being patient, attentive, and totally creative. Michael's words have wound their way alongside mine throughout this book—he's coaxed my ideas into prose, and edited and tidied up as we've gone along. All the women who read this book (including me) should particularly thank him for the inside track on how a man likes to be made love to by a woman. Michael, you're a hero—may the Goddess continue to look after you as one of her favorite sons.

I'd also like to thank my other collaborator, the incredibly talented Ann Field, who once again has brought my words to life with her truly extraordinary and life-enhancing illustrations. Long may we work together!

In addition, thanks go out to the many Gorgeous Real Original Women, ages 6 to 96, who have allowed me to hear their stories, have given me some great guidance, and have shown me the beauty of a woman's mind. They include my mother (of course), Angela Franks, who gives me her wisdom unfailingly every day; my daughter, Jessica Howie, who constantly amazes me with her understanding and strength; my totally delightful daughter-in-law, Monique Duffy, whom I'm so grateful to have in my life; my sister, Sue Spivak, for her good humor and support; and my nieces Adina and Sarah.

I'm also indebted to the wise women of Mallorca, including the truly wonderful Frances Graves; Jackie and Talis Waldren and the indefatigable matriarch Rosa Brown; Lydia and Mia Coric; Marilyn and Aniko Naji; Anki and Tila Delnegro; the extraordinary Lou Landreth; my generous walking companions, Joanna James and Isabelle Rogers, who strode up and down the mountains with me, living this book as it got written; Sybilla, for always being so inspiring; Mitey Roche and Natasha Zupan for their single-girl stories and laughter; Seraphine Klarwein, Gloria Fein, Katharine Hamnett, Annie Lennox, Tina Radcliffe and my many other island friends who are constantly there for me; and finally, always in my memory, Lady June.

From the rest of the world, thanks to Anita Roddick, Denise Linn, Gabrielle Roth, the Zappa women, Trudie Styler, Peggy Horan, Amber Dodd, Rose Rouse, Joanna Rahim, Hazel Henderson, Francine Shera, Ruby Wax, Sinéad O'Connor, Christina Vierra, Gaby Schneider, Janet Street-Porter, and Lucinda Drayton for inspiring me with their creativity, wisdom, and friendship; my buddy Norma Bishop for managing me so brilliantly; Antonya Allen for all her hard work researching the resources; Caren Owen for her good-hearted support; Laura Golden Bellotti for her keen editing in the early stages; Francesca and Isabelle Forristal, Angelina and Gabriella De Cassis, Tiger Hutchence, and India Rose Catto for showing me the wisdom of the girl child; and finally, Om Shanti to my spiritual sisters, Dadi Janki, Sister Jayanti, Sister Maureen, Lucinda Drayton, and all the Brahma Kumaris.

There are many Gorgeous Real Original Men who constantly support my life, and I'd like to thank, in particular, Reid Tracy of Hay House for having faith in this book from the beginning (together with the entire Hay House team in the U.S. and the U.K.); my son, Joshua Howie, whom I love very much and am deeply proud of; and my son-in-law, Jamie Catto, for his constant intelligence, humor, and devotion to my darling daughter. For their encouragement, friendship, and support, thanks also go to Mike George, Geoff Russell, Jasper Conran, Peter Lennig, Renè Carayol, Ahmed Suleiman, Marcello Palazzi, Paul Howie, and Michel Bocandé, to whom I'm especially grateful for his beautiful photographs. There's so many more . . . but you know who you are.

• • • • •

About the Author

As a child of the '60s, **Lynne Franks** grew up with many of the expectations of a woman of her generation. She took it almost for granted that she would have a career, children, and a secure marriage. As the grandchild of immigrants to her native England, she accepted entrepreneurship as a natural part of living and working. After helping in her father's butcher shop in her early teens, she left school at 16, working her way up the typist ladder to her dream of journalism. After working on several British magazines with other young, pioneering female journalists, she started her first public-relations agency when she was just 21 years old. Acclaimed in both the U.K. and overseas as the "PR guru," she created a company that led the way in cutting-edge communications. Lynne Franks PR created London Fashion Week, launched designer jeans, and introduced Swatch watches, while working on many environmental and human-rights issues at the same time.

Lynne sold her agency after 23 years, got divorced, and became a single mother to her two children, Joshua and Jessica, while committing herself to using her communication skills to create positive awareness of feminine values in the world. She created the London event "What Women Want" to draw attention to the changing position of women in society, prior to attending the 1995 United Nations' Conference for Women in Beijing; she chaired the U.K.'s first women's radio station and has become a spokesperson on women's issues and socially responsible business practices all over the world.

Now based between London and Spain, Lynne is committed to growing SEED, a learning and personal-development program for female entrepreneurs in the first and third worlds, based on her book *The SEED Handbook: The Feminine Way to Create Business.*

Lynne Franks believes that the future of a healthy society is based on women moving into their full feminine power, alongside men, as local and global community leaders. *GROW* is her fourth book and will also be developed into training programs for women everywhere. Website: **www.growexperience.com**

• • • • •

Also by Lynne Franks

Absolutely Now!*

The SEED Handbook: *The Feminine Way to Create Business**

The SEED Manifesto*

• • •

Hay House Titles of Related Interest

Books

Archangels & Ascended Masters, by Doreen Virtue, Ph.D.

The Body "Knows," by Caroline M. Sutherland, Medical Intuitive

Inner Peace for Busy Women, by Joan Z. Borysenko, Ph.D.

The Love and Power Journal, by Lynn V. Andrews

Love Your Body, by Louise L. Hay

Menopause Made Easy, by Carolle Jean-Murat, M.D.

The Relationship Problem Solver for Love, Marriage, and Dating,
by Kelly E. Johnson, M.D.

Sacred Ceremony, by Steven D. Farmer, Ph.D.

Secrets of Attraction, by Sandra Anne Taylor

Soul Coaching, by Denise Linn

A Very Hungry Girl, by Jessica Weiner

The Western Guide to Feng Shui: Room by Room,
by Terah Kathryn Collins

325.

Card Decks

Juicy Living Cards, by SARK

Magical Spell Cards, by Lucy Cavendish

Men Are from Mars, Women Are from Venus Cards,
by John Gray

Money Cards, by Suze Orman

All of the above are available at your local bookstore; those without asterisks may be ordered by visiting:
Hay House USA: **www.hayhouse.com;** Hay House Australia: **www.hayhouse.com.au;**
Hay House UK: **www.hayhouse.co.uk** • Hay House South Africa: **orders@psdprom.co.za**

• • •

We hope you enjoyed this Hay House Lifestyles book.
If you would like to receive a free catalog featuring additional
Hay House books and products, or if you would like information about the
Hay Foundation, please contact:

Hay House, Inc.
P.O. Box 5100
Carlsbad, CA 92018-5100

(760) 431-7695 or **(800) 654-5126**
(760) 431-6948 (fax) or **(800) 650-5115 (fax)**
www.hayhouse.com

• • •

Published and distributed in Australia by:
Hay House Australia, Ltd. • 18/36 Ralph St. • Alexandria NSW 2015
Phone: 612-9669-4299 • *Fax:* 612-9669-4144 • www.hayhouse.com.au

Published and distributed in the United Kingdom by:
Hay House UK, Ltd. • Unit 202, Canalot Studios • 222 Kensal Rd., London W10 5BN
Phone: 44-20-8962-1230 • *Fax:*44-020-8962-1239 • www.hayhouse.co.uk

Published and distributed in the Republic of South Africa by:
Hay House SA (Pty), Ltd., P.O. Box 990, Witkoppen 2068
Phone/Fax: 2711-7012233 • orders@psdprom.co.za

Distributed in Canada by: Raincoast • 9050 Shaughnessy St., Vancouver, B.C. V6P 6E5
Phone: (604) 323-7100 • *Fax:* (604) 323-2600

• • •

Sign up via the Hay House USA Website to receive the Hay House online newsletter
and stay informed about what's going on with your favorite authors. You'll receive
bimonthly announcements about: Discounts and Offers, Special Events, Product Highlights,
Free Excerpts, Giveaways, and more!

The GROW Commitments

I, _____ , commit that I will . . .

- Take off the mask of illusion and see the beauty and feminine grace that is the true me.

- Every day in every way nurture my body to create optimum health and vitality.

- Acknowledge the Goddess within me, and welcome the power and wisdom of the sacred feminine into all areas of my life.

- Be grateful for my beloved family and friends, and send them unconditional love always.

- Be ready to give and receive true love and partnership into my life.

- Embrace my feminine sexuality and acknowledge the divine connection with my lover.

- Entrust that my work creates value in my life and the lives of others.

- Recognize my community and contribute to it in every way I can.

- Adhere to the feminine principle of cooperation and do my part in creating a world based on harmony and peace.

- The Final Commitment:
  I am dedicated to living my life's purpose by _____

  _____

  _____

  [fill in the action to be taken]

  _____   _____
  Signature   Date